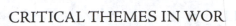

CRITICAL THEMES IN WOR

Sanctified Violence

Holy War in World History

Series Editor: Alfred J. Andrea
Emeritus Professor of History
University of Vermont

Sanctified Violence

Holy War in World History

Alfred J. Andrea
Andrew Holt

Hackett Publishing Company, Inc.
Indianapolis/Cambridge

24 23 22 21   1 2 3 4 5 6 7

For further information, please address
Hackett Publishing Company, Inc.
P.O. Box 44937
Indianapolis, Indiana 46244-0937

www.hackettpublishing.com

Cover design by Rick Todhunter
Interior design by E. L. Wilson
Composition by Aptara, Inc.

Cataloging-in-Publication data can be accessed via the Library of Congress Online Catalog.
Library of Congress Control Number: 2020945947

ISBN-13: 978-1-62466-961-3 (cloth)
ISBN-13: 978-1-62466-960-6 (pbk.)

The paper used in this publication meets the minimum requirements of American National Standard for Information Sciences—Permanence of Paper for Printed Library Materials, ANSI Z39.48–1984.

∞

CONTENTS

ABOUT THE SERIES

Critical Themes in World History focuses on phenomena that have had a profound impact on the course of world history. The first two books in the series, *Shackles of Iron: Slavery Beyond the Atlantic* and *Protests in the Streets: 1968 Across the Globe*, respectively considered, within a global context, human bondage over the past four thousand years and mid-twentieth-century efforts to break the bonds of institutional subordination. Each book, including this newest addition to the series, has employed a combination of narrative and primary sources aimed at helping students and general readers alike to discover and analyze how the phenomenon under consideration has played a critical role in the unfolding of human history through time and across the globe.

Driving this series is the philosophy that analysis of data and an unconstrained commitment to follow wherever that analysis leads are key elements in any meaningful study of the past. For this reason, the authors of each book have labored to raise as many questions as possible and offer select packages of visual and documentary sources, thereby challenging readers to take an active role in exploring the issue under consideration. Current pedagogical research stresses the benefits of active learning—learning that leads to the sharpening of one's critical faculties. The publisher, this editor, and all authors contributing to the series are committed to offering books that encourage readers to probe, in a meaningful way, the events, institutions, and ways of thought and action that have contributed to the shaping of our world.

Alfred J. Andrea
Series Editor

PREFACE

The origins of this book lie in a question raised by a student in Alfred Andrea's 2003 seminar on the crusades in world history at the Global History Center in Beijing: While the crusades were a form of holy war that traveled around the world in the sixteenth century (and whereas the student had also heard about jihads), were there any other types of holy war that students of global history should be aware of? Momentarily stumped, Andrea promised to devote serious thought to the issue and, once class had ended, began formulating a list of the general types of holy war that have existed and persisted over the last five millennia.

The categories he offered the seminar the following day differed somewhat from those articulated in the chapters that follow, for what began as a response to a student's query turned into a research obsession that went through numerous iterations and revisions. For the next fifteen years, Andrea was ever ready to present his evolving ideas to any audience that would listen. This included universities and other learned associations in the United States, China, Taiwan, Turkey, Germany, Greece, England, and Australia, as well as less-formal gatherings at local libraries and in the classes of tolerant (one suspects long-suffering) colleagues. All the while he refined his thoughts on the issue and expanded his collection of holy wars.

A turning point came in 2017, when Adam Knobler invited him to the University of the Ruhr in Bochum, Germany, to participate in "Holy War: Comparative Perspectives," a two-day academic workshop consisting of eleven colleagues representing a variety of disciplines and views. The meeting convinced Andrea that there was a need for a book on holy war in world history that could serve as a starting point for further investigation.

Other commitments intervened until late 2019, when he decided that it was time to begin the project. When Andrew Holt, a specialist on crusades, jihads, and contemporary jihadists' use of social media, received Andrea's invitation to join the project, he accepted an offer that could not be refused. And so here we are.

In choosing the holy wars and other forms of sacred mayhem that appear in these chapters, the authors were forced to be selective, a selectivity that will disappoint many readers because some holy war is absent, given undeserved short shrift, or cursorily treated. Although Cromwell's invasion and "pacification" of Ireland appears briefly in these pages, there is no mention of the English Civil War, even though religion played a significant role in the conflict. This is lamentable because its absence precludes our borrowing that excellent digest of the war as "*the utterly memorable Struggle between the Cavaliers (Wrong but Wromantic) and the Roundheads (Right but Repulsive).*"[1] Alas. We can only throw ourselves on the mercy of the reader.

Because this book cannot hope to be and does not pretend to be all-inclusive, and because the categories of holy war that appear in these chapters are open to challenge, we hope the ideas that we offer might serve as a basis for reflection and further study of this particular type of warfare that has vexed humanity for more than five thousand years. Whatever one thinks of holy war and however one defines it and divides it into types, there is no denying that it has played and continues to play a significant role in world history.

Alfred J. Andrea
Andrew Holt

---

1. Walter Carruthers Sellar and Robert Julian Yeatman, *1066 and All That* (New York: E. P. Dutton, 1931), 63.

ACKNOWLEDGMENTS

In contrast to the "all hands on deck" ethos of the natural sciences, in which multi-authored studies are the norm, historians cherish the image of the solitary researcher, laboring in splendid isolation in musty archives, who then emerges to shed light on a once-dark corner of the human past. The historian as independent academic hero is an attractive figure, but exists only in myth.

Every historian depends on the work of those who have gone before as well on the knowledge, insights, and frank criticisms of colleagues. This is especially true of those who label themselves "world historians." By its very nature, world history is a field of inquiry that demands cooperation and access to the wisdom of many others. Mindful of this reality, we gratefully acknowledge the generous assistance of the following.

Felipe Fernández-Armesto of the University of Notre Dame read an entire late draft of the book and provided numerous comments and suggestions, many of which influenced our final text. John Hosler of the U.S. Army Command and General Staff College read an early draft of the Introduction and offered extensive points to ponder. Kevin Trainor of the University of Vermont has been willing on countless occasions to discuss obscure aspects of Buddhist belief and ritual. C. Matthew Phillips of Concordia University Nebraska shared his expertise in the matter of Martin Luther's evolving ideas regarding war against the Turks, and Wesley Moody of Florida State College at Jacksonville enlightened us about the sixteenth-century massacre at Fort Caroline. Rick Todhunter, serving as Hackett Publishing Company's editorial guru, provided invaluable guidance and warm encouragement, and in like manner, Liz Wilson performed her magic as production director. Without Liz and Rick's professional expertise this book would not have been possible. Likewise, Leslie Connor's careful copyediting and Laura Clark's final review of the text before it went to the printer proved once again that Hackett is blessed with first-rate editors at every level. Finally, but certainly not last in our hearts, there are the many students whose questions and challenges have helped us to sharpen our skills as interpreters of the past. The stimulus of the classroom has been essential in the formulation and evolution of our ideas on holy war in world history.

Our wives, Juanita and Michele; daughters, Kristina, Isabella, and Claire; sons, Peter and Jack; and daughter-in-law, Gretchen, have earned infinite good karma for their forbearance in the face of our eccentric enthusiasms. Our debt to them is beyond adequate expression. All we can say is thank you and we love you.

INTRODUCTION:
WHAT IS HOLY WAR?

War is brutal and compels those waging it to engage in actions that are debasing and dehumanizing. Faced with this reality, societies around the world have sought to justify martial violence by investing it with values that transcend such ignoble motivations as greed and bloodlust. For this reason and in multiple ways and instances, people have sanctified—made holy—various wars.

What Is Holy War?

The simplest definition of holy war, which we shall test throughout this book, is that *holy war is sanctified violence in service to a deity or a religious ideology*. In its broadest sense, *religion is any spiritual or pragmatic connection with a transcendental Other*. In most instances, that transcendental Other is a deity—a specific god or goddess or pantheon of divine beings—but that is not necessarily so. It can be sacred forces, such as the spirits of nature and ancestors as revered in Japanese Shinto. It can be a supreme cosmic spirit, such as Brahman, Hinduism's Ultimate Reality, that transcends the unreality of the physical world but governs the natural world and the lives and destinies of all beings. It does not even have to be a spirit. Buddhist Dharma, the universal Law that leads to Enlightenment and Infinite Compassion, suffices.

This definition of holy war is our baseline, our starting point from which we intend to go off in multiple directions. The overriding thesis of this book is that holy wars have taken on a variety of forms throughout history, and as we proceed in our exploration of the various types of sanctified warfare in Chapters 1–4, we will refine and expand that definition or, better, offer multiple ways of understanding these wars. Not everyone will agree with our reasoning and interpretations, and that is fine. Above all else, we aim to stimulate thought that leads to further inquiry.

We begin our investigation by acknowledging that there have been many wars and reigns of terror throughout history in which religious factors have been so intertwined with secular elements that it often is unclear whether a particular instance of violence merits placement in the category of holy war. We shall investigate instances of this ambiguity throughout the book. Further complicating the issue is the tendency of many to conflate righteous, or just, wars with holy wars.

Holy War or Just War?

Political theorists and theologians, as well as historians, distinguish between a just war and a holy war, although the boundaries often overlap and they can be easily confused, one for the other. At least in the eyes of persons promoting and fighting a holy war, that struggle is, by its very nature, "just," but conversely, just wars are not necessarily holy wars. Moreover, cultures that reject the idea that any war can be holy usually defend their wars as just. In fact, the need to justify war is so basic to the human spirit that sophisticated theories of the just war are embedded in the traditions of many cultures around the world. One commonality they share is the principle that for a war to be just, those engaged in it must have a righteous reason for fighting and must conduct themselves according to certain moral standards.

Just War Traditions

Just War in India

The Indian epic known as the Mahābhārata (The Great Story of the Bharata Clan), which is further discussed in Chapter 1, narrates the struggles between two rival branches of a royal family, and in the process articulates two basic criteria for a *dharmayuddha* (righteous war). Such a war is fought selflessly to uphold Dharma, which for Hindus is the cosmic law of right conduct and proper social order, and combatants must fight honorably. They cannot kill defenseless or unequally armed opponents or prisoners, women and children, holy persons, and a wide variety of other protected individuals. Righteous warriors should so conduct themselves that they do not create an evil greater than the one they seek to remedy. All too often in the epic, heroes and gods violate these norms, but such aberrant behavior stands in stark contrast to the ideal of warfare waged righteously for a just cause.

The Mahābhārata and other Hindu texts that affirmed the code of the just warrior traveled from South India into the lands of coastal Southeast Asia, where Indian cultural traditions merged with indigenous ways of life and belief in the early centuries of the Common Era.

Much later, in an area of northern India known as the Punjab, Guru Gobind Singh, the tenth and last guru, or spiritual master, of the Sikh faith went further. Sikhism (*Sikh* means "disciple" or "seeker") emerged from the teachings of Guru Nanak (1469–1539), who sought to reconcile the tensions between Muslims and Hindus in Mughal northern India with a message of love, virtue, and the full dignity, equality, and inclusion of all peoples centered on worship of a single God

1.1. An early nineteenth-century Sikh war helmet. The unusual shape is due to the need of the Sikh warrior to roll his uncut hair into a topknot. Uncut hair, a symbol of devotion to God and respect for all creation, is one of the five symbols of faith that Guru Gobind Singh mandated for all Sikh men in 1699. A "purified" man committed to the Sikh way of life always carries a dagger known as a *kirpan*. It is to be used solely for self-defense, as well as the defense of all victims who cannot protect themselves.

of the universe. Sikhs in the late seventeenth century, however, became victims of Emperor Aurangzeb's assaults, which included the public beheading in 1675 of the community's spiritual master, Guru Tegh Bahadur. In 1699, the martyred guru's son and successor, Gobind Singh, institutionalized a community of warriors known as the *Khalsa* (the Pure) and taught the principle of the *dharam yudh*, or war in defense of righteousness.

The code underlying the dharam yudh is that it must be an action of last resort and it must not be for territorial gain. In addition, its warriors must be committed Khalsa, whose motives are unpolluted by any desire for gain or revenge or by hate and who conduct themselves according to the highest standards of ethical behavior as taught by the ten Gurus, and they must employ minimum force.

Buddhist Just War

Buddhism, which derives from moral principles articulated by Siddhartha Gautama, the Buddha or Enlightened One (ca. 480–400 B.C.E.), teaches compassion for all living creatures and maintains that violence toward another is *aksula*, an unwholesome state of mind that frustrates one's search for escape from the shackles of the physical world and entry into Nirvana. For this reason, many perceive Buddhism to be a religion fully committed to peace. Yet, as we shall see, Buddhists have engaged in warfare on many occasions.

The classic explanation for Buddhist participation in war is that the duty to preserve the life of the innocent or to protect the Buddhist religion overrides the obligation to refrain from harming another. But in performing this duty, soldiers must act without passion and without seeking to kill, even though their actions might result in someone's death. The proper state of mind and intention are everything.

In the mid-twentieth century, the Chinese monk Taixu (1890–1947) reacted to the Japanese invasion of China that precipitated the Second Sino-Japanese War (1937–45) by publicly proclaiming that fighting to save one's country is an act of compassionate preservation of a people and therefore a just war by Buddhist standards.

The Confucian Just War

Likewise, Chinese philosophers, from the Warring States Era (475–221 B.C.E.) to the Tang dynasty (618–907), composed a body of works that, when collected, became known as the *Seven Military Classics*. When they addressed the issue of when and how one conducted a *yizhan* (just war), they agreed on basic principles, regardless of however else they might disagree. Such a war must be aimed at restoring justice (*yi*) and must meet at least one of the following criteria: it rises to the level of a moral obligation to restore a proper and stable social and economic order to a beleaguered people; it aims to relieve a population of a tyrant; it serves to stop aggression. In conducting such a war, soldiers must conduct themselves according to the principles of *ren* (benevolence; humaneness).

Just War in the Greek and Roman Traditions

In the West, the idea that a war can be just goes back to the fourth-century-B.C.E. Greek philosopher Aristotle, who taught that a just war is an endeavor that establishes or protects a just and peaceful *polis* (city-state). Roman theorists, such as Cicero (106–43 B.C.E.), articulated a series of just causes for waging war that boiled down to defending against or punishing a guilty party. Moreover, they insisted that a just war must be formally declared by a competent authority, fought honorably, and have as its goal the restoration of public order and civic peace. With the acquisition of an empire, the Roman theory of righteous military conduct took on an ecumenical tinge insofar as soldiers were theoretically expected to conduct themselves in accord with the *ius gentium* (the law of peoples), those rules of conduct common to all cultures. More often than not, however, this theory of an unwritten universal law that governed human behavior counted for little or nothing in Rome's wars of conquest and suppression of rebellious dissent.

Christian Just War

The earliest Christians divided on the issue of whether their faith prohibited armed violence. When, however, the Christian Church became identified with the Roman Empire in the fourth century, it became necessary to create a theological reconciliation between the message of the Sermon on the Mount that beatifies peacemakers with the cruel necessities of imperial warfare. The Christian emperor was now the God-anointed defender of the Church and its Christian people. Augustine, bishop of Hippo in North Africa (r. 396–430), provided the Latin Church of the West with its classic answer to this conundrum by articulating the theory of the Christian just war.

Augustine began with the premise that war is both a consequence of sin and a remedy for it. Moreover, the true evil of war is not violence but a violent spirit—the love of carnage, revengeful cruelty, implacable hatred, and a lust for dominion over other people. A just war is a final attempt, after all other means have been exhausted, to avenge, in a non-revengeful manner, an injury that is both a crime and a sin. Moreover, a competent authority must declare the just war and a legitimate army, acting as the minister of the law, must wage it. No individual Christian has a legitimate right to engage in violence, even in self-defense. In this way, Augustine combined Jesus's instruction to "turn the other cheek" with the Roman tradition that the *imperator* (emperor) held and was expected to exercise unlimited *imperium* (supreme military and judicial power). Beyond that, soldiers must fight dispassionately, not hating their enemies but seeking to correct the sin in a proportional and charitable manner, thereby being true to Jesus's command to love one's enemies. The just war is an act of love, but love clothed in benevolent severity. Righteous soldiers might kill bodies, but they aim to save souls.

Augustine did much more than articulate the spiritual and ethical grounds on which the wars of emperors and other legitimate secular authorities might be deemed just. As a Christian, he believed that the entire Bible is divine revelation. That meant he had to explain how the often-genocidal wars that the ancient Israelites reputedly waged in response to God's directives were just. In his commentary on the Book of Joshua's account of God's commanding the Israelites to attack and kill all of the inhabitants of the Canaanite city of Ai (a biblical story that we will examine in Chapter 2), Augustine noted that any war waged on divine command is, by the very nature of God's perfect justice, a just war. With this analysis, Augustine joined holy war to just war and provided a theological basis for Christian holy wars.

Jewish Just War

War commanded by God figures prominently in the early books of the Hebrew Bible, as we shall see in Chapter 2, yet for most of the centuries of the Common Era Jewish holy wars were rare, for reasons that we shall investigate in Chapter 4.

For most of the Common Era, until the founding of the state of Israel in 1948, Jews were a people without a homeland, a diaspora people. During these centuries of statelessness, Diaspora Judaism's religious teachers, its rabbis, wrote extensively on a vast array of legal, ethical, ritual, and spiritual issues but devoted little time and effort to righteous warfare. They did, however, generally agree that just wars should be divided into two categories, obligatory wars and permissible (or optional) wars. The former are of two types: wars commanded by God in the Bible, which became moot when the peoples whom God had commanded the Israelites to eradicate ceased to exist as identifiable entities; and wars to defend the people of Israel. This second type is predicated on the principle that self-defense is not only a right but a duty. Permissible wars are conflicts undertaken for a good reason and when negotiation is no longer possible. They could include preemptive strikes against a threatening opponent and possibly wars to extend the boundaries of Israel, but the righteousness of this latter type of war is problematical, and its justification depends on circumstances. Before waging or declaring a war, good-faith efforts must be made to resolve the issue peacefully. Moreover, in waging war, Jews must acknowledge the humanity of their opponents and act accordingly. Because, however, war inevitably involves soldiers in the sordid business of killing, permissible wars require penance and purification.

Islamic Just War

Muhammad al-Hasan al-Shaybani (d. 804) was the first Muslim legal scholar to articulate a coherent theory of international law. In his effort to establish guidelines governing the conduct of True Believers who wage jihad (holy struggle) against unbelievers, al-Shaybani set clear limits on the manner in which Muslims could set in motion and fight such wars. According to him and all who followed his interpretation of Shari'a (religious law), only legitimate authorities, normally the heads of states, can initiate a jihad. Moreover, this "struggle in the path of God" requires a just cause and righteous intention, which means that the purpose of the war must be either the establishment or the proper governance of an Islamic state. Moreover, war cannot be the initial means employed to realize these just goals. Nonbelievers, for example, must first be given an invitation to either convert to Islam or submit to its authority and protection by becoming tolerated non-Muslim subjects (*dhimmis*) who pay tribute (*jizya*) to the state. Fighting, therefore, is allowed only when other means have proved fruitless. Once war against unbelievers, apostates, heretics, rebels, or brigands has commenced, its goal must always be peace, order, and justice. The holy warriors must also act honorably. Although commanders in the field have wide tactical latitude, they must not intentionally or directly attack children, women, the elderly, slaves, the lame and blind, and the helplessly insane. Unavoidably or unintentionally killing or injuring such protected persons, however, does not incur guilt, as long as this "collateral damage" is proportionate with the military objective.

Chapters 2–4 and the Epilogue will examine various manifestations and moments of jihad over the past fourteen centuries.

Just War Theory in the Aztec Empire

The divergence between theory and reality is strikingly significant in all cultures that have developed a theory of just warfare, and that was certainly true in the Valley of Mexico during the years 1428–1521, when the Aztec Triple Alliance was the region's dominant political-military force.

During the sixteenth and seventeenth centuries, a fair number of converted Natives and Catholic missionaries collected and composed accounts of the history and culture of the Aztec Empire and its neighbors. Even though these reports sometimes present sanitized and idealized views of the past, it is possible to gather from them a picture of an indigenous just war theory, although other evidence clearly suggests that practice rarely, if ever, conformed to principle.

According to that theory, a just war could be launched against an independent polity if Aztec or allied merchants or emissaries had been killed within its borders. A just war could be waged against a tributary state or city if it rebelled and refused to render due tribute after being given the opportunity to do so. Once the precipitating act for a just war had taken place, it was still necessary to send three separate embassies to the offending state or city—the first to the ruler, the second to the nobles, the third to the people—to seek redress and to avoid conflict. But it must be emphasized that first and foremost, war was primarily a practical and brutal affair for an empire that used warfare and intimidation for expansionistic purposes.

Just Wars or Holy Wars?

The interplay between just and holy wars is sufficiently complex for us to ask the question: Can a just war that begins for essentially secular reasons be transformed into a holy war? Consider two examples of wars that many participants on both sides sacralized in the course of conflict.

The American Civil War

The U.S. Civil War was ignited by the secession of the Confederate states, whose leaders feared that President Lincoln and the Republican Party threatened the

Southern way of life, primarily the enslavement of African Americans. Although abolitionism was a moral movement frequently underpinned by appeals to the Bible, and although defenders of slavery often used that same Bible to justify human bondage, the war began as a secular conflict. Yet, given the intensity of religion throughout the United States, the war soon took on a religious aura. In the course of the war, both North and South declared national days of fasting in order to seek God's favor and to atone for sins that led to defeats. In the South, preachers railed against the godlessness of the North. In Fayetteville, North Carolina, in 1862, Reverend Joel Tucker informed his congregation that "your cause is the cause of God, of Christ, of humanity. It is a conflict of truth with error—of the Bible with Northern infidelity—of a pure Christianity with Northern fanaticism—of liberty with despotism—of right with might."[1] In the North, the war took on a millenarian cast, whereby the Kingdom of God on Earth, as promised in chapter 20 of the New Testament's Book of Revelation, would be ushered in by a Union victory. In the stirring words of Julia Ward Howe's *Battle Hymn of the Republic*, God "has sounded forth the trumpet that shall never call retreat / He is sifting out the hearts of men before His judgment seat. / Oh, be swift, my soul, to answer Him; be jubilant, my feet! / Our God is marching on."[2]

The First World War

A more recent example of religion employed to sustain a secular war effort is World War I. The Allied and Central Powers stumbled into war in August 1914 due to a lethal mixture of imperial ambitions, narrow national interests, misguided military alliances, and gross political miscalculations. Yet the populations of several Christian nations and empires embroiled in the Great War almost immediately transformed the struggle into a holy war, indeed a crusade, with profound messianic overtones and replete with prophecies, visions, and miracles. And this religious vision pervaded the popular media of England, France, Germany, Austria-Hungary, and Russia, as well as several lesser combatant nations, for the next four years and even beyond the Armistice. When the United States entered

---

1. Cited in Drake Smith, "The Coming of the Lord: An Analysis of Religious Rhetoric in the American Civil War," *Explorations: The Journal of Undergraduate Research and Creative Activities for the State of North Carolina* 12 (2017): 47–57, at 52, https://uncw.edu/csurf/Explorations /Volume%20XII/The%20Coming%20of%20the%20LORD.pdf (accessed February 21, 2019). 2. The complete lyrics can be found at https://www.austincc.edu/dlauderb/1302/Lyrics /BattleHymnoftheRepublic.htm (accessed June 16, 2020). Terrie Dopp Aamodt, *Righteous Armies, Holy Cause: Apocalyptic Imagery and the Civil War* (Macon, GA: Mercer University Press, 2002), studies the manner in which apocalypticism pervaded the cultures of all parties— North, South, and African American—in this conflict.

the war in 1917, many of its citizens likewise embraced the rhetoric and reputed miracles of holy war.

A single example must suffice. One of the most popular visions on the Allied side of the Western Front was the spectral, Christ-like White Comrade who brought aid and comfort to wounded and dying soldiers. In 1920, American Robert Haven Schauffler, a wounded veteran of the war, composed "The White Comrade," a poem that was widely reproduced. According to the poet, as he lay wounded in No Man's Land, a White Comrade boldly came to his assistance, despite a hail of deadly enemy fire. After his wounds were dressed and his pain

I.2. Heavenly succor on the battlefield. George Hillyard Swinstead, *The White Comrade* (1915).

relieved, the wounded man perceived that this comrade bore apparent bullet wounds in his hands, feet, and side, and he remarked on the fact. In the poem's concluding stanza, the White Comrade replies in words redolent with Christian redemption theology: "These are old wounds," said he, "But of late they have troubled me."[3]

Holy war language, imagery, and tropes also crept into the official propaganda networks of these nations and empires but only in a minor way. The vast majority of state-generated propaganda played on such time-honored themes as the nobility and courage of the soldiery, the indispensable support of the home front, the barbarism of the enemy, and national honor.

There was one major exception to official state media's emphasis on the nonreligious reasons for prosecuting the war. When the Ottoman Empire joined the war on the side of the Central Powers in November 1914, the Shaykh al-Islam,

---

3. Robert Haven Schauffler, *The White Comrade and Other Poems* (Boston: Houghton Mifflin, 1920), 3–6, at 6; reproduced at https://archive.org/details/whitecomradeothe00scha (accessed August 20, 2019).

the empire's highest-ranking mufti (chief jurist and religious advisor to the sultan), declared a jihad against all the Allied Powers. In the words of his proclamation: "Of those who go to the *Jihad* for the sake of happiness and salvation of the believers in God's victory, the lot of those who remain alive is felicity, while the rank of those who depart to the next world is martyrdom. In accordance with God's beautiful promise, those who sacrifice their lives to give life to the truth will have honor in this world, and their latter end is paradise."[4]

The call for jihad went largely unheeded in the Muslim world, but in 1915 the Ottoman government initiated a genocide of its Christian subjects. The numbers of the slain will never be known with certainty, but an estimate of 1.5 million Armenian Christians out of a total population of about 2.5 million is not unreasonable and added to that were at least several hundred thousand Syriac-rite and Greek Orthodox Christians. Although the government appears to have authorized the slaughter out of a deep paranoia that was fueled by military and political fears, one wonders how many perpetrators of the mass killings and other inhumane acts, such as crucifixion and rape, justified their actions as God-pleasing punishment of infidels. Might not the forced conversion of some children to Islam suggest religious motivation?

There is no way of knowing how many soldiers and sailors on all sides and fronts died believing that they were embroiled in a God-sanctioned holy war,

I.3. A call to holy war? A Russian poster of 1914 depicting the Allies' Triple Entente. Beneath the inscription СОГЛАСІЕ (Concord) stand allegorical representations of Russia, Great Britain, and France. Russia holds an Orthodox cross aloft. The woman representing Great Britain holds an anchor. The anchor is a double symbol: it signifies the Royal Navy but it is also the ancient Christian symbol for hope. Marianne, the female symbol for the French Republic, holds a heart. Collectively, they represent the three Christian virtues enumerated in I Corinthians, 13:13: faith, hope, and charity.

---

4. History.com, "This Day in History, November 14," https://www.history.com/this-day-in -history/ottoman-empire-declares-a-holy-war (accessed August 14, 2019).

but given that combat deaths alone for military personnel totaled somewhere between seven and eight million, their number must have been large.

So, were the American Civil War and the First World War holy wars created from below, that is, sanctified by popular sentiment? We conclude that neither rose to the level of holy war, but you might legitimately disagree.[5]

Praise the Lord and Pass the Ammunition: Military Chaplains

Shamans, diviners, priests, imams, preachers, and military chaplains of every sort have accompanied armies for millennia, ministering to the religious, spiritual, and moral needs of soldiers and boosting their morale. What role, if any, do they play in sanctifying war?

Distinguished American Chaplains in Wartime

In 1942, Frank Loesser composed the song "Praise the Lord and Pass the Ammunition" to commemorate the supposed call to arms by Presbyterian chaplain Lieutenant (j.g.) Howell M. Forgy, aboard the USS *New Orleans* on December 7, 1941. Whether or not Chaplain Forgy uttered those words as Japanese planes attacked Pearl Harbor, the tune soon became a runaway favorite on the home front. The catchy lyrics of the song struck a respondent chord throughout the country. The image of the chaplain as "a sonofagun of a gunner" confirmed a widespread belief that the clergy supported and participated in this righteous war.

In the course of another righteous conflict, the American Civil War, four Protestant chaplains received the Medal of Honor for heroism in the field. Lasting honor of another sort was accorded a Catholic chaplain, Rev. William Corby, CSC, who on the morning of the second day of the Battle of Gettysburg stood on a high rock at Cemetery Ridge and bestowed a general absolution of sins on the soldiers of the Irish Brigade. A statue of Father Corby, administering that absolution with upraised right hand, was placed on the same rock at Gettysburg in 1910, and a copy stands on the campus of the University of Notre Dame, where it is known as "Fair Catch Corby."

Since 1946, five U.S. chaplains, all Catholic priests, have received the Medal of Honor for saving lives "above and beyond the call of duty" during conflicts in the Pacific in World War II, Korea, and Vietnam. Three of them died while performing their heroic actions. The Roman Catholic Church has named two of the three, Vincent Robert Capodanno, M.M., and Emil J. Kapaun, as Servants

---

5. Philip Jenkins, *The Great and Holy War: How World War I Became a Religious Crusade* (San Francisco: HarperOne, 2014).

of God, the first of three steps toward canonization as a saint. Additionally, the Church is considering naming Captain Kapaun a martyr because of his self-sacrifice as a prisoner of war during the Korean War.

Numerous other instances of extraordinary valor can be told of Jewish, Muslim, Buddhist, Sikh, Shinto, and Hindu chaplains and religious counselors around the world and across time. And numerous chaplains (or religious teachers, as they are called in the Indian Army) have died in military service. But does the presence of chaplains, whose primary function is to raise morale by rendering religious solace and service, by itself make a war holy or even just? Again, we argue that it takes more than just the presence of chaplains to make a war holy.

Clerical Promoters of War

What if clerics, either chaplains or others who present themselves as spiritual or religious counselors to members of an armed force, openly preach the sacredness of a war? Does that, of and by itself, make the war holy in the eyes of those promoting and fighting the war?

I.4. "Fair Catch Corby." A copy of *Father William Corby*, the bronze statue by Samuel Murray (1909–10) on the campus of Notre Dame.

A Zen Buddhist Advocate of Japanese Militarism

We have already seen the Chinese Buddhist monk Taixu, who opposed the Japanese invasion of China. On the other side of this Sino-Japanese War, Zen master Yasutani Hakuun (1885–1973) was one of the most outspoken supporters of imperial Japan's militarism. In early 1943, as the Asia-Pacific War (1937–45) was turning against Japan, he published *Zen Master Dogen and the "Treatise on Practice and Enlightenment,"* in which he endeavored to explain the teachings of the thirteenth-century Buddhist teacher Dogen. In doing so, he marched Master Dogen to war. In its opening lines, Yasutani set out the purpose behind the book:

> Asia is one. Annihilating the treachery of the United States and Britain and establishing the Greater East Asia Co-prosperity Sphere is the only way to save the one billion people of Asia so that they can, with peace of mind, proceed on their respective paths. Furthermore, it is only natural that this will contribute to the construction of a new world order, exorcising evil spirits from the world and leading to the realization of eternal peace and happiness for all humanity. I believe this is truly the critically important mission to be accomplished by our great Japanese Empire. In order to fulfill this mission it is absolutely necessary to have a powerful military force.... Furthermore, it is necessary to employ the power of culture, for it is most especially the power of spiritual culture that determines the final outcome.... It is impossible to discuss Japanese culture while ignoring Buddhism.... For this reason we must promulgate and exalt the true Buddha Dharma making certain that the people's thought is resolute and immoveable. Beyond this, we must train and send forth a great number of capable men who will be able to develop and exalt the culture of our imperial land, thereby reverently assisting in the holy enterprise of bringing the eight corners of the world under one roof.[6]

The Buddhist virtue of Selfless Compassion was, in his eyes, synonymous with military aggression. His influence throughout Japan was profound, and as we shall see in Chapter 3, his was not the only clerical voice in the Land of the Rising Sun that advocated aggressive militarism. So, let us defer judgment on this issue until we study that second Japanese example.

Clerics in Arms

What about clerics or other persons committed to a religious life, such as monks and nuns, who take up arms? Does their participation in combat sanctify a battle or war?

The Templars

The most famous (and arguably infamous) group of Christian "clerical warriors" is undoubtedly the Order of the Poor Fellow-Knights of Christ and of the Temple of Solomon, popularly known as the Templars. The Templars were the first of a substantial number of military orders that arose within the Church of Rome,

---

6. Quoted in Brian Daizen Victoria, *Zen War Stories* (London: RoutledgeCurzon, 2003), 68–69.

largely during the twelfth and thirteenth centuries, in order to combat the perceived enemies of Christendom, namely Muslims, pagans, and supposed heretics. Templars, Hospitalers, Teutonic Knights, Knights of Santiago, and members of the myriad other military orders lived in communal houses and were subject to papally approved religious rules that regulated their daily lives. Most also took the three traditional monastic vows of poverty, chastity, and obedience. But they were not monks. What set them apart from cloistered monks and members of other religious orders was that they combined an ordered religious life with a military mission. Moreover, most members of the military orders were not ordained clerics. Membership within the various military orders was divided into three classes: knight-brothers, who were often of noble birth; sergeant-brothers of humbler origin, whose duties ranged from serving as infantry and lightly armed cavalry to functioning as artisans and laborers; and priest-brothers, the orders' only ordained clerics, who devoted themselves to ministering to the spiritual needs of the brotherhood. As was true of all the brothers, the priests were subject to the authority of the orders' masters and commanders, who came from the ranks of the lay knight-brothers.

Buddhist Bhikkhus in Battle

Outside of the Christian tradition, the Buddhist *bhikkhus* (ordained monks) of medieval Korea, Tibet, Bhutan, and Japan often mixed military service with the search for Enlightenment. The Buddhist monastic code forbids monks to carry weapons or to engage in battle on any level, even as spectators, and violators are subject to expulsion from the *sangha* (monastic community). Yet, on multiple occasions, the kings of Korea enlisted tens of thousands of monks in irregular units known as "righteous armies" to fight invading armies from China, Mongolia, Manchuria, and Japan. Across the Sea of Japan, numerous Buddhist monasteries housed *sohei* (warrior monks), especially between the tenth and sixteenth centuries, who were often employed in defending or extending the monastery's lands. It is no exaggeration to say that armies wielded by Buddhist monasteries were a constant and important fact of political life in Japan until the suppression of the warrior-monks by the Tokugawa shogunate (1603–1868).

China also witnessed monks marching to war. Despite efforts by Buddhist authors over the past thousand years and more to hide the embarrassing fact, it is clear that Chinese monks have historically participated in armed revolts and have been drafted for military service by emperors and other authorities. Monks of the Shaolin Monastery, which is famous for its development of martial arts, were key warriors in the campaigns that brought the Tang dynasty to power in 618. In the sixteenth century, the Ming imperial government organized monks from Shaolin and elsewhere in its successful campaign against Japanese pirates who were ravaging the empire's coasts. Indeed, the last half of the Ming era (1368–1644) was the high point of China's imperially employed monastic armies, which were evident in every corner of the land ruled by the Son of Heaven.

So Were They Holy Warriors?

The Christian West's military orders were fashioned in the crucible of the crusades, and at times their members participated in crusades that were clearly holy wars. Yet they also waged campaigns and fought battles that were ambiguous in origin and motivation, and they further engaged in struggles that were manifestly self-serving and not at all motivated by religious concerns. Consequently, their battles must be judged on a case-by-case basis.

The same is true of Buddhist warrior monks, who often fought for causes that were less than religiously motivated. But, as we shall see in Chapters 3 and 4, members of the sangha, women as well as men, have been active in a number of holy wars in East Asia. Whether or not it was their participation that made those wars holy is another issue.

Holy War vis-à-vis Just War Revisited

Perhaps we need to further define holy war by way of distinguishing it from a just war. Consider five possible differences: (1) A holy war is called and fought for religious reasons, whereas a just war is called for a mixture of moral and political reasons. (2) Authorization for a holy war comes from a deity or a spirit, or by way of a religious authority, even if that authority is a self-proclaimed prophet or a "God-anointed" king or sultan who presides over a sanctified state. Authorization for a just war comes from a political authority, either an individual or a corporate body, acting with an understanding of the ethical and political factors driving this decision. (3) Participants in a holy war perceive it as a struggle between a saintly army defending piety and a demonic one promoting sacrilege. Warriors engaged in a just war perceive it as a battle between the political-military agents of righteous and unrighteous causes. (4) The mood of holy warriors is religious zeal fueled by a sense of their furthering the wishes or design of a deity. The mood of soldiers fighting a just war is, in theory, sober, given the realization that they are embroiled in a necessary conflict that is the lesser of two evils, the greater evil being further toleration of the injustice they seek to defeat or correct. (5) The holy warrior expects to gain a spiritual reward by virtue of this service and sacrifice and might even court martyrdom. Even if the holy warrior does not seek martyrdom, he or she usually expects to receive a martyr's reward if killed in the struggle.

When martyred, the holy warrior's death is perceived as having been not that of a passive victim, but as the bellicose action of a crowned victor. The just warrior is performing a civic duty, expects civil recognition, and wants to survive. If killed, his or her death is commemorated as a "heroic sacrifice" but is, nonetheless, tragic.

Does this sum up and clarify their differences? Possibly the case studies that appear in the chapters that follow might cause you to question these distinctions and to develop your own understanding of the relationship of just war to holy war. We hope you do.

While we mull over these distinctions between just and holy wars, another related issue arises. What about wars waged in the name of a secular religion? Can they be considered holy?

Wars Driven by "Secular Religions"

Political ideologies such as fascism, communism, and democracy are often defined as secular religions, and there is justification for doing so. Much like religions that center on the worship of a deity or respect for the supernatural, political ideologies focus on something greater than the individual believer. Fascism sacralizes the state. Nazism deified *das deutsche Volk* (the German people) and the myth of Aryan blood. Communism posits the dynamics of history as the prime mover. Democracy worships the collective spirit, will, and interests of "the people." All have a sense of mission. Consider nineteenth-century American democracy's Manifest Destiny. Consider the lyrics of the "Internationale," sung by socialists, anarchists, and communists alike: "Enslaved masses, stand up, stand up. / The world is about to change its foundation. / We are nothing, let us be all."[7] In addition to their sacred music, rituals bind these communities of "believers." *Triumph of the Will*, a documentary celebrating the 1934 Nazi Party Congress in Nuremberg, provides a disturbing, although artistically brilliant, example of that phenomenon. They also have their holy sites and saints, such as Washington D.C. and Abraham Lincoln. They have doctrines and a sense of what is orthodox belief and virtuous conduct and what is heresy and illicit behavior. Most, possibly all, also have a notion of a better world to come. And they have their wars. In requesting that Congress declare war on imperial Germany in 1917, President Wilson declared America's involvement was necessary because "the world must be made safe for democracy."[8]

---

7. The original lyrics in French with an English translation can be found at https://en.wikipedia.org/wiki/The_Internationale#Original_lyrics (accessed May 29, 2020).

8. President Wilson's address to Congress on April 2, 1917, can be found at http://historymatters.gmu.edu/d/4943/ (accessed May 29, 2020).

Although a case can be made for placing wars driven by political ideologies under the umbrella of "holy," we choose not to do so, falling back on our initial definition, "*holy war is sanctified violence in service to a deity or a religious ideology.*" And "*religion is any spiritual or pragmatic connection with a transcendental Other.*" Some will see this as too narrow, but this interpretation of holy war and religion satisfies us.

Can Terrorists Be Holy Warriors?

Our basic definition of holy war might strike many as wrongheaded because it does not take into consideration the scale of violence. How, one might ask, can we equate an all-out war with acts of terrorism perpetrated by a single person or a small group of individuals? And we agree that generally, if we wish to identify a conflict as a war, size matters. An isolated skirmish along an otherwise quiet frontier is not a war. Yet, we argue that even an apparently random and isolated act of violence perpetrated by a single, religiously motivated warrior or small cell of terrorists constitutes holy war. It is holy war because that person or group perceives the act as not only validated but mandated by a transcendental Other. Moreover, when such acts devolve to the level of terrorism, their perpetrators are often persons who, rightly or wrongly, look upon themselves as a "righteous remnant"—a small group who have kept the faith in the midst of persecution.

Righteous-Remnant Terrorists

Jewish Sicarii and Zealots: Terrorists in the Name of God

One of history's earliest recorded groups of holy terrorists are the Sicarii, the "dagger men," who operated in and around Jerusalem in the mid-first century C.E. Most of the little we know (or think we know) about the Sicarii comes to us from the account of the First Jewish-Roman War (66-73) by the historian Titus Flavius Josephus (37–ca. 100), a former Jewish rebel leader who went over to the side of the Romans. Given his subsequent identification with the cause of Titus, the re-conqueror of Jerusalem and future Roman emperor, Josephus had no sympathy for the Sicarii, whom he characterized as bandits.

According to Josephus, the Sicarii emerged in the 50s and carried curved daggers (*sicae* in Latin; sing. *sica*) concealed in their cloaks. These early cloak-and-dagger men used their weapons to assassinate high-ranking Jews whom they considered to be too friendly with Roman authorities. The fact that many of the assassinations were boldly carried out in crowded venues and even during religious holidays suggests that the Sicarii hoped that their brazen acts would incite a Jewish holy war against the Roman occupation that profaned their sacred land and the priestly hierarchy that had partnered with the Romans.

Like the Sicarii, another group of religiously motivated Jewish rebels, which history identifies as the Zealots, worked to sweep away the Jewish collaborationist elite. The term "Zealots" is often wrongly applied to the entire body of Jewish rebels, a mistake that proceeds from an inability to see the ideological and social divisions among the rebel factions. Josephus, who wrote in Greek, identified only one faction as Zealots. The Greek word *zelotai* means "devoted followers." We do not know for certain what the so-called Zealots called themselves (surely they did not use a Greek term), but it seems likely that it was something like " Disciples of God," and clearly the Zealots, who largely came from the countryside, saw themselves as God's faithful followers. More than that, they appear to have accepted the teachings of Eleazar ben Simon, who apparently preached the imminence of a Jewish theocratic state.

The rebellion that the Sicarii, the Zealots, and other groups sought to ignite broke out in 66. In that same year, Jerusalem fell into the hands of rebels who set up a government ruled by a moderate priestly aristocracy. By mid-68, however, the Zealots and their allies managed to take control of the city and initiated a reign of holy terror in which they killed thousands of aristocrats. The Zealot victory did not last long. The Romans began new siege operations in mid-April 70 and retook the city in early September, destroying the city and its Temple in the process. The inhabitants were either killed or enslaved. Josephus estimated that more than a million died in the battle for Jerusalem, most of whom were Jews. That number seems to be wildly inaccurate, but undoubtedly tens and maybe hundreds of thousands lost their lives during those four frantic months.

Meanwhile, the Sicarii, who had occupied the fortress of Masada in 66, held out against the Romans until finally, with all hope of a successful resistance gone, they committed self-martyrdom. At some unknown time, either before or after the fall of Masada in 73, other Sicarii were attempting, with the same tactics employed in Judea, to incite religious rebellion within the sizeable Jewish populations of Alexandria (in Egypt) and Cyrene (in present-day Libya), but were repressed by the Jewish and Roman authorities. Allegedly, the Jewish council in Alexandria handed over to the Romans more than 600 Sicarii, who were tortured to death.

The Assassins: Shi'a Holy Terrorists or Political Murderers?

The best-known terrorist community of the Middle Ages loaned its nickname to all killers who seek out and slay targeted victims. "Assassins," a name bestowed on them by their opponents, derives from the Arabic *hashishiyya* (users of hashish), a derogatory term that, in the context of late eleventh-century Egypt, where the sect arose, probably meant "urban-slum lowlifes." Correctly, they were Ismaili Nizaris, a sect of Shi'a Islam that sprang up in 1094 in opposition to the Fatimid caliph al-Mustali, the religious-political leader of an opposing Shi'a sect. Because the Nizaris soon produced bands of killers who assassinated enemies holding opposing religious beliefs—Sunni Muslims, members of other branches of Shi'a Islam, and Christians—and because these attacks were sometimes suicidal, carried out by men known as *fidayeen* (they who sacrifice themselves), many commentators have concluded that the Assassins were religious terrorists. But were they? Complicating the issue is the fact that we lack sufficient evidence from medieval Nizari sources. Most of what we know or think we know about the Assassins comes from the pens of their opponents.

Despite this paucity of evidence, one thing is clear: what began as a dynastic schism became a struggle waged by a terrorist ministate. The Nizaris had two political-military bases, the cliff-top fortress of Alamut in Iran and the mountain fortress of Masyaf in Syria. From these two bases, Nizari leaders dispatched their killers. The Assassins' most eminent Sunni Muslim victim was the Abbasid caliph al-Mustarshid in 1135, and their most famous Frankish Christian victim was Conrad de Montferrat, the elected, uncrowned king of the Latin Kingdom of Jerusalem. Their best-known near miss was Saladin, the sultan of Egypt and Syria, against whom they made several unsuccessful attacks. There is good reason to conclude that the murders of al-Mustarshid and Montferrat were political killings carried out by Assassins in the pay of others. The attempts on Saladin's life also seem motivated largely by the political concerns of the Syrian Nizaris and their leader. The motives behind other assassinations and attempted murders are far more ambiguous. After all, religious animosities ran deep. Given the fog of insufficient evidence, the best that we can say is that there is no compelling reason to categorically label the Assassins "holy terrorists" or to unequivocally deny them that distinction. If pushed to choose one or the other, we would say that yes, religious zeal drove some but not all Assassin attacks.

Sikh Terrorism: In Search of a Land of the Pure

On October 31, 1984, two of Prime Minister Indira Gandhi's elite Sikh bodyguards assassinated her and died for their effort. Why? In June of 1984, the prime minister had launched Operation Blue Star to drive a group of armed rebels out of Amritsar's Golden Temple, the religious heart of Sikhism. This small but formidable faction of Sikh extremists, led by Jarnail Singh Bhindranwale, who died in the course of the fighting, maintained that the Sikh religion and its culture were under attack by India's Hindu majority. Consequently, Bhindranwale and his followers had initiated a campaign of assassination and other terrorist acts in an effort to usher in an independent nation, Khalistan (Land of the Pure).

According to official reports, 492 militants and bystanders were killed in the assault. In the weeks that followed, some Sikh military units mutinied, and thousands of Sikh men throughout India were rounded up, with many of them tortured. Shortly thereafter, in response to the prime minister's assassination, anti-Sikh riots broke out throughout India, with the epicenter at Delhi, where about 2,000 Sikhs died at the hands of mobs. Months later, in June 1985, a Canadian Sikh group blew Air India Flight 182 out of the sky, killing all 392 aboard. Murderous tensions thereafter abated, but some Sikhs continue to commemorate Bhindranwale and Indira Gandhi's two killers as martyrs, and the dream of Khalistan remains alive both in India and among Sikh diaspora communities around the world.

Sikh terrorism of this sort and celebration of it comprise a fairly recent phenomenon. As noted above, in 1699, Guru Gobind Singh institutionalized a community of warriors known as the Khalsa and taught the principle of the dharam yudh, or war in defense of righteousness. Before his own death in 1708, Guru Gobind Singh's Sikh soldiers fought thirteen major battles against both Mughal forces and the armies of neighboring Hindu rajas. Two of his four sons were killed in battle, and the other two were captured, tortured, and buried alive. Although just war theory underlies dharam yudh, the wars waged by the Khalsa in Guru Gobind Singh's day (and well beyond) would appear to be full-scale holy wars inasmuch as they were in defense of a religious community and its unique faith and culture, a mode of holy war we shall study in Chapter 3.

Following the Second Anglo-Sikh War (1848–49), which resulted in a total victory by the British East India Company, the collapse of the Sikh Empire, and the transformation of the Punjab into Britain's North-West Frontier in India, the Sikhs lacked the wherewithal to wage righteous wars on a large scale. This remained the case when the Republic of India emerged in 1947. Given this state of affairs, extremist Sikh dissidents seeking a homeland turned to terrorism.

The Khalistan movement began in the late 1970s. Launched initially by expatriate Sikhs in the United States, by the 1980s, it had spun off several terrorist groups in India and abroad, with most of the movement's funding coming from Sikhs living outside of India. In 1986, the Khalistan Liberation Front (KLF) emerged in the wake of the events of 1984 and was responsible for several bombings of Indian military targets. On June 17, 1991, KLF militants attacked two trains in the Punjab, killing anywhere from 80 to 126 passengers. In the following years, the KLF claimed responsibility for a few targeted killings, but its activities had been largely blunted by the government following the Punjab train massacre. Moreover, the vast majority of Sikhs do not support it. Finally, in what must be a classic example of delayed reaction, in December 2018, the Ministry of Home Affairs declared the Khalistan Liberation Force to be a banned organization.

Are these terrorist actions by persons seeking an independent Khalistan the tactics of holy warriors, or are they the desperate acts of political revolutionaries? They certainly are not dharam yudh.

Holy War beyond Holy Terrorism

It would be easy to multiply many times over our list of terrorist movements, both large and small, that have been or are driven by religious ideologies, and we shall see some additional ones in the chapters and Epilogue that follow. But now it remains for us to consider the various faces, or forms, of holy war.

A Seventeenth-Century Attempt to Catalog the Types of Holy War

In 1622–23, while much of continental Europe was embroiled in the Thirty Years' War (1618–48), the most destructive of its many wars of religion, and a number of Catholic states were simultaneously engaged in on-again, off-again military operations against the Ottoman Empire, Sir Francis Bacon, an English statesman, jurist, essayist, and philosopher, penned *An Advertisement Touching a Holy War*. Presented as a dialogue among five characters who represent a variety of opinions on holy war, it stands as Bacon's subtle but telling attack on religious fanaticism. The implied message is that the only holy war worth waging is a cultural holy war against Christian extremists of every stripe—Catholics and Protestants alike. Is it any wonder that the work was published only after Bacon's death in 1626?

In the midst of this back-and-forth discussion, one of the five, Zebedaeus, "a Romish Catholic Zelant [Zealot]," lists the five causes, or types, of holy war: (1) a war on infidels for the purpose of propagating the faith; (2) a war for the recovery of lands that had once been Christian; (3) a war to liberate enslaved Christians; (4) a war to recover polluted holy sites; and (5) a war to punish the blasphemies of infidels and to wreak vengeance on their cruelties.[9] This catalog made sense within the context of early seventeenth-century Western Europe, but

---

9. Francis Bacon, *An Advertisement Touching a Holy War*, with an introduction, notes, and interpretive essay by Laurence Lampert (Prospect Heights, IL: Waveland Press, 2000), 29.

it fails to encompass the types of holy war that have arisen throughout the history of humankind.

The Types of Holy War from a World History Perspective

Taking a world history perspective, we propose a catalog of four that encompasses Zebedaeus's list but also considers holy war more broadly. We should note immediately that none of these four categories is exclusive; each overlaps in some way with one or more of the other forms of holy war, and each also has its secular stimuli because all wars, holy wars included, are complex phenomena that are the consequences of multiple factors. Moreover, the four categories that we offer are simply convenient models and little more. No model or theory should be understood as the definitive and last word on what it purports to describe. Put another way, no model or theory should be an intellectual straitjacket.

All of this duly noted, the four forms of holy war that we offer for consideration are: (1) ritualistic sacred wars; (2) holy wars of conquest in the name of a deity; (3) holy wars in defense of sacred space, holy objects, the faith, or believers; and (4) millenarian holy wars. Added to these four broad categories of wars waged by human holy warriors in historic times are wars that deities and deified heroes have waged against cosmic evil forces in mythic time.

Chapter 1 begins our investigation of holy wars not in historical space and time but in the world of the supernatural as we consider cosmic holy wars waged by deities, spirits, and demigods against evil as well as metaphorical holy wars waged by humans against evil. But it does not end there. Returning us to Earth and physical reality, the chapter then focuses on ritual holy wars, the least common and probably least lethal form of sanctified violence—at least so far as total body count is concerned. In many respects, ritual holy war is a rare species unto itself and deservedly is linked with cosmic holy war. Chapter 2 considers wars of conquest in the name of a deity, a form of holy war for which we have the oldest extant evidence. This does not mean it is the most ancient type of holy war; it is simply the one for which we have the earliest graphic and written evidence. Chapter 3 studies holy war waged in defense of sacred space, sacred items, a religious cult or faith, or coreligionists. Many will argue that this is the most common form of holy war, and that might be true. But millenarian holy wars, the subject of Chapter 4, might well have outnumbered holy wars of defense across the ages. If not, they certainly have proven to be some of history's most destructive wars. Violence engendered by expectation of the End Times is a powerful force.

Chapter 1

Holy Wars in Mythic Time, Holy Wars as Metaphor, Holy Wars as Ritual

1.1. Durga on her lion mount battles Mahishasura. A seventh- or early eighth-century relief, *Mahishasuramardini Mandapa (Crusher of Mahishasura Hall)*, Mamallapuram, Tamil Nadu, India.

Religious rituals serve many purposes. Ablution before prayer signifies the purity that a Muslim or upper-caste Hindu brings to the act of worship, just as a Japanese worshipper rinses mouth and hands before approaching a Shinto temple. On another level, some rituals are the means by which an entire religious community commemorates or replicates a moment in sacred history. India's joyful spring festival of Holi, which celebrates love, devotion, and the triumph of virtue over evil, memorializes a number of legends regarding various beneficent actions performed by one god or another. In North India the festival celebrates Vishnu's preservation of his devotee Prahlada from a burning pyre onto which Holika, a female demon, had lured him and which Vishnu then used to destroy her. On the eve of Holi, worshippers burn an effigy of Holika in a bonfire.

Almost all rituals that replicate in symbolic fashion the actions of a deity or spirit are innocuous and many are fun. On Holi people toss colored water and

1

powders on one another as a means of affirming love and life, thereby painting the town red, yellow, blue, purple, pink, and green—each color a symbol of a specific life force that wards off evil.

All of that is interesting. But are myths and the rituals that commemorate them relevant to this book? Our reply is simple: religious myths have at times served as stimuli or paradigms for holy wars waged on Earth, and they deserve a brief survey. The same is true for war used as a metaphor for spiritual struggle. Calls for taking up arms against a spiritual threat have, at times, been taken all too literally and have become rallying cries for physical combat against what is perceived to be an existential threat. For that reason, we shall first consider mythic holy wars, then look briefly at holy war as metaphor, and finally consider a few examples of ritual holy wars in which human blood has been spilled.

Mythic Time

Mythic time is not time within once-upon-a-time fables; it is supernatural time. Moreover, a myth in this sense is not a lie or a piece of deliberate fiction. It is a story containing a hallowed principle or religious truth. Because that principle or truth is of prime importance, the culture embracing it has created, preserved, and transmitted its myth across generations. In this sense, mythology is theology.

Consider the stories in the Bible's Book of Genesis, such as the account of the Deluge and Noah. Most devout Jews and Christians do not accept these tales as absolutely accurate accounts of historical events; rather, they view them as a means, crafted in a prescientific age, to convey divinely inspired religious truths. The physical impossibility of placing all of Earth's animals into a single ark is irrelevant. Equally irrelevant, so far as the core religious ideas are concerned, is the fact that many of these stories were adapted from tales already circulating throughout the ancient Near East. Using those stories, the authors of Genesis and other books within the Hebrew Bible reworked them to reflect their view of the special relationship that the God of Israel has with humanity at large and particularly with his Chosen People.

Storm Gods of the Ancient Near East: Cosmic Battles and Metaphorical Conquests

The ancient Near East, which we shall study in greater detail in Chapter 2, was a complex cluster of cultures in an area extending from Egypt to Iran. Chronologically, its origins lie in predynastic Egypt and Sumerian Mesopotamia (present-day southern Iraq) around 3500 B.C.E., and a convenient end point is the rise of the Persian Achaemenid Empire around 550 B.C.E. Despite the vastness of the region, networks of roads and waterways allowed merchants and armies to travel from end to end, resulting in tremendous cultural interchange and cross-fertilization over these three thousand years.

One deity whom many shared was a storm god who battled evil forces. As a divine being who brought life-giving rains, this god was worshiped as the beneficent deity of agriculture and fertility. But he also could bring life-depriving storms and floods and as such was a fierce and fearsome god of war.

The origin of this deity can likely be traced to the lands of the eastern Mediterranean, where Baal (the Lord) held prominence as the god of storms. He was not the head of the pantheon; El, the creator god, played that role. Baal's centrality lay in the fact that he was the champion of cosmic order by virtue of his mastery over chaotic drought, which was represented by Mot, the god of death. Like the Mesopotamian Adad (with whom Baal became interchangeable), he was associated with a bull, and thunderbolts were his weapon.

The fact that so many texts in the Hebrew Bible vehemently condemn the worship of Baal is testimony to the threat his cult represented to those who promoted the exclusive worship of the God of Israel, Yahweh, himself a god of storms. In Canaanite texts dating roughly from

1.2. Adad, Mesopotamian god of storms. *The Stele of Adad.* This basalt stele (upright stone monument) was discovered in northern Syria, which was under the control of the Neo-Assyrian Empire when it was created during the reign of Tiglath-Pileser III (r. ca. 744–727 B.C.E.), one of the ancient Near East's great conquerors. It depicts Adad, who holds thunderbolts in his left hand and is in the act of hurling another with his right hand. Adad, who in some texts is referred to as "radiant bull," is associated with the bull, which is a symbol of both his awesome power and the roar of thunder. The starred sun disk above his head associates Adad with Shamash, the solar deity, who holds power over darkness and evil.

the fifteenth to thirteenth centuries B.C.E., Baal defeats Lothan, a seven-headed serpent from the sea. In the Hebrew Bible, a psalmist sings of Yahweh's splitting the sea in two and smashing the heads of the monsters on the waters as a prelude to creation. Yahweh also crushes the multiple heads of Leviathan (a variant of Lothan), thereby releasing springs and brooks.[1] Moreover, the prophet Isaiah, probably writing in the late sixth century B.C.E., foretells the day when Yahweh will emerge from his dwelling place to punish Earth's guilty. On that day, "Yahweh will punish / with his unyielding sword, massive and strong / Leviathan the fleeing serpent, / Leviathan the coiling serpent; he will kill the dragon that lives in the sea."[2] Yahweh's slaying of Leviathan was transformed from a cosmic battle sung by a psalmist to a prophetic metaphor.

Hinduism's Cosmic Wars

India is home to several of history's most spiritually rich religions. Yet when speaking of religion in India, one immediately thinks not of Buddhism, Sikhism, or Jainism, but of Hinduism. Hinduism is not a discrete religion unto itself, namely a single belief system with a clearly delineated and limited body of doctrines, ceremonies, rules, and scriptures. Rather, it is a complex family of religious beliefs, spiritual traditions, rituals, and sacred texts with which the vast majority of the Hindu, or Indian, people identify in one form or another. Among Hinduism's many deities and spirits, quite a few are warriors battling evil.

Indra's Victory over Vritra

India's earliest known god of rain, storms, and war is Indra. With the collapse of the Indus civilization—which rose, flourished, declined, and vanished between roughly 3300 and 1300 B.C.E. in an area that today encompasses most of Pakistan and northwestern India—a people known as the Aryans (nobles) emerged as the dominant force in northern India. The Aryans, who probably began migrating into the region around 1500, were a warlike people, and their chief god was Indra, "the mighty one." Although he later would be demoted in the Hindu pantheon, Indra reigned supreme in the Aryans' *Rigveda* (*Verses of Knowledge*), the first and most basic body of Hindu sacred literature. Transmitted orally until they were set down in writing around 600 B.C.E., more than one-fourth of the *Rigveda's* 1,028 hymns sing the praises of Indra.

---

1. Psalms, 74:13–17.
2. Isaiah, 27:1 (New Jerusalem Bible, 1990), 1228.

One of its most famous hymns recounts Indra's victory over Vritra, an evil demon-dragon that has locked up all water (shades of Leviathan!). Taking in his hand a heavenly bolt of thunder, Indra, "the many-slaying hero," who was also known as *Maghavan* (Lord Bountiful), kills the dragon, letting loose "the channels of the mountain torrents" and also "giving life to sun and dawn, and heaven" as well as Earth. Thus, "Indra is king of all that moves and moves not."[3]

Durga Defeats the Demon of Disguises

Later, a more fully developed Hindu tradition created a new myth of a cosmic battle between the forces of good and evil—the heavenly battle between the warrior goddess Durga (the Invincible) and Mahishasura (Buffalo Demon). The *asuras* (demons) wage a timeless struggle against the *devas* (deities), and the most malevolent of all is Mahishasura, noted for his shape-shifting, which enables him to use deception as a tool for evil. A consummate liar, he is ignorance and chaos disguised as knowledge and order. When his attacks threaten the tripartite world of Heaven, Earth, and Hell, the gods Vishnu, Shiva, and Brahma combine their powers to create an ultimate divine force embodied in the warrior goddess Durga. Riding forth on her lion and carrying all of the gods' mighty weapons, she advances to save the universe from Mahishasura. Because she is a "mere woman," he does not fear her. Fatal mistake. For fifteen days she battles him as he continuously changes forms. When finally he takes on the appearance of a buffalo, she runs him through with Shiva's trident and decapitates him. As the savior of the gods and humanity, she is now the protective Mother Goddess of all creation, gods and humans alike. One of the grandest annual festivals in India, the Durga Puja, ritualizes the restoration of Dharma, or cosmic right order.

Christian and Zoroastrian Victors over Evil

Michael the Archangel, God's Heavenly Warrior

Christianity also has a myth of victory over cosmic evil led by a heavenly warrior. The Hebrew Bible's Book of Daniel ascribes a vision of the End Times to Daniel, a Jew in exile in Babylon during the sixth century B.C.E. Internal evidence, however, allows us to date the book to the period 167–164 B.C.E., a time of

---

3. All quotations are from *The Rig Veda: An Anthology of One Hundred and Eight Hymns Selected, Translated, and Annotated*, trans. Wendy Doniger O'Flaherty (Harmondsworth, UK: Penguin, 1981), 160–62.

tremendous religious, political, and cultural upheaval in and around Jerusalem, as Chapter 3 will demonstrate.

In the revelation, Daniel is promised that Michael, a great prince, will rise up to defend the Jews against the "kings of the Persians."[4] Michael re-appears in the Christian New Tes-tament's Book of Revelation (also known as the Book of the Apoca-lypse), which purports to be a series of visions of the End Times conveyed to a Christian named John. But now Michael is an angel who leads the heavenly host against the legions of the Devil, whom he defeats and hurls to Earth. Moreover, the Epistle of Jude provides Michael's rank: he is an arch-angel.[5] This prince-turned-archangel became one of the preeminent warrior saints throughout Christendom.

In Chapter 3, we shall investigate further the Christian belief in and ven-eration of warrior saints, and in Chapter 4, we will return to the Book of Dan-iel, the Book of Revelation, and Judaic-Christian concepts of apocalyptic bat-

1.3. Michael the Archangel. Normally shown with a sword, Michael in this seventeenth-century Coptic (Egyptian) Christian repre-sentation wields a lance, which he thrusts into the mouth of the Devil.

tles and the End Times, which have profoundly influenced the rise and course of multiple holy wars over more than two thousand years of history.

Zoroastrianism's Cosmic Struggle against Evil

The notion of Michael the Archangel as the heavenly champion who fights the Devil and, more significantly, the Christian doctrine of the End of Time and the Last Judgment appear to have been influenced by Zoroastrianism, an Ira-nian faith pronounced by the prophet Zarathustra (later called Zoroaster by the Greeks), who might have lived as early as the eighteenth century B.C.E.

The religion, which today lives among the Parsis (Persians) of India and elsewhere, is based on the cosmic struggle between the all-good creator

---

4. Daniel, 10:13, and 21; 12:1.
5. Revelation, 12:7–9; Epistle of Jude, 9.

divinity Ahura Mazda (Lord Wisdom) and the evil Angra Mainyu (Destructive Spirit). These supernatural beings, who later became known respectively as Ohrmazd and Ahriman, personify two principles. One is *asha*, which translates to "order" but means much more, specifically goodness, holiness, truth, and righteousness. The other is *drug*, which translates to "chaos" and implies all that is opposite asha. In the course of this struggle, Ahura Mazda created, as an emanation of himself, Spenta Mainyu (Holy Spirit), who battles the Liar, Angra Mainyu. Spenta Mainyu is aided in this struggle by other divine beings as well as human devotees who, through their combined good thoughts, good words, and good deeds, will eventually defeat all manifestations of evil and annihilate all demons. Victory in this spiritual battle, which is equally fought on the celestial and terrestrial planes, will result in the renovation and cleansing of the universe and in the eternal redemption of all humans. Even grave sinners will be redeemed through a purgation in Hell and the ordeal of molten metal. The only being who will not escape Hell is Angra Mainyu/ Ahriman, who will be shut in it forever.

Buddhism

Victory over evil is a motif found in every religion based on a moral code. This includes a religion that arose in India in the fifth century B.C.E. and deviated from the main currents of Hindu belief and practice by rejecting the Vedas as scripture and the caste system. At the same time, it accepted other basic Hindu beliefs, the most important being reincarnation, the unreality of the physical world, and the imperative need to escape rebirth and enter the Reality of Nirvana. It was Buddhism.

1.4. Manjushri. This fifteenth-century Chinese sculpture depicts the bodhisattva seated on a lotus, the Buddhist symbol of Enlightenment and release from rebirth. In his primary right hand he holds his characteristic sword. His primary left hand holds a lotus, on which rests the Perfection of Wisdom Sutra (scripture). He has the Buddha's elongated earlobes and forehead protuberance (*urna*), a third eye that allows vision beyond the physical world. His jewelry, however, marks him as a princely bodhisattva and not the Buddha.

In its original form, Buddhism was a moral movement that lacked a complex cosmology, a theology, and formal rituals, and it also considered irrelevant the question of whether or not gods exist. In time, however, it became a multi-branched religion with elaborate cosmologies, abstract theologies, myriad myths, numerous rituals, and seemingly endless heavenly beings. It was in this form that Buddhism became the dominant religion in Central Asia (until replaced by Islam) and East Asia, even as it became a minor religion in its Indian homeland.

Siddhartha Gautama, who became the Buddha (the Enlightened One), established Buddhism's basic principles, which, as fascinating as they are, need not concern us. Moreover, source 2 focuses on Prince Siddhartha's triumph over temptations presented him by the legions and daughters of Mara, the demonic deity of desire, death, and rebirth, and we need not explore here his journey into Buddhahood. It suffices to consider briefly Buddhism's two major branches, Theravada (The Doctrine of the Elders) and Mahayana (The Great Vehicle), and a significant offshoot of the latter, Vajrayana (The Vehicle of the Thunderbolt or Diamond), which is also known variously as Tantric Buddhism and Esoteric Buddhism.

1.5. A Tibetan vajra. Thunderbolts (or diamonds) are used in tantric rituals. Today Vajrayana Buddhism is the dominant form of Buddhism in Tibet, Nepal, Bhutan, Mongolia, and parts of China.

By the first century of the Common Era, Buddhism was a widespread, multi-ethnic religion that divided along theological and ritual lines. Theravada, which centers on monasteries, emphasizes that the journey across the river of painful rebirth toward Nirvana (a perfect state of being and nonbeing) is an individual's solitary voyage under the tutelage of a monastic master who offers guidance that accords with the teachings of the Buddha. Mahayana, which became (and remains) far more popular, offers a pathway to Nirvana that is paved by the perfection of countless *bodhisattvas* (enlightened beings), who have achieved Enlightenment but out of compassion for all suffering humanity delay Buddhahood and entry into Nirvana until they can bring all humans with them. Although the numbers of bodhisattvas are beyond measure, early on, several emerged as especially popular and widely worshipped. One such heavenly being is *Manjushri*, the bodhisattva of supreme wisdom and insight, who wields a sword that cuts through ignorance.

Yamantaka, Destroyer of Death

The Mahayana tradition produced a wide number of different schools and sects, one of which was the Vajrayana, which emerged around 500 C.E. and subsequently divided into distinctive regional and cultural variations. *Vajra*, which means both "thunderbolt" and "diamond," symbolizes the speed and destructive power of lightening and the hardness and indestructability of a diamond. Through its esoteric rituals known as tantras, devotees seek to strip away the illu-

sion of dualism, which falsely causes one to think that a binary physical world is "real," and to perceive the Reality of nondualism, where there is no male or female, yes or no, good or evil, thereby becoming enlightened. Along the path to Enlightenment, Vajrayana's devotees worship a vast number of fierce spirits, deities, and bodhisattvas who battle chaos-producing ignorance. One such celestial being is the emanation of Manjushri known as *Yamantaka* (Destroyer of Death).

The statue that appears here portrays a multiheaded, six-armed, six-legged, fanged, and tongue-protruding Yamantaka sitting astride a water buffalo. A skull diadem sits atop his forward-facing head and a flaming

1.6. Yamantaka. A bronze statue from the Dali kingdom (937–1253), which was located in present-day southwestern China.

circle surrounds his heads. On his forehead is the Buddha's third eye. Vipers wind around his neck, upper arms, wrists, and ankles, and a garland of decapitated heads encircles his midriff. In his six hands he holds a vajra, a sword, an arrow, a noose, a skullcap bowl, and the remnants of a bow. The hand holding the noose makes the *tarjani mudra* (symbolic hand gesture), a warning sign that signifies caution, respect, or attention.

In this wrathful state, Manjushri/Yamantaka vanquishes Yama, the demon-god of death, thereby breaking the cycle of rebirth that prevents Enlightenment and entry into Nirvana.

Christian Metaphorical Battle

Jesus in the Gospels

Swords, often a metaphor for bloody battle, appear several times in words as-cribed to Jesus. In the Gospel of Matthew, Jesus is quoted as saying: "Do not suppose that I have come to bring peace to the earth; it is not peace I have come to bring, but a sword. For I have come to set son against father, daughter against mother, daughter-in-law against mother-in-law; a person's enemies will be the members of his own household."[6] The Gospel of Luke quotes Jesus at the Last Supper counseling his apostles that if they have no sword, to sell their cloak to purchase one.[7] The general consensus of biblical scholars is that Jesus was using poetical imagery in both instances. In the first he metaphorically describes how his difficult message will divide people, even family members. In the second in-stance, Jesus employs vivid imagery to warn the apostles that because he will be charged with rebelliousness, hard times are immediately ahead. A third mention of swords occurs at the moment of Jesus's arrest, when one of Jesus's followers draws a sword and cuts off the ear of the high priest's servant. According to Mat-thew, Jesus exclaims, "Put your sword back, for all who draw the sword will die by the sword."[8] That is unambiguous.

The Pauline Epistles

The earliest New Testament texts are letters that the Apostle Paul sent to various churches before his death around the year 65. Those letters, as well as several oth-ers that scholars largely agree were written later and ascribed to Paul's authorship, are known collectively as the Pauline Epistles. An important source for the be-liefs and practices of the early Church, the epistles contain five instances in which faithful Christians are compared with soldiers. Clearly all are metaphorical allu-sions. In the letter to the Church of Ephesus, for example, Paul or someone else (scholars divide on the issue) instructs the Ephesians to "put on the full armour of God so as to be able to resist the devil's tactics," to always carry "the shield of faith," and to "take salvation as your helmet and the sword of the Spirit, that is, the word of God."[9]

---

6. Matthew, 10:34–36 (New Jerusalem Bible, 1626). Compare Luke 12:49–53, where Jesus is quoted as claiming that he has come to bring fire and division to Earth.

7. Luke, 22:36–38 (New Jerusalem Bible, 1727).

8. Matthew, 26:51–52 (New Jerusalem Bible, 1654).

9. Ephesians, 8:10–17 (New Jerusalem Bible, 1938).

Christ Triumphant

Our last instance of cosmic warfare wrapped in metaphor is a mosaic known as *Christ Triumphant*, created for the palace chapel of the archbishop of Ravenna around the year 500. In Chapters 2 and 3 we will examine some of the consequences of the Roman Empire's adoption of Christianity as its state religion in the course of the fourth century, but this work of religious art will serve as a prelude to that study.

Here we see Jesus in the military uniform of a Roman emperor. But like a legionnaire carrying a two-meter-long *pilum* (javelin), he almost carelessly slings his thin cross over his right shoulder. He stands atop a lion and a snake, bringing to mind Psalm 91, verse 13: "You will walk upon wild beast and adder, you will trample young lions and snakes." That psalm, which promises safety to all who trust in Yahweh,

1.7. *Christ Triumphant.*

employs quite a bit of military imagery, assuring the faithful that "though a thousand fall at your side, ten thousand at your right hand, you yourself will remain unscathed."[10] The book Christ holds is a Gospel on which are emblazoned (in Latin) the words "I am the Way, the Truth, and Life" (John, 14:16).

We view this mosaic and see an allegory with a spiritual message. But did the archbishop who commissioned it, and who clearly rejoiced in the embrace of the Roman Empire, understand it as a work of religious art that solely offered a spiritual lesson? Or was it for him and others a metaphor carrying a more bellicose message?

---

10. Verse 7.

Ritualistic Sacred Wars

All holy wars are ritualized, often with blessings extended to the holy warriors, and more often than not with the fighters carrying into battle a sacred talisman, such as a cross, or wearing distinctive attire or a badge that has spiritual or religious value. Quite often these items are believed to be guarantors of victory, and they might even be credited with ensuring the invincibility of those who carry or wear them, such as the ghost shirts worn by certain Lakota Sioux in the 1890s or the holy water dispensed to warriors in the Maji Maji War in German East Africa of 1905–7. Anthropologists term these ritualistic aspects of war "the magical technologies of war." But only some wars are sacred rituals from start to finish.

Sacramental Flower Wars

The most-oft-cited example of ritualistic holy war is the Flower War, a form of combat that some Native American peoples of central Mexico waged before the arrival of the Spaniards in 1519. These special wars, which constituted only a small percentage of pre-Conquest Mexico's many wars, were mainly conducted by the Aztec Triple Alliance and its neighbors. Descriptions of the wars indicate that they were primarily religious and ritualistic, and their main reason for existence was the capture of enemy warriors for sacrifice to the ever-hungry appetites of Mexico's deities. There is also evidence of secondary motives, namely, to train young men in the skills of combat and for more seasoned warriors to display their prowess. For all of these reasons, flower-war armies were relatively small and participation was generally limited to nobles and elite fighters because each side had to consider its opponents to be worthy of sacrifice.

More so than any other form of combat, a Flower War was replete with formalities and ritual. An agreed-upon day was established for the battle, and its location was on consecrated ground that the two states set aside exclusively for such an event. Both sides also agreed on the equal number of fighters who would participate. Fighting was inaugurated by setting alight a large pyre of bark paper between the two forces and tossing into it copal, an aromatic tree resin that the Aztecs called "the blood of trees." Unlike other battles, combat did not begin with mutual barrages of missiles; rather, everything was hand-to-hand fighting, which made it all the easier for a warrior to capture an opponent and to display his prowess.

Although prisoners were the primary goal, death was a constant reality, but warriors who fell or were captured in a Flower War were regarded differently than combatants killed in regular battle. They suffered a "flowery death" that was fortunate and blissful because they went to reside in the House of the Sun.

1.8. Sacrificial combat. An illustration from Diego Durán, *History of the Indians of New Spain*. During the early March festival of Tlacaxipehualiztli (the Skinning of Men) honoring Xipe Totec, the god of agricultural renewal, more men were sacrificed than at any other festival, with a ritualized battle preceding the sacrifice of each captive. The naked captive was bound by a rope to a stone and given as armament a shield, four wooden balls, and a stick that had feathers in place of what normally would be the sharp obsidian blades of a battle ax. Note the flowers in his hair. Facing him was an elite warrior (shown here is a jaguar warrior) armed with a shield and a bladed weapon. Once the captive was sufficiently wounded, he was taken to another stone where his beating heart was cut out and offered to the sun god. His body was then flayed and the skin given to his captor, who wore it for twenty days as it decayed on his body. Removal of the rotted skin symbolized the slow but eventual germination of maize seed.

Diego Durán, a sixteenth-century Dominican missionary, provides a detailed description of a Flower War undertaken toward the end of the reign of the Aztec ruler Axayacatl (r. 1468–81). Following the Aztecs' devastating defeat in a war against Mechoacan and after the mandatory eighty-day period of mourning, Axayacatl decided that there was now all the more reason to gather sacrificial captives for the upcoming ceremonies for the stone that was revered as the Likeness of the Sun. Consequently, the Aztecs arranged for a Flower War with Tliluhquitepec. In the ensuing battle, the Aztecs and their allies lost 420 soldiers, but counted 700 prisoners. Axayacatl consoled those who had lost relatives by reminding them that the Sun wished to eat warriors on both sides. Before the Aztecs departed, nobles from Tliluhquitepec came to Axayacatl to acknowledge that both sides had acquitted themselves bravely and to wish the Aztecs good fortune on their journey home. The king replied in kind, stating that he would leave in peace until once again the gods summoned both sides to another battle.

Upon reaching Tenochtitlan, the Aztec capital, the prisoners were made to eat some earth at the feet of the statues of Huitzilopochtli, the Aztec god of the sun, war, and sacrifice and the patron of Tenochtitlan. Now known as "Sons of the Sun," they were given abundant food and drink, flowers, and tobacco. After the required period of mourning for those killed or captured in the fight, the ceremonies for the Great Sun Stone reached their climax with the sacrifice of all seven hundred captives.[11] Elsewhere Durán describes the sacrificial ritual. Each victim is bent over on a pointed stone. The chief priest then rips open his chest and tears out his heart. The heart is lifted to the Sun and then flung into the face of an idol. The bleeding body is rolled down the stairs of the temple. The person who had captured the victim retrieves the body and carries it away for ritual consumption, thus bringing the ceremony to a conclusion.[12] After the flesh is eaten, the victors carry the victims' skulls to the temple, where they are placed on a skull rack; the remainder of the skeleton is displayed in front of the captor's home as a trophy.[13]

Indigenous Ritual Warfare in North America

The confluence of religion and ritual warfare was not unique to precolonial Meso-america. The same phenomenon was continent-wide across North America both before and after contact with European settlers.

Numerous societies have intricately linked war and fertility. As far as ancient America is concerned, archeological and ethnographic evidence from the present-day Four Corners region of the United States (where Arizona, New Mexico, Utah, and Colorado meet) strongly suggests that its Pueblo peoples have for centuries, and well before the coming of the Spaniards, had a belief system that connected ritualized warfare with rainmaking. More specifically, scalps taken from fallen enemies were rainmakers. In Zuni poetry, for example, a bloody scalp trophy (usually of a Navaho) metaphorically became a "rain-filled covering." On their part, the Hopi went campaigning seasonally, after the harvest, in order to obtain fresh scalps for an abundant rainfall that would ensure the next growing season was bountiful. Upon returning to the pueblo, the scalps would be handed to the women, who ceremoniously threw them onto drawings of clouds that had been placed on the earth. In both cultures, scalp-taking as a rain-producing act had cosmological origins. Among the Hopi, the Heart-of-the-Sky god, Sotuqnangu, "who kills and renders fertile," initiated scalping.[14]

---

11. Diego Durán, *The History of the Indies of New Spain*, trans. and ed. Doris Heyden (Norman: University of Oklahoma Press, 1964), 286–90.

12. Diego Durán, *Book of the Gods and Rites* and *The Ancient Calendar*, trans. and ed. Fernando Horcasitas and Doris Heyden (Norman: University of Oklahoma Press, 1971), 91–92.

13. Durán, *Book of the Gods*, 79–80.

14. Polly Schaafsma, "Documenting Conflict in the Prehistoric Pueblo Southwest," in *North American Indigenous Warfare and Ritual Violence*, ed. Richard J. Chacon and Rubén G. Mendoza

Evidence from the eighteenth century indicates that the Lowland Cree of southern Hudson Bay in present-day Ontario and Quebec regularly waged war against neighboring Inuit settlements in order to negate the misfortunes they suffered as a consequence of what they believed to be the supernatural invasion of Inuit sorcery. A bad season of hunting or an outbreak of disease provided sufficient reason to wage a war of counter-sorcery in the spring.[15] These seasonal raids, which had a history long predating the appearance of French and British traders and settlers in the region, ended in the last decade of the eighteenth century. One explanation for this sudden cessation is the expansion of Hudson's Bay Company trading posts that kept the Cree busy as a labor force throughout spring and summer months as well as providing them with greater security and fewer times of hardship.[16]

On the other side of the continent, the Kwakiutl people of the Pacific Coast region of present-day British Columbia divided the year in half, with an everyday, warm-weather season dedicated to food gathering and social interchange and a sacred winter season, during which the spirits of death and war returned. To mark this season, secret societies conducted the Winter Ceremonial, during which slaves were sacrificed and which often precipitated their warring against and killing enemies and taking human-body trophies.[17]

The days-long Winter Ceremonial, which began in November, was a shamanistic festival in which the entire community participated as a means of communing with the spirits, thereby inviting in supernatural forces and transforming themselves into these spirits. In this season of death and the growing weakness of the sun, the ceremony affirmed life and power. As Man Eater, the spirit of death and war, around whom the entire Winter Ceremonial revolved, proclaims, "I do not destroy life, I am the life-maker."[18] But that life was only purchased by offer-

---

(Tucson: University of Arizona Press, 2007), 114–28, at 123; Polly Schaafsma, "Head Trophies and Scalping Images in Southwest Rock Art," in *The Taking and Displaying of Human Body Parts as Trophies by Amerindians*, ed. Richard J. Chacon and David H. Dye (New York: Springer, 2007), 90–123, at 107–10.

15. Charles A. Bishop and Victor P. Lytwyn, "'Barbarism and Ardour of War from the Tenderest Years': Cree-Inuit Warfare in the Hudson Bay Region," in Chacon and Mendoza, *North American Indigenous Warfare*, 30–57, at 49.

16. Ibid., 54. According to a mid-eighteenth-century traveler to Hudson Bay, some of the labor force at these company posts consisted of Inuits whom the Cree had enslaved: Henry Ellis, *A Voyage to Hudson's Bay, by the Dobbs Galley and California, in the Years 1746 and 1747* (London: H. Whitridge, 1748), 133.

17. Joan A. Lovisek, "Aboriginal Warfare on the Northwest Coast: Did the Potlatch Replace Warfare?" in Chacon and Mendoza, *North American Indigenous Warfare*, 58–73, at 69.

18. Irving Goldman, *The Mouth of Heaven: An Introduction to Kwakiutl Religious Thought* (New York: John Wiley & Sons, 1975), describes the Winter Ceremonial on pages 86–121; the quotation is at 109.

1.9. A petroglyph representing life-giving rain. Beneath the jagged-edged clouds on this petroglyph (rock carving) is a symbol of a summer thunderhead with projectile lightning bolts emerging from it. The birdlike figure to its left (our right) appears to be an early representation of the warrior spirit Knifewing, who presides over both lightning and scalping. Half-human and half-eagle, his weapons include razor-sharp flint feathers, the sky bow (rainbow), and lightning arrows. The square probably symbolizes agricultural land, and the tall figure with arms pointing down and the double-crossed figure, both of which are immediately below the thunderhead, probably symbolize maize. The three stepped glyphs within the square represent rain clouds. A second birdlike creature merges into the bottom of the larger stepped glyph. Likewise, stars (see the four-pointed star in the lower left as we view it) were associated with war and scalping. Petroglyph National Monument, New Mexico.

ing human sacrifices, slaves and slain enemies, to Man Eater. Moreover, as representatives of Man Eater, Kwakiutl warriors were eaters of men.

Archaeological evidence strongly suggests that such ritual warfare had existed for thousands of years and only significantly declined due to nineteenth-century depopulation and British attempts in the early 1860s to suppress indigenous warfare.[19]

Ritual Human Trophy Taking in South America

Since the early sixteenth century, accounts of the warriors who inhabited the Gran Chaco, a dry plain extending into portions of Paraguay, Bolivia, Argentina, and Brazil, described them as fierce takers of human trophies. This practice continued into the early or even mid-twentieth century.

Scalping raids were conducted for a variety of reasons, often in revenge for scalps taken by an enemy, and complex rituals preceded each raid to ensure supernatural protection. While engaged in the campaign, warriors were bound by certain taboos—such as not eating the heads or paws of animals that they killed

---

19. Ibid., 72.

along the way—and as they marched toward the enemy, they pierced their bodies with the bones of select animals, such as jaguars, to gain their powers.

A warrior able to secure a scalp wore it back as a trophy, and upon returning to his village participated in a celebratory scalp dance. But he also underwent a purification ceremony for having taken a human life. Although victors would sometimes ornament themselves with hair from defeated enemies as they went into battle, the scalps themselves were stored in either a bag or basket.

Because the scalp was believed to contain the soul of the defeated enemy, the victor would converse with it in order to gain spiritual advice and protection. In effect, a former enemy became a supernatural ally. The more scalps won in raids, the greater one's spiritual wisdom and protection. Upon a warrior's death, the scalps he had collected were burned over his grave in the belief that the rising smoke would carry his spirit into the otherworldly land of warriors.[20]

Asmat Headhunting

Until the 1960s, the Asmat people of West Papua, New Guinea, conducted ritualized headhunting raids to secure a departed one's safe passage to the Other Side. The Asmat believed the death of an adult occurs only through magic or murder; there is no such thing as death by natural causes for a person in the full vigor of life. Consequently, such a death required the taking of an enemy's head in order to conduct the ceremonies that appease the spirit of the departed and allow it to travel to *safan*, the spiritual land of the ancestors. As part of the ritual, carvers crafted intricate *bisj* poles believed to embody the spirit of the recently departed and replete with symbols signifying virility, fertility, physical and spiritual health, head-hunting, and transit to the other world. Raised before the communal men's house, the pole served as a reminder of the obligation to avenge the murder. Once a head was taken, it was placed in a receptacle at the base of the pole and a celebration was held, with everyone feasting on the flesh of neighboring enemies known collectively as *manoewe* (eatables). Following the feast, the poles were taken out to a sago palm grove to rot and thereby fertilize it. Once again, death renewed life.

Life out of Death in All Holy Wars

As suggested here and as the following chapters will further illustrate, life out of death is a recurring theme in all forms of holy war. In cosmic holy wars waged by deities, more often than not an evil being or force is killed and dismembered in

---

20. Marcela Mendoza, "Human Trophy Taking in the South American Gran Chaco," in Chacon and Dye, *The Taking and Displaying of Human Body Parts*, 575–90.

1.10. Asmat bisj poles.

order to bring either new life or order out of chaos. On an earthly plane, it can be the death of old deities and the emerging life of a new religious cult when a victorious holy war results in the imposition of a new god or gods on a defeated people. In pre-Columbian Mesoamerica the victory of one state or city over another, in essence the triumph of one deity over another, was represented pictorially as the defeated enemy's major temple in flames—fire that both destroys and, for an agricultural people, brings forth new life. The defense of a people's beliefs and practices, sacred spaces, cultic items, or coreligionists often results in new life. A prime example is the sacrifice of martyrs who have fallen in defense of the sacred. Out of their self-sacrifice comes eternal life for them and life and prosperity on Earth for what or whom they fought and achieved victory in death. Life out of death can also be the ushering in of a Heaven on Earth or some other form of millenarian New Age through the destruction of the old order, as we shall see in Chapter 4.

SOURCES

Source 1. The Sacred Duty of Holy War

The *Bhagavad Gita*[21]

In the Introduction's section on just war, we briefly examined the Mahābhārata, where we defined the dharmayuddha (righteous war) as a war "fought selflessly to uphold Dharma," and we defined Dharma as "the cosmic law of right conduct and proper social order." All of that is correct, but if we probe deeper, we see that

---

21. *Bhagavad Gita*, trans. Stanley Lombardo (Indianapolis, IN: Hackett Publishing, 2019), 11–12, 14–15, and 19.

the dharmayuddha is a sacred duty imposed by Dharma, the eternal order that makes possible, governs, and sustains the universe and all life within it, including that of the gods. From all eternity, Dharma has established the rules of proper divine, human, and animal behavior.

One of the most unambiguous articulations of how Dharma governs human actions in regard to the waging of sanctified war appears in a spiritual text known as the Bhagavad Gita (Song of the Blessed Lord) that appears within the Mahābhārata. The epic itself centers on the complicated story of the mythic Kurukshetra War between two rival families, the Kauravas and Pandavas, both of which belonged to the Bharata clan.

The epic has roots in ancient oral traditions but was essentially constructed as a complex but coherent whole between about 200 B.C.E. and the beginning of the Common Era. But this was not the final text. Revisions and alternate versions continued to issue forth until a definitive Sanskrit text was set down sometime between about 300 and 450. During that long period of composition, some author or authors crafted the Bhagavad Gita as a means of explaining why the brutalities of war (and the epic is gruesomely graphic in its depiction of inhumane violence) are cosmically necessary, spiritually liberating, and blessed.

In the Gita, the all-powerful god Vishnu, who embodies within himself the three divine qualities of Creation, Preservation, and Destruction, explains the cosmic necessity of war and how a member of the Kshatriya caste, the class of princes and warriors, can serve as an agent of cosmic order by selflessly waging war. "Selflessly" means without any thought or desire whatsoever as to the consequences of his actions. He must not even seek spiritual merit.

The Gita opens on the plain of Kurukshetra as two massive armies—one led by the five Pandava brothers, the other by their cousins, the one hundred Kaurava brothers—prepare for mortal combat. Suddenly the Pandava family's greatest warrior, Arjuna, enters the space between the opposing forces, driven there by his charioteer, Krishna, an avatar (incarnation) of Vishnu. Arjuna, the half-divine son of Queen Kunti and Indra, has been avidly preparing for this conflict. Suddenly, however, upon seeing his relatives, former comrades, and teachers in the opposite battle lines, he shrinks in horror at the thought of the coming battle, for he now cannot see what good will come of his killing kinsmen and friends. A battle of this sort can, in his eyes, only be evil. It now becomes Krishna's task to educate Arjuna on certain timeless truths and to spur him into holy action.

Before reading the excerpts below, we should understand that the Gita is holy scripture, and more than that it is the most venerated of all of the sacred texts of India. Moreover, as is true for all scripture, it has been variously interpreted.

Mohandas Gandhi, the twentieth-century apostle of nonviolence, embraced its message of selflessness and read it as an allegory that calls for a spiritual war with our baser instincts. After you read these excerpts, see if you agree with him.

Questions for Consideration

Krishna presents several reasons why Arjuna must fight. What are they? To recapitulate, if Arjuna is to become a holy warrior, what must he do? Is this battle that Krishna tells Arjuna to join a holy war? If so, why? If not, what is it?

◆◆◆◆◆

Chapter 2

And the Lord[22] said:
"You mourn those who should not be mourned,
and yet speak as if you were wise.
But those who truly are wise mourn
neither the living nor the dead.

Never have I not existed,
nor have you ever not existed,
neither have any of these lords.
Nor will we ever cease to exist . . .

Know that what pervades the cosmos
is in fact indestructible,
No one is able to destroy
this imperishable being.[23]

Only the bodies of the eternal,
indestructible, embodied Self
are said to die, to come to an end.
Therefore, Arjuna, join battle!

---

22. Krishna/Vishnu.

23. *Atman*, the spark of Brahman, the Universal Soul and Ultimate Reality (or cosmic divine energy). All living creation, including gods, animals, and plants, have atman. Upon death, one's atman migrates to a different body. Where it inhabits another life form depends on *karma*, the fruit of one's actions in the previous incarnation. This transmigration of a soul (the real Self as opposed to the false self of ego) is known as *samsara*, and it is something to be escaped because of the inescapable pain of existence. Escape into Brahman, thereby returning an atman to the Universal Soul, is Nirvana, the goal behind all action.

Whoever thinks this embodied Self
is either the slayer or the slain
simply has not comprehended
that it neither slays nor is slain. . . .

Perceiving your own proper duty,
you should not tremble or waver.
Nothing is nobler than rightful war
for those in the warrior class. . . .

If, however, you should refuse
to fight in this rightful battle,
shunning duty and glory both,
you will incur iniquity. . . .

Slaughtered, you will attain heaven.
Victorious, you will enjoy earth.
Therefore rise up, son of Kunti,
Resolved now to enter battle! . . .

Treating pleasure and pain the same,
gain and loss, victory and defeat,
join battle and engage in war!
Doing so you will incur no guilt. . . .

The person who casts off desires,
who acts free from craving and lust,
indifferent to "I, my, me,"
that person will arrive at peace.

This is the divine, Arjuna.
Attain this, free of delusion,
firm even at the hour of death,
and in *Brahman* reach *nirvana*."

Source 2. The Buddha-to-be Defeats Mara

According to the received biography of the Buddha, as Prince Siddhartha Gautama sat meditating under a sacred pipal tree and was on the cusp of Enlightenment, the demonic Mara, god of death and the desires that lead to rebirth, made an all-out assault on the *Bhagavathi* (Blessed One) in order to deflect him from his path. Accounts vary, but most include a series of attacks by Mara upon

Siddhartha. The images below, both created by Theravada Buddhists, depict two of Mara's attempts to defeat the Buddha-to-be. The first, a nineteenth-century lithograph print from the island nation of Sri Lanka (formerly Ceylon), depicts the attack on Siddhartha by Mara's army of the tenfold vices, vices such as sloth, false glory, and ignorance. Within the Theravada tradition, Mara challenged Siddhartha's right to achieve Enlightenment, whereupon the prince called upon Earth to bear witness to his deeds. At that moment, the giant elephant, Girimehkala, who carried Mara, knelt down in reverence to Siddhartha. In a second challenge (and accounts vary as to the sequence of events), Mara sent his three daughters, Tanha (desire), Arati (discontentment), and Raga (attachment and passion), to tempt the *Shakyamuni* (Sage of the Shakya clan). They also failed. Our second image, a twentieth-century painting from a temple in Thailand, depicts that temptation.

It is tempting to claim that the Gospel accounts of Satan's temptation of Jesus in the wilderness (Matthew, 4:1–11; Mark, 1:12–13; Luke, 4:1–13) can be traced back to this story of Mara's challenging the Buddha, but no solid evidence exists to support the theory. Likewise, the fourth-century leader of the Egyptian Church, Saint Athanasius of Alexandria, composed an account of the life and miracles of Saint Anthony of the Desert, in which he related how the Devil unsuccessfully assaulted the holy man with apparitions of monsters and tempted him with visions of wanton women. Again, there is no unambiguous connection between these stories and that surrounding the Buddha and Mara. But an absence of evidence is not evidence of absence.

Questions for Consideration

Where is Mara in our first image? How has the artist made it possible for us to recognize him, and what is the artist's message? What is the message behind the many demons depicted here and the nature of their assault? Who or what are those seven figures in the upper right of the print? What is the message here? Compare the Buddha-to-be with all that is happening around him. What is the message? In the second image, Siddhartha performs the *abhaya* (fear not) mudra with his right hand. How does it relate to the entire composition? In the painting, we see not a Buddha-to-be but the Buddha. This is a deviation from the story. So what is the artist's message? How do these two works of art, which are apparently so different, relate to one another? Does either or do both symbolize life emerging from death? If so, how so?

1.11. Mara and his demons attack Siddhartha.

1.12. Mara's daughters tempt the Buddha.

Source 3. Ritual Warfare Set in Stone

Questions for Consideration

In addressing these questions, refer back to information provided in the caption for illustration 1.9 (p. 16). Who or what is the large figure located in the center of this photo? What is that strange contraption that juts out of its head? Consider the bird in the upper right corner as we face the rock. What does it symbolize? Consider the "horned" being in the lower right corner of the photo and the pouch-like symbol that is located in the middle of the three creatures. What might it be and what relationship might it have with these three beings? Why is it reasonable to infer that this carving was created later than the one that we studied earlier?

1.13. Rock art at Petroglyph National Monument.

Source 4. An Anthropologist Describes Kwakiutl Warfare

Franz Boas, *Kwakiutl Ethnography*[24]

Franz Boas (1858–1942), widely recognized as "the father of modern anthropology," devoted a lifetime to attacking in detail the then-fashionable theories of race and cultural evolution that placed the Caucasian "race" and Western European cultures at the apex of human development. His work went far in undermining

---

24. Franz Boas, *Kwakiutl Ethnography*, ed. Helen Codere (Chicago: University of Chicago Press, 1966), 109–10.

the fundamental assumptions that propped up white supremacy and the early twentieth-century eugenics movement. A passionate advocate of cultural relativism, Boas also dedicated years of study to the indigenous peoples of the Pacific Northwest coast, especially the Kwakiutl of the Fort Rupert region of British Columbia.

Beginning in the late nineteenth century, he spent a total of twenty-eight and one-half months with this First Nation and committed many more years to working on the Kwakiutl in other venues. The result was numerous publications about its language, ways of life, and beliefs. Upon his death, he left an unfinished manuscript, *Kwakiutl Ethnography*, which finally was edited and published in 1966. It is from the section titled "War" that we have chosen our text.

Questions for Consideration

Carefully consider the meanings behind each of the rituals that preceded a large war expedition. Were they more than just symbols? If so, what were their individual and collective purposes? Next, does this form of warfare appear to have been inspired by religious or spiritual considerations? Or was it just the practice of magic in the service of aimless killings used to assuage grief and to honor the dead? Compare the reasoning behind Kwakiutl warfare as described here with that practiced by the Asmat people. Does either qualify as ritual holy war?

◆◆◆◆◆

War

The reason that led to warfare was generally the murder or even accidental death of a member of a tribe. The size of the war party depended entirely upon the social importance of the person whose death was involved or upon the depth of feeling of a relative of high standing. It would be entirely wrong to call this "revenge," because it was quite immaterial whom the war party might attack and kill. The feeling underlying the desire to kill had a double origin.

The loss of a relative was felt as an insult to one's dignity, as a cause of shame and sorrow. The reaction to this feeling was the wish to make someone else, no matter who, feel sorrow and shame at least equal to one's own. A typical case was that of a family consisting of a husband, wife, and daughter who had been drowned. Probably their canoe had capsized. Then the woman's brother, a man of high rank, called his tribe together and asked them, "Who shall wail? I or someone else?"

Another feeling prompting retaliation was the desire to do honor to the deceased. A person killed became the "pillow" of the first victim. He was "pulled under" him or was "cause or means of lying face down." The survivor might also sacrifice himself and commit suicide to become the "pillow" of the deceased. This was not called "war," unless a whole war party was organized to do honor to an important person who had been killed. . . .

A larger war expedition was preceded by a number of rituals. The men who went on the war expedition, both warriors and crews, had to purify themselves for four days and nights. The description of one ritual was given as follows: They were called into the chief's house, where a pole was set up on the floor. Each warrior carried one or more hemlock wreaths, representing wreaths of slain enemies, which he put on the pole with appropriate words, referring to the winter ceremonial positions:[25] "This is one head hung on the post as a keeper of my promise. Very hungry for men is this great raven";[26] or "I will sit in front of the steersman of your war canoe, Chief. I am not afraid of this new world. This is one head obtained in war. I put it around this pole as keeper of my promise." Another might have said, "I want to eat men, really hungry for men is this cannibal." Finally, the chief put two wreaths around the pole, uttered his cry as a fool dancer,[27] and said, "These are my heads which I pull under my sister and my niece."

Next, the men of lower rank who were not warriors offered themselves individually as members of the crews.

Before the warriors started, neckrings made of preserved bottle kelp were prepared. They selected a piece, preferably next to the end of the bladder and blew it up so that it was filled with their breath. The end into which they had blown was twisted so that it was air-tight, and the bladder end was crumpled and twisted until the body of the tube was taut. Then a ring was made by tying the ends together.

When the men were taking their seats, they wore these neckrings. As soon as they were seated, a man who stood in front of the leader's house shouted, "wai," while someone in the house or he himself, began to beat fast time. At this signal, the women rushed out of the houses, their faces blackened, and ran into the water where the canoes lay. The men threw their neckrings over the necks of their wives, and the women ran back into their houses. . . .

---

25. Poles had supernatural powers and meaning and figured prominently in the Winter Ceremonial and in other aspects of Kwakiutl life and belief. One of the major meanings of the Winter Ceremonial pole was the bringing of wealth—the wealth of slain enemies. The Kwakiutl apparently chose hemlock for these wreaths because hemlock eradicates human scent, and the slain were now spirits.

26. The Great Raven is one of Man Eater's attendants.

27. Fool dancers (*nutlmatl*) played an important role in the Winter Ceremonial. Acting in destructive and obscene ways, they represented the wildness, even madness of war. They provided recompense for their destructiveness and foul behavior by giving out property, an act that symbolized a return to good order through reverse action.

While the warriors are away, these rings were decorated with red cedar bark and bird's down and hung over the bed of the warrior's wife. The bursting of a ring was believed to show that the man whose breath it contained was killed; its gradual collapse, that he was wounded.

The Indians avoided open warfare but endeavored to surprise the helpless or unsuspecting and unarmed victim. In an entirely unprovoked attack upon the people of the southern part of Vancouver Island, waged to obtain a "pillow" for some drowned Kwakiutl, a camping party was attacked while asleep. The tents under which they lay were thrown down over them, and they were stabbed to death while unable to extricate themselves. Individuals also attacked their enemies, not in open combat, but from ambush, or when they lived in the same village, they tried to kill them by witchcraft.

Chapter 2

Holy Wars of Conquest in the Name of a Deity

2.1. Eanatum, warrior-king. A fragment from the *Stele of the Vultures*, so called because one fragment displays vultures feasting on battlefield corpses. Eanatum, ruler of Lagash, erected the stele around 2450 B.C.E. to commemorate a victory over the city of Umma. In the upper register he carries a sickle-sword while leading a phalanx of soldiers who trample on the bodies of defeated enemies; in the lower register he stands in a chariot, holding a spear in his left hand and a sickle-sword in his right hand, with a quiver of arrows placed before him, and leads a group of spear-bearing infantry.

Holy wars of conquest waged in the name of a deity are as old as civilization. They include wars driven by a sense of mission to spread a divine being's cult; wars undertaken because a god or goddess wills one's possession of a particular land; wars engaged in because a deity demands the submission or eradication of a particular people; wars embarked on to prove the superiority of one's divine protector; and wars to rectify or avenge wrongs done to one's god.

We shall consider this form of holy war in a roughly chronological manner as we look around the globe over the past five millennia, and as far as evidence is concerned, we must look first at the ancient Near East.

The Ancient Near East: History's First Holy Warriors?

Holy war is religious worship and sacrifice. The earliest cultures, for which there is clear evidence, practicing this form of devotion were active in Egypt around 3100 B.C.E. and in southern Mesopotamia about 2450 B.C.E.

2.2. The *Narmer Palette.*

The Unification of Egypt: The Land of Two Lands

According to Egyptian tradition, around 3100 B.C.E., Menes, the king of Upper Egypt (the southern desert region that the Nile irrigates and fertilizes), conquered Lower Egypt (the northern delta area), and created united Egypt's first royal dynasty. Menes is a shadowy figure, for whom there is only a single piece of ambiguous archeological evidence. But there is plenty of evidence for the historical figure of Narmer, who flourished sometime around 3100 B.C.E. and is generally regarded as the first king of the "Land of Two Lands." Consequently, most Egyptologists conclude that Menes and Narmer were one and the same.

One of the artifacts identifying this king is the *Narmer Palette*. The Egyptians used stone palettes as bases on which they ground cosmetics. The size and artistic qualities of this artifact indicate that it was no ordinary palette, and it probably was never used as such. The weight of learned opinion is that it dates from the reign of Narmer and celebrates the unification of Egypt. Moreover, it was probably dedicated to the deities Bat and Horus and deposited as an offering in a now-unknown temple.

Both sides of the palette are carved in raised relief, with the side shown on our left known as the *recto* (front) and the side on our right as the *verso* (rear). On the recto side, Narmer wears the white domed crown of Upper Egypt and wields a mace, which he uses to subdue a kneeling prisoner, whose hair he grasps in his left hand. Behind Narmer a servant carries his sandals, and to the king's left is the falcon-god Horus, the sky god and god of war.

Horus was believed to have been born in the delta region and in time became the protector deity of Lower Egypt, but his cult was universal throughout Egypt, and it appears that the predynastic kings of Upper Egypt worshipped him as their special deity. With the unification of Egypt, the living god-king became identified with Horus. Here, Horus (Narmer?) pulls on a rope that is inserted into the nose of a human-headed creature, apparently pulling out its life force. One symbol of Lower Egypt was the cobra. Can this be a cobra with a human head? In support of that theory, notice the papyrus reeds, symbols of Lower Egypt, growing out of the creature. Might the number of reeds, six, represent the thousands killed or the holy sites captured?

In the lowest register are two naked men, who appear to be sprawled in death. In the center of the topmost register is a *serekh*, a crest reserved for kings, that bears the phonetic symbols for "Narmer." Flanking it are two human-headed bovine creatures representing the cow-goddess Bat, a deity of Upper Egypt who bestowed royal authority on kings.

Representations of Bat also adorn the top register on the verso side, where they flank another serekh with the king's name. Beneath them is a busy register. On the far left is a sandal-bearer walking behind Narmer. The king wears the red crown of Lower Egypt and carries a flail and mace, symbols of absolute royal authority. Five persons precede the king. The long-haired person closest to Narmer carries what appear to be two drooping lotus flowers. Is this a symbol of defeated Lower Egypt? Preceding him are four standard-bearers, carrying an animal skin, a jackal, and two falcons. The jackal represents Anubis, the god of death and mummification. Might the animal skin also represent death? If so, do the falcons of Horus represent life? To the far right are ten decapitated corpses, their heads stuck between their feet. The next register shows us two men holding the halters of two mythical serpopards—half-serpent, half-leopard beasts. Their intertwining apparently represents the conquest that transformed Egypt into the Land of Two Lands. Finally, in the bottom register a bull tramples a fallen, naked individual and simultaneously knocks down a city's walls. The bull was a universal symbol of male potency and the power of kingship throughout the ancient

Near East and beyond into bordering regions. Clearly the palette is filled with symbols of a god-directed conquest and the new life of unification that came out of the deaths occasioned by a sacred war. As we turn to Mesopotamia and the early civilizations watered there by the Tigris and Euphrates Rivers, we find another type of holy war of conquest.

Eanatum, Sumer's First-Known Holy Warrior

In the mid-third millennium, the Sumerian city states of Lagash and Umma, which were located in present-day southern Iraq, engaged in a long series of struggles over possession of a fertile piece of land, water rights, and payment of rent. Around 2450, Eanatum I achieved a victory commemorated on the *Stele of the Vultures*. This chapter's opening image presents Eanatum leading soldiers into battle. From the stele's other side, we have a fragment portraying Lagash's chief deity, Ningirsu, the god of war, agriculture, and healing. In his left hand he holds "the great battle net of the god Enlil," which has caught up the naked bodies of Umma's soldiers. One pokes his head out of the net, but Ningirsu crushes him with the mace that he holds in his right hand. Closing the net is the eagle-headed lion Anzu, gripping two lions in its talons. Anzu was strongly associated with Ningirsu, being both his agent and a manifestation of him.

An inscription on the stele describes Ningirsu's connection with Eanatum. Although some words are missing or broken, there is no ambiguity in the boast:

2.3. Ningirsu, warrior-god. The celestial side of the *Stele of the Vultures*.

> [Lor]d [Ni]ngirsu, [war]rior of [En]lil.[1] [Ni]n[gir]su [imp]lanted the
> [semen] for E[a]natum in the [wom]b . . . [and] rejoiced over [Eanatum].
> Inana[2] accompanied him, named him Eana-Inana-Ibgalakakatum,[3] and set
> him on the special lap of Ninhursag.[4] Ninhursag [offered him] her special
> breast. Ningirsu rejoiced over Eanatum, semen implanted in the womb by
> Ningirsu. . . . Ningirsu, with great joy, [gave him] the kin[gship of Lagash].[5]

Given this relationship between Eanatum and Ningirsu, it is not surprising
that the king served as this god's champion. As noted above, one of the major factors in the war between Lagash and Umma was a land dispute, but this was not
just any land. In the opening lines of the inscription, we read, "Ningirsu . . . spoke
angrily: 'Umma has my forage, my own property, the fields of the G[u'ede]na.'"[6]
Gu'edena, "the beloved field of Ningirsu,"[7] was land sacred to the god and given by
him to Lagash. For this reason, the god came to the king in a dream:

> He followed after him. Him who lies sleeping, him who lies sleeping—He
> approaches his head. Eanatum who lies sleeping—[his] be[loved] master
> [Ningirsu approaches his head]. Kish[8] itself must abandon Umma, and,
> being angry, cannot support it. The sun-(god) will shine to your right, and
> a . . . [crown?] will be affixed to your forehead. O Eanatum, you will slay there.
> Their myriad corpses will reach the base of heaven. [In] Um[ma] . . . will rise
> up against him and he will be killed within Umma itself.[9]

And so, "he defeated Umma. . ." and "restored to Ningirsu's control [his] belov[ed
fi]eld, the Gu'eden . . . [and] erected a [monument] in the grand temple of
Ningirsu."[10]

Here, in one of history's earliest-known holy wars, we see the inherent problem with the models of holy war that we are examining in these chapters. As
noted in the Introduction, rarely does a holy war conform exclusively to one type.
There is a good deal of overlap, and in this case, Eanatum's war against Umma

---

1. The chief god of Sumer.

2. The goddess of war, fertility, and love.

3. "Worthy in the Eana of Inana of the Ibgal." The Eana, located in the city of Uruk, was Inana's chief temple and main cultic center. The Ibgal was her temple in Lagash.

4. The mother of the gods and humans.

5. Jerrold S. Cooper, *Presargonic Inscriptions* (New Haven, CT: American Oriental Society, 1986), 34.

6. Ibid.

7. Ibid.

8. The sacred city, founded by the gods, that gave birth to sanctified kingship.

9. Cooper, *Presargonic Inscriptions*, 34.

10. Ibid., 35.

could just as easily be categorized as a war in defense of sacred space—"the beloved field of Ningirsu." Moreover, this war was not without its secular concerns, namely the economic value of the disputed land. Rare (or nonexistent) is the holy war that is devoid of all worldly motives.

The Assyrians

Ancient Assyria, in Upper Mesopotamia, was a major force in the Near East from around 2025 to its total collapse in 605 B.C.E. At its height, an era known as the Neo-Assyrian Empire (911–612), it carved out an empire encompassing all or parts of seventeen present-day nations. For almost three hundred years, Assyria was the Near East's dominant power.

Between 2025 and 605, Assyrian imperial fortunes experienced peaks and troughs. One of its high points was the reign of Tukulti-Ninurta I (r. ca. 1243–ca. 1207) in an era known as the Middle Assyrian Empire (1366–1050). The king's name translates as "My trust is in Ninurta," Ninurta being another name for the Sumerian god Ningirsu. The Assyrians were not Sumerians. In fact, the cities of Sumer had ceased to be a significant military-political force around 1700 B.C.E., but the Sumerians' cultural imprint on the soul of Mesopotamia endured for many centuries thereafter.

Despite his name, Tukulti-Ninurta's primary devotion was focused on Assyria's chief deity, Ashur, whom the king claimed to serve as vice-regent. In one of the many royal inscriptions enumerating his conquests and other acts of piety that the king scattered about his lands, Tukulti-Ninurta boasted of his victory over the king of Babylon around 1225 B.C.E.:

> Tukulti-Ninurta, king of the universe, king of Assyria, king of the four quarters,[11] sun(god) of all people, strong king, king of Karduniash,[12] king of Sumer and Akkad,[13] king of the Upper (and) Lower Seas,[14] . . . the king whom the gods help to obtain his desired victories and who shepherds the four quarters with his *fierce* might. . . .
>
> With the support of the gods Ashur, Enlil and Shamash,[15] the great gods, my lords, (and) with the aid of the goddess Ishtar, mistress of heaven (and) underworld, (who) marches at the fore of my army,[16] I approached Kashtiliash, king of Karduniash, to do battle. I brought about the defeat

---

11. Of the world.
12. Babylon. See note 17.
13. Akkad lay north of Sumer and south of Assyria.
14. The Mediterranean Sea and the Persian Gulf and all lands between them.
15. A sun deity and the champion of justice.
16. Known to the Sumerians as Inana. See note 2.

of his army (and) felled his warriors. In the midst of that battle I captured Kashtiliash, king of the Kassites,[17] (and) trod with my feet upon his lordly neck as though it were a footstool. Bound I brought him as a captive into the presence of the god Ashur, my lord. (Thus) I became lord of Sumer and Akkad in its entirety (and) fixed the boundary of my land as the Lower Sea in the east.[18]

A second source, known as the *Tukulti-Ninurta Epic*, provides further detail. According to the poem, King Kashtiliash violated a long-standing treaty with Assyria, and Tukulti-Ninurta called upon Shamash, the god of treaties and defender of justice, to witness this treachery. After favorably comparing the king's warlike abilities with those of the divine Ninurta, the poet states that he was "cast sublimely from the womb of the gods" and was "the eternal image of Enlil," who had appointed him to lead troops and had exalted him as if he were his own son.[19] The epic further states that all the gods were enraged at the Kassite king's betrayal of a treaty that Shamash had witnessed and sealed. Consequently, each deity fled from the particular city within Kashtiliash's kingdom where his or her cult reigned supreme. Even Marduk, Babylon's chief god, "abandoned his sublime sanctuary, the city."[20] Presented in this light, Tukulti-Ninurta's campaign certainly appears to be a war of conquest countenanced by the gods. Did this Assyrian monarch actually believe that the gods blessed and even demanded the war that he was waging? We will never know for certain, but is there any good reason to doubt the king's piety?

The Israelites: "Yahweh Is a Warrior"[21]

The origins of the Israelites are murky but not totally unknown. Based largely upon archeological evidence, the story that emerges is that around 1200 B.C.E. waves of Canaanite agriculturalists from the lowlands of Palestine began to migrate into the thinly settled highlands, where they merged with newcomers who

---

17. Kashtiliash IV (r. ca. 1232–ca. 1225), the king of Babylon/Karduniash in Mesopotamia. The Kassites had gained control of Babylon around 1531. The Assyrian army destroyed Babylon's walls, massacred many of its inhabitants, and carried off the statue of Marduk, Babylon's chief deity. Tukulti-Ninurta then sent Kashtiliash into exile.

18. Albert Kirk Grayson, *Assyrian Royal Inscriptions*, vol. I (Wiesbaden: Otto Harrassowitz, 1972), 108.

19. Vladimir Sazonov, "Some Remarks Concerning the Development of the Theology of War in Ancient Mesopotamia," in *The Religious Aspects of War in the Ancient Near East, Greece, and Rome,* ed. Krzysztof Ulanowski (Leiden: Brill, 2016), 23–50, at 32.

20. Ibid., 34.

21. Exodus, 15:3.

had come in from various directions. Over time, these highlanders developed a sense of ethnic commonality and became the Israelites. From the highlands, they moved back onto the coastal plain, where they assimilated with the region's urban inhabitants. Archeological research also strongly suggests that although bloody conflicts were part of the process, the conquest was nowhere near as total and sudden and its battles not anywhere near as genocidal and destructive as portrayed in chapters 1–11 of the Book of Joshua in the Hebrew Bible.

The eleventh century B.C.E. was a period of turmoil in which major powers in the Near East suffered eclipses. This vacuum allowed the development of smaller, independent polities, such as the kingdom of Israel, which emerged toward the end of the century. A significant turning point in its fortunes was the occupation of Jerusalem, possibly around the year 1000. Jerusalem became the capital of a theocratic monarchy, a reality expressed sometime in the tenth century B.C.E. by construction of the Temple, Israel's sanctuary for the cult of its God, Yahweh.

For all of the alleged brilliance of tenth-century Israel (a brilliance that some historians dispute), the kingdom suffered from internal weaknesses it could not overcome, and around 924, it split in two, with a northern kingdom known as Israel and a southern kingdom, known as Judah, centered on Jerusalem.

Israel and Judah were fairly weak at the start, and they further weakened themselves through ill-considered warfare. Moreover, because they were strategically located within a region connecting Mesopotamia with Egypt, the aggressive Neo-Assyrian Empire loomed large in the minds of the inhabitants of these two small states, and this obsession is evident in various books of the Bible. The fear was not unfounded. Between 745 and 721, the Neo-Assyrian Empire first annexed and then obliterated Israel, sending into permanent exile thousands of its inhabitants. The kingdom of Judah avoided Assyrian conquest and enjoyed a precarious existence for the next 136 years. During that period of grace its priests began to articulate a vision of sacred history and holy warfare that has echoed down through the centuries.

Deuteronomic History and Holy Genocide

The Hebrew Bible is textually complex. Its earliest books, such as Genesis and Exodus, underwent centuries of composition, transmission, and editing, and its later books, such as Esther and Daniel, were composed in a world that was quite different from the time when the Israelites coalesced into an identifiable people. Consequently, it is impossible to conclude that the Hebrew Bible contains only one notion of holy war. There are several, a fact reflecting developments that responded to and grew out of changing social, political, and religious realities.

The most comprehensive picture of holy war in the early books of the Hebrew Bible emerges out of a body of sacred scripture that biblical scholars term "Deuteronomic history." The term derives from Deuteronomy, the final book of the Torah (the instruction or law), which encompasses the first five books of the Bible. Collectively, the five books define in detail the obedience and worship due Yahweh, the God of Israel, and "Deuteronomy" means the second, or supplementary, body of laws, specifically the laws that Yahweh gave Israel on the plains of Moab (Deuteronomy, 29) that complemented the earlier laws given on Mount Sinai (Exodus, 19–31).

According to this academic construct, a theory that has stood the test of almost eight decades of research and debate, five books of the Hebrew Bible—Deuteronomy, Joshua, Judges, Samuel, and Kings—constitute a single work that went through two editions, the first in the late seventh century and the second in the sixth century B.C.E. Each edition, although drawing from far-earlier oral traditions and written sources now lost to us, reflects pressing contemporary concerns. The first edition took shape in the reign of the religious reformer King Josiah of Judah (r. 640–609), who attempted to eradicate all forms of pagan worship in his lands. The compilers of the second edition did their work against the backdrop of the conquest of Jerusalem and destruction of the Temple in 587/86 by the army of Nebuchadnezzar of Babylon and the carrying off into captivity of large numbers of Judah's elites, a phenomenon known as the Babylonian Exile.

The Deuteronomic depiction of and justification for holy war is consistent throughout the five books and consists of two basic elements: possession of the land that Yahweh promised to the people of Israel, and cleansing that land of all false gods, idolatry, and all other practices abhorrent to God. Behind the promise of a Chosen Land for a Chosen People is the threat that should they fail by forsaking their Covenant, or binding agreement, with Yahweh, they shall suffer dire consequences. According to the Book of Deuteronomy, just prior to his death and before the Israelites would pass over the Jordan into Canaan, Moses delivered a detailed discourse on God's Law, in which he promised and admonished them:

> When Yahweh your God has brought you into the country which you are going to make your own, many nations will fall before you. . . . Yahweh your God will put them at your mercy and you will conquer them. You must put them under the curse of destruction. You must not make any treaty with them or show them any pity. You must not intermarry with them. . . . Instead, treat them like this: tear down their altars, smash their standing stones, cut down their sacred poles and burn their idols. For you are a people consecrated to Yahweh your God; of all the peoples on earth, you have been chosen by Yahweh your God to be his own people. . . . Do not be afraid of them, for

Yahweh your God is among you, a great, a terrible God. Little by little, Yahweh your God will clear away these nations before you.... Yahweh your God will put them at your mercy, and disaster after disaster will overtake them until they are finally destroyed. He will put their kings at your mercy and you will blot out their names under heaven; no one will be able to resist you—until you have destroyed them all.[22]

Hebrew Holy Warfare before Deuteronomy

Such a radical vision of God-mandated, genocidal warfare did not emerge suddenly and without precedent in the seventh century B.C.E. As we have seen, god-directed-and-assisted holy war had been part of the cultural environment of the ancient Near East for more than two thousand years before the authors of the Book of Deuteronomy sat down to write. If we look carefully within both the Torah and the books of Deuteronomic history, we can find echoes of traditions of holy warfare among the Israelites that long predated the seventh century.

The Book of Exodus details the escape of the Hebrews from Egyptian slavery and their subsequent wandering for forty years before entering Canaan. In chapter 15, following their miraculous escape from the pursing Egyptian army that culminated in the drowning of Pharaoh's army, the Hebrews break out in a victory chant that is variously known as "The Song of the Sea" and "The Song of Moses and Miriam." In its opening lines, the Hebrews sing out:

> I shall sing to Yahweh, for he has covered himself in glory,
>> horse and rider he has thrown into the sea.
> Yah[23] is my strength and my song,
> to him I owe my deliverance.
> He is my God and I shall praise him,
> my father's God and I shall extol him.
> Yahweh is a warrior;
> Yahweh is his name.
> Pharaoh's chariots and army he has hurled into the sea; ...
> Your right hand, Yahweh, wins glory by its strength,
> your right hand, Yahweh, shatters its foes,
> and by your great majesty you fell your assailants;
> you unleash your fury, it consumes them like chaff.[24]

The Book of Exodus is multilayered. Scholars have concluded that its composition took place from the tenth to as late as the sixth century B.C.E., and they further

---

22. Deuteronomy, 7:1–6, 21–24 (New Jerusalem Bible, 1985), 233–34.
23. Another form of the God of Israel's name.
24. Exodus, 15: 1–4, 6–8 (New Jerusalem Bible), 99.

agree that it is composed of several traditions, some quite ancient. The oldest of all appears to be "The Song of the Sea," which is noted for its archaic language. It probably dates from the twelfth or even thirteenth century B.C.E., about the time in which Moses purportedly lived.

Herem: Destruction and Devotion

A second piece of evidence appears in the Book of Joshua, chapters 6 and 7. In order to understand the story, we must investigate the principle of *herem*. Herem is normally understood as "the ban, or curse, of destruction," such as the curse of destruction that Moses instructed the Israelites to place on the people of Canaan. However, herem also meant "devotion" and could refer to items, usually war booty, set aside for Yahweh alone. In a sense, destruction and devotion intersected insofar as people and items that would otherwise corrupt the Israelites were either destroyed totally or exclusively and irrevocably dedicated to Yahweh, and thereby sanctified. Once sanctified, the items lay under a ban, and to violate that ban was sacrilege and incurred the punishment of total obliteration.

According to the story, the Israelites' initial victory upon crossing the Jordan River was at Jericho, a major city that barred its gates to the immigrants. Upon the command of Yahweh, the Israelites marched around the city for six days. On the seventh, priests blew rams' horns and the city's walls collapsed, whereupon the Israelites entered the city. Before assaulting Jericho, Joshua placed the city and everyone in it under the curse of destruction. The only exception was Rahab and her family because she had provided a safe refuge for Joshua's two spies who earlier had reconnoitered the city. He further warned the Israelites that all gold, silver, bronze, and iron items taken from the city would be consecrated to Yahweh and placed in his treasury. If anyone defied this second herem, disaster would befall the entire camp.

Sure enough, in their initial assault on Ai, the next town on their itinerary of genocidal destruction, they were repulsed. When Joshua bewailed this setback, Yahweh informed him that the Israelites lay under herem because the booty taken at Jericho had been violated and hidden away. The curse would not go away, and Israel could not stand up to its enemies until the purloined objects were discovered and the malefactor, along with the desecrated items and all his possessions, consumed in fire. The Israelites cast lots to reveal the perpetrator, and discovered it was Achan, who confessed to stealing a fine garment and large quantities of silver and gold. Achan was taken outside the camp, along with his children, livestock, all his other possessions, and the stolen objects. He and his children (and presumably the livestock) were then stoned to death. Their bodies and all his possessions, including the items he had stolen, were burned, and a large mound of stones was raised over the ashes. In this way, the curse of destruction was lifted.

We do not know the source for this story, but it has the ring of a past that was far distant from the seventh century B.C.E. Similar curses, bans, and consecrations had been common enough for many centuries among the various peoples of the ancient Near East. And this leads us to conclude that whatever else he was, Yahweh of the early Israelites, the Israelites of the twelfth century and probably earlier, was a god of war. We shall further explore Yahweh's role as a warrior-god when we study source 2, which describes the capture of Ai.

Greco-Roman Antiquity

Warfare for the Greeks and the Romans was a profoundly religious affair. The numerous religious rites that were embedded in all aspects of warfare from the declaration of hostilities to the commemoration of victory and the fallen were focused on winning the favor of the gods. Both cultures also had a notion of holy wars of conquest, but it was far less pronounced than that of the Deuteronomic authors.

The Hellenic World

The Greeks had a god and a goddess of war, Ares and Athena. Whereas "manslaughtering" Ares embodied the irrational side of war and its carnage, Athena represented war's more strategic aspects, but not always. She also bloodied her hands. In the *Iliad*, she plots the destruction of Troy, even though she was its guardian deity from the day of its foundation. In book 5, she gives the Greek hero Diomedes a measure of supernatural strength and daring that drives him to feats that no mortal could otherwise perform. She even allows him to wound two deities, Aphrodite and Ares, who have intervened on the side of Troy. In the latter case, she deflects Ares's spear away from Diomedes and guides the Greek's spear deep into Ares's belly, causing the bleeding god to leave the field of battle.

That was holy war crafted by poets (assuming Homer was not a lone individual). Greek historians also dealt with war's sacral motives and manifestations. According to Herodotus, the Persians destroyed and looted all of the shrines on the acropolis of Athens in 480 B.C.E. in retaliation for the Athenians' burning down the temple of the Anatolian mother goddess Cybele in Persian-held Sardis in 498. Later, in a cycle of vengeance, the Athenians cited the burning and destruction of their gods' statues and homes as the reason for their fighting on against the armies of Xerxes, because they were "duty bound to avenge them."[25]

Avenging the gods also served as a reason or, better, pretext, for intra-Hellenic warfare. Thucydides reports that on the eve of the Peloponnesian War (431–404) fought between Athens and Sparta and their respective allies, Sparta maintained that it was going to war "for the honor of the gods," in order to drive out a curse that certain Athenians had long ago incurred through an act of sacrilege. Thucydides, ever the rationalist, claims that this was a pretext that camouflaged Sparta's desire to discredit the Athenian leader Pericles, an archenemy of Sparta, whose family was associated with the curse.[26] Regardless of whether or not politics was the prime factor behind Spartan aggressiveness, the fact remains that "avenging the gods" made sense within the context of Hellenic society's religious values.

The Romans

The Romans considered themselves to be the most pious of people, believing that all life is in the hands of the gods. They were also unapologetic imperialists whose foreign policy reflected the principle that might makes its own right. Their god of war, Mars, was very much like ancient Lagash's Ningirsu. Also a god of agriculture, fertility, and spring, he was far less bloodthirsty and uncontrollable than Ares but was nonetheless an aggressive deity. As the putative father of the mythical founder of Rome, Romulus, Mars had a paternal connection with the eternal city. Emblematic of this was the city's *Campus Martius* (Field of Mars). In the days of the early Republic (509?–27 B.C.E.), it was where the city's militia mustered in March, Mars's month, before it set off to fight surrounding Italian tribes. There the Romans also celebrated religious services at the god's altar—services predicated on the belief that Mars sanctified war.

The most characteristic Roman celebration, the triumph, provides insight into how the Romans intertwined religion and war. A triumph was the three-day celebration accorded a victorious general and became a characteristic of Rome's imperial era.

On the first day, about 250 chariots carry the defeated people's cultural artifacts, especially religious statutes, from the Field of Mars into the city. As the chariots wind through the streets, placards displaying key moments in the campaign are displayed to the cheering crowds. At dawn on the second day, the

---

25. Herodotus, *Histories*, 8:144.
26. Thucydides, *The Peloponnesian War*, 1:126–27.

military equipment of the defeated enemy receives a similar parade, and then the riches of the enemy, gold and silver vessels, silken tapestries, masses of coins, and similar riches are carried to the Capitoline Hill, the center of Roman civic-religious activity, on which stood the Temple of Jupiter Optimus Maximus (Jupiter, the Best and Greatest). On the third day, the triumphant general enters the city. Trumpeters playing calls to battle followed by large numbers of richly garlanded oxen destined for sacrifice lead the parade. They are followed by a second display of captured wealth. After that comes the general's empty chariot, followed by important prisoner-slaves, such as royal children. The captured enemy king or general comes next. Finally the triumphal general arrives in a special two-wheeled chariot drawn by four white horses. In his right hand is a laurel branch and his left hand holds a scepter. He wears bright scarlet robes, rather than the white toga of citizenship, and his face is painted bloodred. Above his head, a slave holds a golden wreath. Toward the end of the day, the procession stops at the base of the Capitoline Hill. The chief captives are led off for execution, an act that harkens back to days of human sacrifice, and the triumphant general ascends to the Temple of Jupiter Feretrius (Jupiter of the Spoils), in an act reminiscent of Rome's first triumph, which is offered for your analysis as part of source 3.

Following the adoption of Christianity by Constantine I (r. 306–37) and the increasingly deep penetration of Christianity into the imperial fabric, triumphal celebrations continued, but without the sacrifices and many of the other overtly pagan ceremonies. Rome's civic deities might have been replaced by a Christian God, but the emperor and his generals remained as the champions of a sacred empire that waged divinely sanctioned battles.

Constantine I, the Great

Before Emperor Constantine's conversion to Christianity, the emperor's chief duty was expansion and defense of the sacred empire under the guidance and protection of Rome's civic deities. For Constantine and all of his successors, except one, the Christian God now was the sole divine being who directed and protected the emperor's military actions.

In a letter of 324 to his eastern provinces, in which Constantine justified his prohibition of polytheistic sacrifices, he addressed God directly:

> Now I call upon you, the supreme God. Be merciful and gracious . . . and proffer healing through me your servant. . . . By your guidance I have undertaken deeds of salvation and achieved them; making your seal my protection everywhere, I have led a conquering army. Whatever the public need may

anywhere require, following the same tokens of your merit I advance against the enemy.[27]

The "seal" and "tokens" are surely the *labarum*, a battle standard that consisted of a tall cross surmounted by a wreath of precious stones and gold in which was placed the Greek letter *chi* (X) intersected by the Greek letter *rho* (P), a monogram for Christ. The early fourth-century Christian bishop and historian Eusebius of Caesarea wrote that the emperor devised this standard following a dream in which Christ told him it would protect against enemy attacks. Moreover, "this saving sign was always used by the Emperor for protection against every opposing and hostile force, and he commanded replicas of it to lead all his armies."[28]

Use of a holy talisman as a shield in battle is not sufficient evidence of a belief that one is waging a God-directed war. But Eusebius did not stop there. In the concluding chapter of his *History of the Church*, Eusebius celebrated Constantine's victorious battle in 324 against his co-emperor as a struggle between Christianity and paganism, proclaiming that "God granted, from Heaven above, the deserved rewards of piety—trophies of victory over the unfaithful—and He cast the guilty one . . . prostrate at the feet of Constantine."[29] There is good reason to conclude that Constantine attacked Licinius primarily because he sought sole power over the empire. But the fact that Eusebius and so many other Christian leaders, who were steeped in the pages of the Book of Joshua and similar books of holy scripture, saw this as a God-directed holy war might be sufficient to place it in that category. Constantine himself probably rationalized his assault as directed by the God who had adopted him and his empire.

Islamic Jihad

We looked briefly at the just war aspect of Islamic jihad in the Introduction, but given its importance over the centuries, especially as a holy war of conquest in the name of a deity, jihad deserves additional coverage.

Jihad means "struggle" in Arabic, and Islamic jurists over the centuries have delineated a number of forms of holy struggle that righteous Muslims engage in. There is an oft-cited story, which historians generally agree is spurious, that

---

27. Eusebius, *Life of Constantine*, trans. Averil Cameron and Stuart G. Hall (Oxford: Clarendon Press, 1999), 113.

28. Ibid., 81–82.

29. Eusebius of Caesarea, *History of the Church*, bk. X, trans. A. J. Andrea, *The Medieval Record: Sources of Medieval History*, 2nd ed. (Indianapolis, IN: Hackett Publishing, 2020), 18.

as Muhammad journeyed from battle, he instructed his warriors that they were now leaving behind the Lesser Jihad and returning to the Greater Jihad. That Greater Jihad, according to interpreters of Shari'a, is the individual's struggle to live a pious and moral life in total conformity with the teachings of Islam, and it has many subsets. Jihad of the mouth is prayer and preaching. For Sufi mystics, jihad of the soul is the struggle to put aside all sense of self and to attain a state of innocence whereby one embraces the divine presence in this life. Regardless of the many forms that the Greater Jihad can take, Muslim rulers and intellectuals have normally meant jihad of the sword—holy war on behalf of Allah and Islam—when uttering or writing the phrase "jihad in the path of God."

2.4. The labarum. The Resurrection from a mid-fourth-century sarcophagus. The labarum symbolizes the Risen Christ. Two soldiers flank the standard. An imperial eagle swoops down, with a laurel wreath in its beak. At its wingtips are the sun and moon, symbols for the extent of the empire. The two doves represent the soul of the entombed person released by death.

As is true of all sacred scripture, the Qur'an contains many inconsistences and ambiguities. There are verses that extol peace, or at least nonaggression. Surah 59:23 lists *As-Salam* (Giver of Peace) as one of God's names. Surah 2:190 commands Muslims to "fight in the cause of God those who fight you, but do not commit aggression. God does not love the aggressors."[30] But then there is the so-called Sword Verse: "And when the sacred months have passed, then kill the polytheists wherever you find them and capture them and besiege them and sit in wait for them at every place of ambush. But if they should repent, establish

---

30. The Qur'an, 2:190, at https://www.clearquran.com/002.html (accessed May 1, 2020).

prayer, and give zakah,[31] let them [go] on their way. Indeed, Allah is Forgiving and Merciful."[32] It certainly seems to command offensive warfare and forced conversion, and today's Islamic terrorists often cite it as the divine mandate that governs their actions.

One way of understanding these conflicting verses is that they emerged in different circumstances. Qur'anic revelations at Mecca, where Muhammad preached a religious and moral message that was profoundly revolutionary on several levels, differed from the revelations that he uttered at Medina, where he was also a political and military leader. And it is to Medina that we must look for the origin of jihad of the sword.

The Birth of Jihad of the Sword

The watershed event in the early history of the Islamic *Umma*, or community, was the *hijra* (departure), when in 622, the Prophet and a number of his followers secretly left Mecca and moved to Yathrib (later called Medina) in order to escape a plot on Muhammad's life. Here they developed into a strong community able to engage its Meccan opponents.

From Medina, the Muslims launched several traditional, small-time raiding expeditions on Meccan caravans, as a hopeful means of supporting themselves in their new setting and as a way of putting pressure on the Meccans to relent. The raids reached a new level of seriousness in January 624, when a Muslim scouting party attacked a Meccan caravan, killing its leader. The problem was that this was the pre-Islamic sacred month of *Rajab*, in which all hostilities were forbidden. Understandably, many of Medina's Muslims were initially aghast at this breach of sacred tradition. But then the Prophet uttered the following revelation from Allah:

> Fighting has been enjoined upon you while it is hateful to you. But perhaps you hate a thing and it is good for you; and perhaps you love a thing and it is bad for you. And Allah knows, while you know not. They ask you about the sacred month—about fighting therein. Say, "Fighting therein is great [sin], but averting [people] from the way of Allah and disbelief in Him and [preventing access to] al-Masjid al-Haram[33] and the expulsion of its people therefrom are greater [evils] in the sight of Allah. And *fitnah*[34] is greater than

---

31. The religious tax imposed on Muslims; paying it is one of the Five Pillars of Islam.
32. The Qur'an, 9:5, at https://quran.com/9/5 (accessed May 1, 2020).
33. The Great Mosque, Mecca's Kaaba, a site of pre-Islamic pilgrimage. In 630, Muhammad would turn it into Islam's holiest shrine and the focal point of the Islamic *hajj*, or pilgrimage, after cleansing it of idols.
34. Persecution. A rich word that also means "sedition," "discord," and "civil war."

killing." And they will continue to fight you until they turn you back from your religion if they are able. And whoever of you reverts from his religion [to disbelief] and dies while he is a disbeliever—for those, their deeds have become worthless in this world and the Hereafter, and those are the companions of the Fire, they will abide therein eternally. Indeed, those who have believed and those who have emigrated and fought in the cause of Allah—those expect the mercy of Allah. And Allah is Forgiving and Merciful.[35]

In March 624, the Meccans sent a large force against Medina to avenge the sacrilege of two months earlier. Surprisingly, the outnumbered Muslims won a stunning victory at the Battle of Badr, which proved to be a turning point in the fortunes of Islam. In celebration, Muhammad uttered the following revelation:

And remember when you were few and oppressed in the land . . . but He sheltered you, supported you with His victory. . . . And fight them until there is no fitnah[36] and [until] the religion, all of it, is for Allah. And if they cease—then indeed, Allah is Seeing of what they do. . . . O you who have believed, when you encounter a company [from the enemy forces], stand firm and remember Allah much that you may be successful.[37]

Three points merit notice. First, this revelation mandates the eradication of the enemy's idolatry ("[until] the religion, all of it, is for Allah"). What had been a defensive struggle under the shelter provided by Allah has become an offensive jihad. Second, the words "fight them until there is no fitnah," as well as what we know of the Prophet's actions and teachings before and after Badr, lead to the conclusion that he was urging a war of conversion only against Arab polytheists, especially those of Mecca, and not against Arab Christians and Jews. Third, success is guaranteed to those who stand firm and trust in Allah.

Despite setbacks, the Prophet, largely through diplomacy but also through holy war and, at times, severe measures, was able by 630 to so strengthen the Islamic community, which now extended far beyond Medina, that he marched victoriously into Mecca without a fight, and cleansed it of its polytheism.

Islam's First Century of Conquests

Although Muslims made a few raids into Syria during the caliphate of Abu Bakr (r. 632–34), who succeeded to the headship of the Umma upon the Prophet's

---

35. The Qur'an, 2:116–18, at https://quran.com/2/216-222 (accessed April 30, 2020).
36. See note 34.
37. The Qur'an, 8:26, 30, and 39, "The Spoils of War," at https://quran.com/8/26-39 (accessed August 2, 2020).

death, most of Abu Bakr's brief period of leadership was spent suppressing the secession of some Arab tribes that refused to acknowledge his authority. Records for the "Wars of Apostasy" are scarce, contradictory, and partisan, but it is clear that Abu Bakr's campaign was religious and political. It established on a firm basis an Islamic community that transcended traditional tribal and kin loyalties and cemented the caliph as the ultimate authority in the Arabian Peninsula.

Under the next caliph, Umar (r. 634–44), Arab Muslim warriors exploded out of the peninsula into Syria and beyond. Within a century, the Umayyad caliphs (661–750) could claim an empire that extended from the Atlantic lands of North Africa and Spain to the Central Asian border of China.

Evidence indicates that initially these military excursions were traditional raids and wars of conquest in search of booty rather than holy wars. Moreover, the Muslim armies accomplished as much or more through negotiation and intimidation as through bloody combat. There was also no attempt to force conversion as the Arabs swept through the lands of their weakened neighbors, Byzantium and Persia. The pact that Habib ibn Maslamah gave the Christian inhabitants of Tiflis (present-day Tbilisi, Georgia) in 645 was typical of the first generation of the conquest. It ensured the security of their "lives, churches, convents, religious services and faith, provided they acknowledge their humiliation and pay tax to the amount of one *dinar* on every household." The inhabitants were further told that if they "return to the obedience of Allah" (in Muslim eyes, Christians had perverted the revelation that Jesus gave them), they will be "brethren." Otherwise, they must pay the tax.[38] Earlier, he had provided the same guarantee to the Christians, Jews, and the Zoroastrian inhabitants of the Armenian city of Dvin. Although the Qur'an identifies only Jews, Christians, and an enigmatic group called the "Sabeans" as monotheists who believe in the Last Day and who, if they live righteously, "will have their reward with their Lord,"[39] it was initially easier to guarantee the integrity of the Zoroastrians' fire temples than it was to destroy them.

Several factors prompted the shift from warfare that was not driven by religious fervor to holy war, but probably the most significant stimulus was the work of Muslim scholars, especially the historian Ibn Ishaq (d. ca. 767) and a group of jurists who flourished from the mid-eighth to the mid-tenth century, an era known as the Golden Age of Islamic Jurisprudence.

Sometime after the Prophet's death, the doctrine of *ismah* (incorruptible innocence) became widespread within Islam, whereby it was believed that Allah

---

38. Al-Baladhuri, *Kitab Futah al-Buldan* (*The Origins of the Islamic State*), trans. P. K. Hitti (New York: Columbia University Press, 1916), 316–17.

39. The Qur'an, 2:62, at https://quran.com/2/62 (accessed May 3, 2020).

had granted Muhammad, the most perfect of all humans, immunity from sin and error. It followed, therefore, that he was *the* model of righteous behavior. Tales of his military actions and reputed sayings in favor of God-directed war against polytheism circulated during his life and were repeated, embroidered, and supplemented then and in the generations that followed. When collected by historians and jurists and incorporated into canonical texts, the result was a picture of Muhammad the holy warrior. And given that the Prophet had waged holy jihad against his Meccan enemies, the picture was not incorrect, even though much of the detail was questionable.

Ibn Ishaq's *Life of the Messenger of God* was the first biography of Muhammad and served as the source of all subsequent Muslim accounts of the Prophet's life. In it, the author (and his ninth-century editor), depending in large part on oral tradition, portrayed Muhammad as someone who was propelled from defensive pacificism to offensive holy war by the attacks on him by his pagan enemies in Mecca and by divine revelation.

Muslim jurists completed the work. Tales of the utterances, actions, and silent approvals of the Prophet are called *hadiths* (discourses). Collectively known as Hadith, they have served as an authoritative guide to Muslim life and a useful supplement to the Qur'an. Although Hadith deals with almost every imaginable aspect of proper behavior, such as personal hygiene, a fair number of the hadiths concern war as a religious duty. A typical holy war hadith, as canonized by al-Bukhari (d. 870), the greatest of all hadith scholars, cites the reported testimony of one of Muhammad's Companions:

> Abu Hurairah reported from the Prophet that he said: "Allah takes the responsibility for whosoever goes forth in His way, (saying) 'if nothing causes him to go forth except faith in Me and affirmation of the truth of my messengers, then I will bring him back with what he may gain as a reward or as a booty or make him enter the paradise.' And had it not been hard for my followers, I would not have remained behind an army and it has always been my passionate desire that I be killed in the way of Allah, then given life again, and killed again, and given life again and killed again."[40]

Unlike the Greater Jihad, which is enjoined on all Muslims, the jurists, who evaluated, collected, and commented on this vast body of hadiths, taught that offensive jihad of the sword is a communal not an individual obligation, whereas a defensive jihad is obligatory for every able-bodied man. Moreover, although both

---

40. Aftab-ud-din Ahmad, trans., *Sahih-al-Bukhari: English Translation and Explanatory Notes* (London: Ahmadiyya Anjuman Lahore Publications, 2019), as excerpted in Andrea, *Medieval Record*, 69.

the Qur'an and numerous hadiths delineate rules regarding booty, in order for a jihad to be valid, one must wage it on behalf of Allah and not for gain.

Beyond that, the jurists agreed that there is a permanent state of conflict between Muslims and non-Muslims, which they framed as the House of Islam, or Peace (*Dar al-Islam*), namely Muslim-controlled lands, and the House of War, or Chaos (*Dar al-Harb*), meaning all non-Muslim lands. Although jihad against the House of War is continual, it may be momentarily suspended with occasional truces, which can last up to ten years. With such a suspension, the non-Muslim treaty state becomes the *Dar al-Sulh* (House of Truce). A fourth possibility is when a non-Muslim state becomes a client, or tributary vassal. Then it is a *Dar al-'Ahd* (House of Treaty).

In essence, historians and legal scholars gave Dar al-Islam a universal mission to bring the whole world to confess that "there is no god but God, and Muhammad is His Messenger."

Such is the theory, but reality tends to diverge from theory. Over the past fourteen centuries, peace has been more of a constant than war between the House of Islam and its non-Muslim neighbors, even when we take into consideration the first century of Muslim expansion (634–ca. 750), the era of the crusades (1095–1700?), the Muslim conquest of India (eleventh–sixteenth centuries), the age of Ottoman expansion (ca. 1300–ca. 1700), and numerous other periods of conflict, both holy and secular. Regardless, jihad in the path of God has been a recurring reality throughout these centuries, and Chapters 3 and 4, as well as the Epilogue, will focus on several notable examples.

Medieval Europe

The terms "medieval" and "Middle Ages" are imprecise and misleading when applied to the thousand years of European history that ran from about 500 to approximately 1500. They are based on the mistaken notion that this millennium was a holding pattern in Western history between the ancient world, which supposedly laid the foundations of Western civilization, and the so-called Renaissance that allegedly rediscovered Europe's Greco-Roman origins. In point of fact, by the year 1000, a new civilization had emerged that drew from its Greco-Roman and early Christian roots but was quite different in many essential ways. Many historians term that civilization the "First Europe."

One of the notable characteristics of the First Europe was its creation of a form of holy war known as crusades, which began in the eleventh century and extended well into the early modern era, at least into the seventeenth century, and ultimately touched much of Afro-Eurasia and significant portions of the

Americas. As with jihad, Chapters 3 and 4 will offer additional detail on the crusades, but here it is necessary to look at one aspect of the First Crusade (1095–
99)—a holy war called in the name of God—and for that purpose we will look
at Pope Urban II's call for that expedition to the Holy Land. In like manner, we
will briefly consider the Baltic Crusades, which got underway almost a half century later.

God Wills It!

Several books of the Hebrew Bible, a body of sacred scripture that Christians
revere as the "Old Testament" and believe to be divine revelation, served as inspiration for the crusades. As one can easily imagine, these were the Deuteronomic
books of history, especially the Book of Joshua, that described the Israelites' conquest of the Promised Land.

On November 27, 1095, Pope Urban II preached a sermon at Clermont in
south-central France that ignited the First Crusade. We have no transcript of that
sermon, but six twelfth-century historians composed versions of it, and of these,
three had been at Clermont. One of those in attendance was Robert, a monk of
Saint-Rémi in Rheims, France, whose *History of the Journey to Jerusalem* became
Europe's most widely read account of the crusade. According to Robert, after the
pope had finished his sermon, "all those who were there coalesced into a single
entity whereby they shouted out, 'God wills it! God wills it!'"[41] Whereupon the
pope responded:

> Most beloved brothers, today we demonstrate what the Lord said in the Gos-
> pel: *Where two or three are gathered in My name, I am in their midst.*[42] If the
> Lord God had not inhabited your minds, all of you would not have had one
> voice. To be sure, although your voices were many, they nevertheless had a
> single source. Therefore, I say to you that God, who placed this into your
> hearts, has elicited it from you. Consequently, let this be your war cry in bat-
> tle because it has come from God. When you mass in battle to charge the
> enemy, this single cry from God will be the war cry of all: 'God wills it! God
> wills it!'[43]

Robert composed his version of the events of that day with rhetorical flourishes
that poured forth from his mind and pen. Regardless, there is no doubt that "God

---

41. Robert the Monk, *History of the Journey to Jerusalem*, trans. A. J. Andrea, *Medieval Record*,
309.
42. Matthew, 18:20.
43. Robert the Monk in *Medieval Record*, 309.

wills it," shouted out in a variety of vernacular tongues, was the war cry of the First Crusade, as several other sources that detail the battles of the crusade report.

Whatever else it was, the First Crusade was, in the minds of the vast majority of its more than one hundred thousand participants, a holy war sanctioned and blessed by God. It was, however, not a war of conquest or conversion, at least as far as the Roman Church was concerned. As we shall see in Chapter 3, the pope envisioned this expedition to the East as a means of recovering Christian lands and rescuing coreligionists. Yet, Pope Urban's holy war was only the first of a centuries-long series of crusades. Less than half a century after the "recovery" of Jerusalem in 1099, God-willed crusading took on the mantle of conquest and conversion. And it did so thousands of miles from the Holy Land.

The Baltic Crusades

Conquest and conversion were two principal driving forces in a series of holy wars that Latin Christian Europe waged from 1147 to around 1525 in northern Europe's Baltic region. As had been the case with Charles the Great (Charlemagne), who conducted a thirty-two-year-long series of campaigns of conquest and conversion against the pagan Saxons to the northeast of his Frankish kingdom (772–804), this centuries-long succession of crusading forays had a defensive purpose—to protect Christians from the assaults of the "godless." But first and foremost, the goals of conquest and conversion were King Charles's and the later Baltic crusaders' primary motives.

In March 1147, Bernard, abbot of the monastery of Clairvaux and the dominant clerical voice in the Western Church for the first half of the twelfth century, began advocating for a second theater of operations in the upcoming Second Crusade to the Holy Land (1147–49). That theater would be the lands of a pagan Slavic people known as the Wends, who inhabited a region along the Elbe River that today is northeastern Germany. Bernard convinced the pope to grant crusader status and privileges to all who campaigned against the Wends. Buoyed by this papal approval, Bernard dispatched a letter to "Christian princes" in which he proclaimed:

> [Satan] has raised up evil seed, wicked pagan sons, whom, if I may say so, the might of Christendom has endured too long, shutting its eyes to those who with evil intent lie in wait, without crushing their poisoned heads under its heel. . . . Because the Lord has committed to our insignificance the preaching of this crusade, we make known to you that at a council of the king, bishops, and princes who had come together at Frankfurt, the might of Christians was armed against them, and that *for the complete wiping out or, at any rate, the conversion of these peoples* [italics added], they have put on the Cross, the sign

of our salvation. And we by virtue of our authority promised them the same spiritual privileges as those enjoy who set out toward Jerusalem. . . . We utterly forbid that for any reason whatsoever a truce should be made with these peoples, either for the sake of money or for the sake of tribute, until such a time as, by God's help, *they shall be either converted or erased* [italics added].[44]

Church law and the unanimous agreement of the Church's theologians condemned indiscriminate mass slaughter and forced conversion. That did not stop Bernard or many of the Germans and Danes who prosecuted the Wendish Crusade (1147). The Second Crusade to the East was a dismal failure, and the Wendish Crusade had mediocre results. But now, in the mid-twelfth century, crusading was extended well beyond the boundaries of the eastern Mediterranean, and conquest and conversion of nonbelievers were added to the list of valid motives for undertaking a holy war.

Conversion was not the Baltic Crusades' sole driving force. Lust for land and mercantile opportunism, as well as a dizzying array of geopolitical concerns and ambitions, drove many of these crusades and their crusaders. And then there were crusaders who joined up searching for glory, adventure, and wealth. In many ways, the Baltic Crusades prefigured crusades that the Spaniards launched in the Americas in the sixteenth century. And yet, as with the Americas, regardless of the selfish motives that all too many crusaders flagrantly displayed, the conquest and conversion of pagan peoples was an articulated goal of and justification for this warfare.

A German priest known as Henry of Livonia (d. after 1259), who was active in efforts to Christianize the pagans of Livonia (today Latvia and southern Estonia), composed a chronicle that covered the first thirty-four years of the century-long Livonian Crusade (1193–1290). After describing the capture of the fortress of Mona on the island of Ösel in January 1227, and the killing of almost all of its inhabitants "who deserved to be killed rather than baptized . . . because they vigorously spurned peace," Henry moved on to the capture of the fortified town of Waldia and the forced conversion of its inhabitants by crusaders from Riga, the Christian cathedral city of Livonia. In his words:

When the fortress at Mona had been reduced to ashes, the army hurried to another fortress called Waldia. . . . The army encamped there and prepared its weapons of war. . . . The inhabitants of Waldia . . . noticing the weapons that had been prepared . . . conceived a fear of God. They begged for

---

44. This portion of the letter (without italics) is available at https://www.worldhistory.biz /sundries/41106-bernard-of-clairvaux-s-summons-to-the-wendish-crusade.html (accessed April 6, 2020).

peace, and intensely terrorized by the slaying of the people of Mona, they gave themselves up humbly and spoke words of peace. As suppliants, they begged to receive the sacrament of holy baptism. This was a thing of joy for the Christians....

They demanded as hostages the sons of the better people. The Öselians of Waldia became the sons of obedience—they who formerly had been the sons of pride. He who formerly was a wolf was now a lamb. He who formerly was a persecutor of Christians was now a brother who accepted peace, did not refuse to surrender hostages, faithfully asked for the grace of baptism, did not fear to pay perpetual tribute.... These gifts of God are our delight. The glory of God and of our Lord Jesus Christ and of the Blessed Virgin Mary gave such joy to their Rigan servants on Ösel. To vanquish rebels, to baptize those who come freely and humbly, to receive hostages and tribute, to free all the captives who bear the name "Christian," to return with victory. What kings have to this point not been able to do, this Blessed Virgin, through her Rigan servants, has quickly and easily accomplished to the honor of her name.[45]

As the text makes plain, the crusaders' motives were far from purely religious. Yet, Henry's ascribing this victory to the Virgin Mary would have been understandable to an Incan monarch half a world away and two centuries into the future, who perceived the sun god as his heavenly patron of victory.

Holy War under the Incas

During the fifteenth century, a people of the Andean highlands whom we know as the Incas created an empire that encompassed a vast area of western South America and embraced about ten million people. The rapidity of the Incan Empire's rise and the extent of its conquests is best understood within the context of its religious beliefs and practices.

Within the pantheon of Incan deities, Inti, the god of the sun, held a special place. He was not the supreme creator god. That role was reserved for Viracocha, a pre-Incan deity whom the Incas adopted as the god who created all life and the heavens, including Inti. Although at the top of the divine pyramid, Viracocha removed himself from earthly affairs and left the governance of the cosmos in the hands of intermediary deities.

The Incas believed that Inti was the father of Manco Cápac (royal founder), the first Sapa Inca (sole Inca), or ruler of the people whom the Spaniards (and we) wrongly refer to as "Incas." In fact, the Inca was a divine ruler. Descended

---

45. Henry of Livonia, *Chronicle*, trans. A. J. Andrea in *Medieval Record*, 334–35.

directly from Manco Cápac, he and all of his relatives styled themselves "Children of the Sun" as a way of delineating their heavenly lineage. Moreover, the devotion of these Children of the Sun to the cult of Inti appears to have been a motivating force behind the rise of a dazzling empire that lasted, however, for less than a century, from about 1438 to 1532.

Evidence strongly indicates that it was under Pachacuti Inca Yupanqui (r. 1438–71) that Incan imperial expansion began in earnest, and it had deep religious overtones. All of the sixteenth-century sources that we have for the Incas mention the devotional nature of Incan expansion, and of them, the most telling is by the Spanish priest, historian, and ethnographer Cristóbal de Molina, a careful researcher who interviewed elders who had lived during the reigns of the last three Incas. According to Molina, Pachacuti:

> ordered that in the capitals of the provinces of all the lands that he conquered grand temples should be built for [the Sun and] endowed with large estates. He [also] ordered all the people that he conquered to worship and revere him together with the Creator. Throughout his life . . . everything he conquered and subjected was in the name of the Sun, his father, and the Creator. He said that everything was for them.[46]

The Incas enlarged their empire through diplomacy as well as war, and one factor that contributed to their success in persuading various foreign groups to submit to their rule was their reputation for tolerance. They allowed new subjects to retain their native rulers, customs, and religious practices. According to Molina, Pachacuti had ordered all the peoples whom he conquered "to hold their *huacas*[47] in great veneration and to go to them with their sacrifices, telling [the huacas] not to be angry with them for not remembering to revere and worship them."[48] Despite this tolerance, all who had been absorbed into the empire were required to worship the Sun as their god, and land in each newly acquired area was set aside for a temple to Inti. This was a dual iron-clad requirement laid on all subjects throughout the relatively brief history of the Inca Empire. Universal worship of Viracocha the Creator might have been another matter. The fact that other sources that deal with imperial expansion after Pachacuti focus exclusively on the Incas' insistence on universal worship of Inti suggests that Pachacuti's inclusion of the Creator (as Molina informs us) might have been unique to him.

---

46. Cristóbal de Molina, *Account of the Fables and Rites of the Incas*, trans. Brian S. Bauer, Vania Smith-Oka, and Gabriel E. Canarutti (Austin: University of Texas Press, 2011), 17.
47. Sacred sites, items (such as rocks), and idols inhabited by spirits.
48. Molina, *Account of the Fables*, 17.

When diplomacy failed and the Incas went to war to conquer an alien people, they followed a set of rituals that underscored the religious nature of their undertaking. Two days of fasting, accompanied by the sacrifice of llamas and children, preceded each military expedition, and priests accompanied each army. Upon the return of victorious armies, more human and llama sacrifices were offered up in thanksgiving.

War initiated by a divine ruler in the name of an ancestor sun god, with the express purpose of extending that god's cult, and accompanied by a set of solemn rituals, including human sacrifice: this looks like a war of conquest in the name of a deity, although surely more mundane motives, such as a megalomaniacal love of conquest for the sake of conquest, were part of the mix.

Native American Crusaders in Mesoamerica

With the triumphal conclusion of the *Reconquista* a recent memory, it was natural for the monarchies of Spain and Portugal to view their transoceanic ventures as a continuation on several fronts of the crusading that had become an integral part of Iberian culture over the past four and a half centuries. To be sure, the Spanish conquistadors voyaged to the Americas for gold, glory, and God, and it is easy enough today to say cynically that, of the three, God was a distant third. But that is too simple. In the tradition of the Iberian reconquest, personal profit and service to God and Church were inextricably intertwined. What is more, their monarchs, the chaplains who traveled with them, and even the conventionally pious conquistadors themselves clothed these conquests and the mass baptisms that accompanied them in the righteousness of crusading, despite the fact that the soldiers were not accorded any of the spiritual and other benefits normally given crusaders.

In his letter of July 10, 1519, to Queen Mother Juana and Emperor Charles V, Hernán Cortés, who would conquer the Aztec Empire twenty-five months later, noted that annually thousands of humans were sacrificed in temples that stretched from the island of Cozumel to central Mexico, and the queen mother and emperor should consider putting an end to such evil practices. For, he wrote, "Your Majesties may gain much merit and reward in the sight of God by commanding that these barbarous people be instructed and by Your hands be brought to the True Faith."[49] Additionally, Cortés requested that, through the agency of Charles and his mother,

---

49. Hernán Cortés, *Letters from Mexico*, trans. Anthony Pagden (New Haven, CT: Yale University Press, 1986), 36.

His Holiness may permit and approve that the wicked and rebellious, after having first been admonished, may be punished as enemies of our Holy Catholic Faith. This will be the occasion of a fearsome warning and example to those who are obstinate in coming to the knowledge of the truth; and the great evils which they practice in the service of the Devil, may be prevented.[50]

In other words, Cortés sought papal permission to wage a perpetual crusade against the Natives of Mexico who resisted conversion, using their punishment as a lesson to others down the road who resisted conversion.

His holiness, Pope Leo X, had many other concerns, including his unsuccessful attempt to launch a crusade against the Hussites of Bohemia and a brewing religious rebellion in Germany. Consequently, he never acknowledged the conquest of Mexico as a crusade. But this did not make it any less holy in the eyes of the Spaniards. How the Spaniards' Native allies viewed that struggle is another issue.

Without Native allies, who outnumbered his small army many times over, Cortés would never have been able to take Tenochtitlan. In essence, Cortés benefited from age-old animosities between the Aztecs and their neighbors, and chief among them were the Tlaxcalans. It is not at all likely that the Tlaxcalans saw this struggle as a Christian crusade, even after their chiefs were baptized in 1520, roughly a year before the conquest of Tenochtitlan. They probably saw it as a struggle between their chief deity Camaxtli, a god of war, and the Aztecs' chief deity Huitzilopochtli, a god of war, the sun, and sacrifice—a holy war, to be sure, but not a Christian holy war.

After the Spanish victory, however, the Tlaxcalans quickly learned to present themselves as crusading holy warriors. Around 1550, they crafted three identical renderings of one of the most extraordinary works of art to come out of colonial Mexico, the *Lienzo de Tlaxcala*. A *lienzo* is a graphic narrative on cloth. This particular cloth was canvas, about six and a half feet wide and sixteen feet long, containing eighty-seven scenes depicting the Tlaxcalans' relations with the Spaniards and their role in the war on the Aztecs. They sent one lienzo to the viceroy of New Spain in Mexico City, another to the emperor's court in Spain, and deposited the third in Tlaxcala's new town hall.

It was marvelous propaganda, and as propaganda it was not totally honest. The lienzo fails to record the battles that took place between the Tlaxcalans and the Spaniards before the Indians sued for peace and joined forces with Cortés. It also places the baptism of the Tlaxcalan chiefs out of sequence, making their acceptance of Christianity appear much earlier than it was. But strict adherence

---

50. Ibid., 37.

2.5. The fight for the causeway and the Temple of Toci. *Lienzo de Tlaxcala.*

to historical fact would have detracted from the lienzo's portrayal of the Tlaxcalans as Christian holy warriors. And it worked. Tlaxcala enjoyed special status and privileges under colonial rule.

None of the sixteenth-century originals has survived, but we have reasonable facsimiles created in the eighteenth and nineteenth centuries. The scene depicted here, a copy made in 1773, depicts an amphibious assault on the causeway into Tenochtitlan on which the Temple of Toci, "Mother of the gods," stood. Brigantines carrying Spaniards and Native Americans, including Malintzin, Cortés's interpreter and lover, are in the uppermost register. One of the two bearded Spaniards in the boat is probably Cortés. The lowest register shows Mexica in their watercraft attempting to intercept the invaders. In the middle register is the fight for the causeway. A Tlaxcalan warrior (identified by the golden eagle battle standard and his headband), supported by a second Indian, emerges from the temple (which is identified as "Teçiquauhtitlã"). After having apparently captured the temple (note the disembodied head at the temple's summit), he charges a jaguar warrior. In the midst of the fray, Malintzin, who carries a shield, points two laggard Spaniards to the temple. The Spaniard in the lead appears to be Cortés. The message is unmistakable.

Subsequent Holy Wars of Conquest

From about the middle of the seventeenth century until the early twenty-first century, holy wars of conquest in the name of a deity became rare to nonexistent. There is good reason to catalog the Cromwellian invasion of Ireland by the Puritan New Model Army (1649–53), which defeated the papally sponsored Irish Catholic Confederation, massacred large numbers of Catholics, and conquered the entire island, as the last holy war of this sort waged on European soil.

SOURCES

Source 1. Ashurnasirpal II in Victory

2.6. A panel from the Assyrian royal palace at Nimrud.

The Neo-Assyrian monarch Ashurnasirpal II (Ashur is guardian of the heir, r. 883–859) established his capital at Nimrud, not far from present-day Mosul, Iraq, and there he built the magnificent Northwest Palace, which he decorated with huge carved reliefs that depict several of his many campaigns (he embarked on at least fourteen wars of conquest). Here the king stands under a parasol, a symbol of royalty, and holds arrows with their heads upright, a symbol of victory and peace (arrows pointing down signify enmity and war). He is viewing prisoners, who are not shown here, and converses with a noble. Overhead, Ashur in the form of a winged sun disk, holds a bow in his left hand and raises his right hand in blessing.

Western archeologists carried away from Nimrud a wealth of monumental Assyrian sculptures in the mid-nineteenth century, with much of it going to London's British Museum. Perhaps that robbery had positive consequences. In 2015, ISIL (the Islamic State of Iraq and the Levant) bulldozed the extant ruins of Nimrud, effectively destroying what it considered to be the remnants of pagan idolatry.

Questions for Consideration

Many scholars have noted that war in the ancient Near East was an act of worship in which human agents on Earth not only acted in accordance with the will of a deity but also strove to emulate that deity's actions. Is there anything about this depiction of the king that might support that thesis? As long as we are analyzing artifacts, let's briefly return to the *Narmer Palette* (p. 29) and the *Stele of the Vultures* (p. 31). Some scholars have seen in holy wars of conquest attempts to establish or restore cosmological order in the face of chaos. Does any one or more of these works of art and propaganda support that conclusion? If so, how?

Source 2. The Capture of Ai

The Book of Joshua, Chapter 8[51]

The story of Jericho, where "the walls came tumblin' down,"[52] is well known within Jewish and Christian religious circles. Archeological excavations, however, have unambiguously shown that the site had no fortifications at the time in which the Israelites were presumably moving into the lands of Canaan, namely the early twelfth century B.C.E. In fact, the absence of pottery and tombs strongly suggests that the site was not even inhabited then. This indicates that we must be cautious in accepting uncritically the Deuteronomic account of the conquest of Canaan. If so, what can we make of the story of the capture of Ai? As we saw in the Introduction, this biblical story led Augustine of Hippo to conclude that sacred wars proclaimed by God are, by their very nature, just.

Our story begins just after the death of Achan and his family, which we studied in the body of this chapter.

Questions for Consideration

What roles does Yahweh play in this battle? What roles do Joshua and the Israelites play? What does your answer suggest about the interplay between divine and human agency in these wars? In what way(s), if any, does the story of Ai parallel the story of Achan and the curse of damnation laid upon him?

◆◆◆◆◆

---

51. Chapter 8:1–2; 13–29 (New Jerusalem Bible), 292–93.
52. From the gospel song "Joshua Fit the Battle of Jericho." You can find the lyrics at https://www.lyrics.com/lyric/2125087/Mahalia+Jackson/Joshua+Fit+the+Battle+of+Jericho (accessed March 11, 2020).

Yahweh then said to Joshua, 'Be fearless and undaunted. Take all your fighting men with you. Up! March against Ai. Look. I have put the king of Ai, his people, his town and his territory at your mercy. You must treat Ai and its king as you treated Jericho and its king. The only booty you will take are the spoils and the cattle. Take up a concealed position by the town, to the rear of it.' . . .

The people pitched the main camp to the north of the town and set up its ambush to the west of the town. Joshua went that night into the middle of the plain.

The king of Ai had seen this; the people of the town got up early and hurried out, so that he and all his people could engage Israel in battle . . .; but he did not know that an ambush had been laid for him to the rear of the town. Joshua and all Israel pretended to be beaten by them and took to their heels along the road to the desert. All the people in the town joined in the pursuit and, in pursuing Joshua, were drawn away from the town. Not a man was left in Ai . . ., who had not gone in pursuit of Israel; and in pursuing Israel they left the town undefended.

Yahweh then said to Joshua, 'Point the sabre in your hand at Ai; for I am about to put the town at your mercy.' Joshua pointed the sabre in his hand towards the town. No sooner had he stretched out his hand than the men in ambush burst from their position, ran forward, entered the town, captured it and quickly set it on fire.

When the men of Ai looked back, they saw smoke rising from the town into the sky. None of them had the courage to run in any direction, for the people fleeing towards the desert turned back on their pursuers. For, once Joshua and all Israel saw that the town had been seized by the men in ambush, and that smoke was rising from the town, they turned about and attacked the men of Ai. The others came out from the town to engage them too, and the men of Ai were thus surrounded by Israelites, some on this side and some on that. The Israelites struck them down until not one was left alive and none to flee; but the king of Ai was taken alive, and brought to Joshua. When Israel had finished killing all the inhabitants of Ai in the open ground, and in the desert where they had pursued them, and when every single one had fallen to the sword, all Israel returned to Ai and slaughtered its remaining population. The number of those who fell that day, men and women together, was twelve thousand, all people of Ai.

Joshua did not draw back the hand with which he had pointed the sabre until he had subjected all the inhabitants of Ai to the curse of destruction. For booty, Israel took only the cattle and the spoils of the town, in accordance with the order that Yahweh had given to Joshua. Joshua then burned Ai, making it a ruin for evermore, a desolate place even today.[53] He hanged the king of Ai from a tree till

---

53. In Hebrew, Ai, or *hā-'āy*, means "heap of ruins."

evening; but at sunset Joshua ordered his body to be taken down from the tree. It was then thrown down at the entrance to the town gate and on top of it was raised a great mound of stones, which is still there today.

Source 3. Roman Triumphs

Dea Roma and Livy, *From the Foundation of the City*[54]

This source is a two-for-one. The first half is a relief that dates from the reign of Caesar Augustus (r. 27 B.C.E.–14 C.E.), the first Roman emperor. The second half is an excerpt from the history of Rome composed by Livy (Titus Livius, 64 or 59 B.C.E.–17 C.E.) during the early Augustan Peace.

The relief depicts a helmeted *Dea Roma* (*Goddess Rome*), who resembles Minerva, the goddess of wisdom and war and the Roman counterpart to Athena. In the palm of her right hand, Nike, the Greek winged goddess of victory, hovers above a column. Opposite her on a pedestal are three items, one of which is a caduceus, the entwined-serpents staff of the divine messenger Mercury and a symbol of peace. The rest of the symbols we leave to your interpretation.

Livy's history consisted of 142 books that covered 744 years, from the traditional founding of Rome in 753 down to 9 B.C.E. Of it, only 35 books have survived, 1–10 and 21–45, but we have brief summaries for all but 2 of the 142 books. Livy was a careful historian who consulted and closely read available records from contemporary and near-contemporary times. The traditions and "pleasing poetic fictions" available to him from much earlier days he intended "neither to affirm nor to refute." Rather,

> this indulgence is conceded to antiquity, that by blending human matters with those that are divine, it might make the origins of cities more venerable. And if it might be granted to any people to sanctify its origins and to credit the gods as its founders, such is the glory of the Roman people in war that, when it acknowledges Mars, above all others, as its parent and the parent of its founder, the peoples of the world should acquiesce to this claim in the same spirit that they submit to its rule.[55]

Our excerpt comes from an early chapter in book 1 that revolves around the fabled abduction of the Sabine women. Rome, which served as a place of asylum for a motley crew of lowborn men and former slaves, lacked women, and nearby

---

54. Titus Livius, *Ab urbe condita*, bk. 1, ed. H. E. Gould and J. L. Whiteley (Basingstoke, UK: Macmillan, 1952), 18–19. Translated by A. J. Andrea.
55. Ibid., 2.

tribes refused to send brides. Consequently, the city's founder and leader, Romulus, devised a stratagem to secure wives for his citizens. He announced that Rome would hold games in honor of Neptune, god of the sea. Men, women, and children from neighboring tribes and especially the Sabines, who came en masse, traveled to Rome to view the festival. On the day of the games, by prearranged signal, the men of Rome began grabbing unmarried girls, causing an end of the games and impelling the visitors to run away in distress. Caenina, which had lost young women to the Romans, decided to be avenged and aggressively marched on the city. Romulus surprised the Caeninenses as they were plundering the countryside, routed them, and killed their king, whose body he stripped of armor. With its king now dead, Caenina fell swiftly to the Romans—their first victory and the beginning of their territorial expansion. Our excerpt picks up the story at that point.

Questions for Consideration

Consider the symbols in the relief that have not been explained. What items lie under and behind the goddess's stool? What is in her left hand and what does it signify? Consider the two items on the pedestal that were not identified. What are they and what do they mean? What seems to be in Nike's hands? What do it and the column appear to symbolize? What is the overall message of this scene? The background to Romulus's victory was the abduction of the Sabine women and other female visitors to the city, thereby ensuring Rome's fecundity and

2.7. *Dea Roma (Goddess Rome).*

future. Is there any symbol in the sculpture of *Dea Roma* that also symbolizes fertility? If so, what is the implied message? What is the religious meaning, if any, of Romulus's bearing the spoils of war to Jupiter's temple? Finally, does either or do both of these sources fit the theme of this chapter? If so, how? If not, how does one or both fall short?

◆◆◆◆◆

Book 1, Chapter 10

Romulus then led back his victorious army, and . . . ascended the Capitol,[56] carrying the spoils of the slain enemy's leader hung on a frame that had been especially constructed for the purpose.[57] There, after he had set them down at an oak tree sacred to the shepherds,[58] he marked out the boundaries for a temple dedicated to Jupiter and bestowed a new title on the god: 'Jupiter Feretrius,'[59] he said, 'I, victorious King Romulus, bring you the royal armaments of a king, and I dedicate a temple in these precincts that I have just now marked out in my mind, a place for the spoils of honor,[60] which they who come later, following my example, will bring here, after slaying enemy kings and generals.' This is the origin of the first temple that was ever consecrated at Rome. And so, afterward, the gods saw to it that the words of the temple's founder, which he had publicly spoken regarding those who would come later bearing spoils there, were not uttered in vain, and that the honor of this donation would not be cheapened by large numbers sharing in it. In the course of so many years and so many wars, the spoils of honor have been earned twice.[61] Rare, indeed, has been the good fortune of this distinction.

---

56. Rome's Capitoline Hill (present-day Campidoglio).

57. Known to the Romans as a *tropaeum* (trophy), it was a treelike structure on which enemy armor and weapons were hung.

58. The oak was also sacred to Jupiter, king of the Roman pantheon.

59. The meaning and origin of the title are equally obscure. In his "Life of Romulus," Plutarch (ca. 46–ca.120 C.E.) opined that the word derives from *ferire* (to strike down) because Romulus had pledged to strike down his enemy. Because Jupiter was also the god who witnessed contracts and marriages, some think that the expectation that he will strike down those who swear falsely supports this etymological explanation. Others theorize that it comes from *ferre* (to bring or carry) because the spoils of honor were carried to Jupiter. Livy seems to imply that it derives from either *ferculum* (a wooden frame on which something is carried) or *feretrum* (a litter, or bier, on which war trophies were borne), which supports the *ferre* theory.

60. *Spolia opima*, arms taken from an enemy leader whom, theoretically, the bearer of the spoils had killed in single combat.

61. Aulus Cornelius Cossus, who killed the Etruscan king Lars Tolumnius (437 B.C.E.), and Marcus Claudius Marcellus, who killed the Gallic king Viridomarus (222 B.C.E.).

Source 4. Two Incan Prayers to the Sun

Cristóbal de Molina, *Account of the*
Fables and Rites of the Incas[62]

Cristóbal de Molina (ca. 1529–85), was born in Spain and arrived in Cuzco in 1556, where he served as a priest until his death. In the early 1570s, Peru was in turmoil. The last independent Sapa Inca, Tupac Amaru, was executed in 1572, following the fall of the final Incan stronghold, Vilcabamba, which had held out for almost forty years. Prior to the collapse of this Neo-Incan state, a millenarian-messianic cult had arisen in the 1560s known as *Taqui Onqoy* (also *Ongoy* and *Unquy*), which means "dance or chant of sickness." It appears to have been an indigenous, largely nonviolent, and uncoordinated movement that centered on the belief that because the world had completed its last thousand-year cycle, the ancient huacas, spirit-inhabited sites and idols that the Spaniards had destroyed, had come back to life and were preparing to engulf the Spaniards and their God in a cosmic flood. All Natives who had been baptized would suffer sickness and death. Moreover, these huacas were now inhabiting the bodies of believers who, upon being possessed, would break out into uncontrolled ecstatic dance and chant. As living huacas, these persons themselves became objects of worship.

In the face of this challenge, church and government officials allied to suppress the "heresy" with some severity, flogging, fining, and exiling known leaders. In the course of the 1570s, the movement went quiet, probably going underground. It was against this background, and probably in the period 1573–75, that Molina, who had already composed a now-lost *History of the Incas*, wrote his account of what he termed Incan "fables" and their myths for the bishop of Cuzco. The theory presumably was "know your foe."

As noted above, Molina was an exacting researcher who consulted Native elders who offered the best available oral testimony. What appear here are two prayers that Molina recorded in Quechua and then translated into Spanish. Each was uttered at the *Citua* festival that was annually held in September following the new moon that arrived after the September equinox. Intended to drive away the sicknesses that came with the rains, it was presided over by the Inca and the high priest of the Sun. By the time Molina described the ceremony in its pre-Conquest form, it had largely been stripped of overt "pagan" rites and meaning and, therefore, much of its meaning.

---

62. Molina, *Account of the Fables*, 46–47.

Questions for Consideration

How has Inti become more than just a creation of Viracocha? What does the sentence "Let there be Cuzcos and Tambos" mean? What is the relationship of the sun god to the Inca and his people? If gods of war ensure victory, what else, by extension, do they ensure?

◆◆◆◆◆

First Prayer

O Merciful Creator! [You] who are at the end of the world, who ordered and deemed it proper for there to be a Lord Inca. Keep this Inca, whom you created, in safety and in peace along with his servants and vassals. [Let] him have victories over his enemies [and] always be victorious. Do not shorten his days or those of his sons or descendants. Keep them in peace, O Creator!

Second Prayer

O Sun! My Father who said, "Let there be Cuzcos and Tambos."[63] [Let] these sons of yours be victorious and despoilers of all peoples. [I] pray to you so these Incas, your sons, are blessed [and will] not be vanquished or despoiled, but rather will always be victorious, since you made them for this.

---

63. Cuzco was more than the empire's capital city; it was a living huaca, a divine city. Tambos were inns along the Incan roads that held supplies and housed journeying officials.

Chapter 3

Holy Wars in Defense of the Sacred

3.1. In defense of the Buddha and the Dharma. A temple guardian, Xumishan Grottoes, Ningxia Hui Autonomous Region, China. Constructed between the fifth and tenth centuries, many of the 130 Buddhist caves and shrines at Xumishan have menacing guardians to ward off evil forces. The upraised right hand would originally have held a thunderbolt or a mace. The guardians are believed to be manifestations of Vajrapani (holder of the thunder bolt), a bodhisattva, who originally had been a guardian of the Buddha. Vajrapani, who is represented in numerous fearsome forms as a manifestation of the power of the Buddhist Dharma, or Law, is worshipped in a wide variety of Buddhist sects. His cult is popular at the Shaolin Monastery, a centuries-old Chan (Zen) Buddhist center for Chinese martial arts.

Not all wars are defensive and even fewer are holy, but when the two combine, a powerful force emerges. With the possible exception of millenarian wars, we would be hard pressed to present another type of conflict that has the potential to inspire combatants more than a defensive holy war—a divinely approved defense of one's faith, religious principles, coreligionists, holy items, or sacred spaces.

Defensive holy wars fill the pages of history, spanning the ages from antiquity to today.

Defensive Holy Wars in Antiquity

Egypt and the Expulsion of the Hyksos

The Egyptian expulsion of the Hyksos in the sixteenth century B.C.E. had all the elements of a war in defense of a sacred land. The Hyksos probably were an amalgamation of Semitic peoples from western Asia who invaded and subjugated the delta region of Lower Egypt in the mid-seventeenth century. Roughly a century later, Pharaoh Ahmose I led a series of campaigns from his capital at Thebes in Upper Egypt against the Hyksos to the north and their Nubian trading allies to the south.

In Egyptian eyes, the Hyksos had upset Egypt's divine equilibrium by occupying half of the Land of the Two Lands, a land held in balance by the gods Horus and Set, the deities who reigned respectively over Lower and Upper Egypt. Moreover, the Hyksos had exacerbated this disequilibrium by establishing Set, Upper Egypt's god and the deity who presided over chaos and foreigners, as the chief deity in a land that rightfully belonged to Horus. Ahmose's efforts drove the Hyksos into Syria-Palestine on the eastern Mediterranean coast, where his forces dispersed and destroyed them as an identifiable people.

The Greek Sacred Wars

The expulsion of the Hyksos usually finds its way into world history textbooks, but Hellenic Greece's Sacred Wars in defense of the sanctuary of Delphi are obscure footnotes in the history of the ancient world, although the Greeks waged four so-called Sacred Wars from the early sixth to the late fourth century B.C.E. Three reasonably qualify as wars in defense of sacred space; the fourth, set in motion by Philip II of Macedon in 339, was part of an overall strategy to dominate the entire Greek Peninsula.

Philip's war, also known as the Amphissean War (339–338), was a barely disguised stratagem to humble Thebes and win over Athens to his side. The first three Sacred Wars, however, appear to have been far more religiously motivated, although jockeying for a position of hegemony, a constant fact of life within a politically divided Hellenic world, was clearly a factor. Regardless, it is reasonable to conclude that the combatants thought these three wars were divinely sanctioned, inasmuch as they were contesting the issue of who legitimately and with the blessing of Apollo controlled his sanctuary at Delphi, one of the most sacred Panhellenic holy sites. Guardianship over the shrine was traditionally assigned to the city of Delphi. However, because of the wealth the holy site generated, as well as the goddesslike eminence of its high priestess, who served as Apollo's prophetic intermediary, on several occasions war broke out over the right to protect and thereby control the sanctuary.

The Second Sacred War, which probably took place during the 450s (there is controversy over the dating), is a prime example. The Spartans declared a sacred war to free Delphi from the control of the Phocians, who had occupied it, and restored control of the sanctuary to the Delphians. Yet almost immediately, the Athenians sent troops to restore the sanctuary to Phocian control. According to the contemporary Athenian historian Thucydides, the conflict was eventually resolved in 422/1, which reestablished Delphian control of the sanctuary. Thucydides further makes clear that the Spartans saw their efforts as a means of defending the right of access of all Greeks to sacred Delphi.

The Maccabean Revolt

Perhaps the best-known example of a defensive holy war in antiquity is the Maccabean Revolt (167–ca. 140 B.C.E.), a religious uprising and civil war that turned into a war of liberation. Its immediate cause was the desire of observant Jews to prevent the Hellenization of Judaism and the outlawing of Jewish practices and worship in their homeland, which the Seleucid Empire, a Hellenistic state centered in Syria, then controlled.

The process of Hellenization began in earnest under the high priest Jason (175–172), who attempted to transform Jerusalem into a Greek-styled city-state, which exacerbated the already strained relations between Jews who welcomed Greek culture and strictly orthodox Jews who resisted what they deemed to be an idolatrous alien culture. Tension exploded into armed resistance when King Antiochus IV called for the modification of the Jewish Temple to accommodate pagan worship, prohibited the Sabbath and other Jewish festivals, lifted food restrictions, forbade circumcision, and, reportedly, offered the sacrifice of swine on a newly constructed altar in the Temple.

The Maccabean struggle, so called because its early leader was the priest and guerilla fighter Judah, surnamed Maccabee (the Hammer), eventually resulted in the expulsion of the Seleucids, cleansing of the Temple, restoration of Yahweh's Law, and establishment of the Hasmonean dynasty around 140 B.C.E. The Hasmoneans, who came from Judah Maccabee's family, would reign over a Jewish state until 37 B.C.E. when they were replaced by the Hellenized Herodian dynasty, which the Roman Senate imposed on Judea.

Although the Books of the Maccabees, which detail the revolt, are not part of the Hebrew Bible, celebration of the Jewish holiday of Hanukkah continues to commemorate the rededication of the Temple in 164 after its desecration by the

Syrians, and in that commemoration, the Maccabean Revolt is commonly understood as a war in defense of Judaism.

In Defense of Shinto in Japan

Japan's Asuka (538–710) and Nara (710–94) periods were transformative. During those years and beyond, many of the elites of this emerging island empire willingly imported from China, the dominant East Asian civilization of the day, a wide variety of ideas, religious beliefs and modes of worship, cultural norms, and political structures. Beginning in 630, nineteen missions from Japan made their way to Tang-dynasty China (618–907) to learn the ways of the Middle Kingdom, and for several centuries Japan was a virtual cultural satellite of China. The voyages ended in 839 in the face of a severe weakening of Tang authority and undoubtedly also due to the notion that the Japanese had nothing more to learn from their troubled neighbor. Before the end of this era of apprenticeship, many Japanese elites had learned to drink tea and to worship the Buddha.

Mahayana Buddhism, with its countless bodhisattvas and buddhas, eventually became a dominant force in Japanese life but not without a struggle. Cultural imports are rarely, if ever, adopted wholesale and without some resistance. This certainly was true for sixth-century Japan, where a holy war erupted between champions of the new religion and defenders of the indigenous animistic religion of Shinto, the way of the *kami* (spirits) who inhabit everything.

The conflict, which took place between 552 and 587, pitted the anti-Buddhist Mononobe clan against the Buddhist Soga clan. The clan leader of the former, Mononobe no Okoshi, vehemently opposed the spread of Buddhism, fearing it would offend the local divine spirits, whereas the Soga clan, which enjoyed widespread influence over Kinmei, the leader of the Yamato clan, who later would be retroactively numbered as Japan's twenty-ninth emperor, had already embraced the Buddhist faith and promoted its spread.

The decisive battle came in 587, when the Soga overcame the Mononobe near Mount Shigi. Its army reportedly rallied to victory as a result of the leadership of the Yamato clan's semilegendary Prince Shotoku, an ardent Buddhist, who reputedly inspired his troops by wearing on his forehead an image of Buddhism's Four Heavenly Kings, which had been carved from a tree sacred to Shinto. Following the victory, Shotoku, who served as regent for his aunt Suiko, the Great Queen of Yamato, ordered the construction of Japan's first two Buddhist temples, the first of which was dedicated to the Four Heavenly Kings.

As noted so often, no holy war is devoid of mundane concerns. Modern historians have tended to see the Soga-Mononobe conflict as a dynastic struggle between two powerful families, with each seeking influence over the Yamato clan.

Consequently, one might question, cynically perhaps, whether this was truly a war in defense of the kami. But while historians must always be critical in their analysis, the sources explicitly frame it as a clash between two religious cultures. Among the Mononobe clan's avowed reasons for resisting the Soga and the Yamato clans' rising patronage of Buddhism was the belief that a recent widespread epidemic was due to the kamis' anger at this foreign invasion.

Defensive Holy Wars in Afro-Eurasia, 600–1650

During the millennium stretching from around 600 to about 1650, defensive holy war was a fact of life for major portions of that great landmass we term Afro-Eurasia. This was especially true for the four civilizations to which we now turn: Byzantium, Islam, the European West, and Ethiopia.

Holy War in Defense of the Sacred Byzantine Empire?

By the end of the sixth century, the Eastern Roman Empire that Constantine I had established in the early fourth century was fast becoming something new— an Eastern Christian, Greek-speaking empire that was focused far more on western Asia than western Europe. Historians refer to it as the Byzantine Empire, and that empire persisted down to May 29, 1453, when Constantinople, the imperial capital and last significant vestige of the empire, fell to the Ottoman Turks.

Defended by Heavenly Guardians

Constantinople, "the God-protected city," withstood numerous sieges (and about 120 civil wars) in the 1,123 years of its existence as the capital of the Eastern Roman Empire. The city only succumbed twice to frontal assault: in 1204 to the forces of the Fourth Crusade, who established the brief but consequential Latin Empire of Constantinople (1204–61), and in 1453. To Byzantine minds, one of the major reasons for the city's survival, and that of the empire, was a host of warrior saints, almost all of whom were believed to have been early Christian soldier-martyrs. Within that large army of celestial warriors four stood out as preeminent, two named Theodore (Theodore Tiron, or the recruit, and Theodore Stratelates, or the general), George, and Demetrius.

From Byzantium, the warrior saints traveled west and north, where they were widely venerated within the Church of Rome and in all of the Slavic Orthodox Churches. Farther afield, the military saints found homes in Ethiopia and Iraq. From Iraq, missionaries of the Church of the East (today the Holy Apostolic and Catholic Assyrian Church of the East) brought the cult of Saint George to the

3.2. A heavenly defender. A carved wooden icon of Saint Demetrius, who is credited with saving the city of Thessalonica (present-day Thessaloniki) in northern Greece on numerous occasions. Here Demetrius is portrayed killing Kaloyan, the Christian tsar of Bulgaria. In April 1204, the army of the Fourth Crusade captured Constantinople and shortly thereafter began a campaign to conquer much of the Greek Peninsula and outlying islands. Taking advantage of the instability in the region, Kaloyan launched an offensive against the crusaders and in 1207 besieged Thessalonica, which the leader of the Fourth Crusade, Boniface of Montferrat, had claimed for himself. During that siege, Kaloyan died under mysterious circumstances. According to the French crusader-knight and chronicler Robert de Clari, Kaloyan's death was not due to natural causes. Repeating a story that circulated throughout the Byzantine world and beyond, Robert reports: "John the Vlach [Kaloyan] . . . besieged Salonika. . . . Now the body of my lord Saint Demetrius, who would never allow his city to be taken by force, lay there in this city. There flowed from this holy body such a great quantity of oil that it was a total miracle. And so it happened, as John the Vlach lay one morning in his tent, my lord Saint Demetrius came, struck him with a lance through the body, and thus killed him. When his people . . . realized that he was dead, they broke camp and returned home."[1] According to one popular Greek source, Saint Demetrius was riding a white horse when he speared Kaloyan, and this image became standard in the saint's iconography. Ironically, Demetrius was and is a popular saint within the Church of Bulgaria.

far-eastern regions of Central Asia and northern China during the sixth and seventh centuries.

On their part, the Byzantines transformed the warrior saints from defenders of the empire and its faith into aggressive warriors. According to a widely circulated story, during the Battle of Dorystolon in 971, in which Emperor John I faced a combined Rus'-Bulgar army, Saint Theodore Stratelates appeared on a white horse to rally the emperor's troops. Following the victory, Emperor John renamed the city Theodoroupolis (Theodore's City).

Although the army that Theodore defeated in 971 was pagan, a large percentage of the enemies against whom these heavenly soldiers showed their might were

---

1. Robert de Clari, *La conquête de Constantinople* in *Historiens et chroniqueurs du moyen âge*, ed. Albert Pauphilet (Paris: Gallimard, 1952), 90. Translated by A. J. Andrea.

S GEORGI.

3.3. A universal military saint. A nineteenth-century paint-on-glass icon of Saint George, possibly from Albania. According to tradition, he was a Roman soldier martyred under Diocletian in 303 and was often paired with Saint Demetrius. Popular throughout the Christian world, George is the patron saint of Catalonia, England, Ethiopia, Georgia, Greece, Lithuania, Palestine, Portugal, and Russia. The dragon is a reference to chapter 12 of the Book of Revelation, in which Michael and his angels fight the red dragon, who is Satan. In addition to George, each of the two Saints Theodore was credited with having killed a dragon. The white horse is typical for mounted warrior saints, who include Demetrius and Theodore, as well as the Latin Church's Santiago Matamoros (Saint James the Moor-killer).

not "infidels" but Christians, including Orthodox Slavs, crusaders from the West, and rebellious Byzantines. Moreover, the Byzantine armies that the celestial warriors supported often included significant numbers of non-Christian mercenaries. How did the warrior saints keep the combatants straight?

Did Byzantium Fight Holy Wars?

Does seeking the aid of celestial champions constitute holy war? Some historians have concluded that Byzantium never engaged in holy wars, claiming that not one of its conflicts was called by a religious authority, was an instrument of religion, or offered spiritual benefits to combatants. Our counterargument is that the emperors of Byzantium waged holy wars in defense of a sacred empire and, at least on occasion, held out the promise of martyrdom to those who fell in these conflicts.

Integral to our thesis is the fact that the Byzantine emperor presided over a state and a religion that had a profound Old Testament tone and spirit. He was a priest-king, who was often favorably identified with such Israelite leaders as Moses, Joshua, and David. If, therefore, the emperor was a latter-day King David, any battle in defense of his God-bestowed empire was "holy." This certainly appears to have been how Emperor Heraclius (r. 610–41) viewed his campaign against the Zoroastrian empire of Sasanian Persia.

3.4. The emperor as priest-king? Emperor Justinian I, his army, court, and clerics. Created around 547, this mosaic graces the right side of the high altar in the Church of San Vitale in Ravenna, Italy. Down to 751, the city served as the center of Byzantine imperial authority in Italy (or those portions of the peninsula still held by Constantinople). Above this mosaic, in the center of the apse, or semicircular area of the altar, is a mosaic of Christ as *pantokrator* (ruler of the universe), wearing a purple robe. Emperor Justinian, also wearing imperial purple, holds a basket containing the Eucharistic bread that a priest at Mass will transform into what is believed to be the body of Christ. The basket points toward the mosaic of Christ. To Justinian's immediate left is Archbishop Maximian, who completed construction of the church and holds a bejeweled gold cross. To Maximian's left are two lesser clerics, one holding a gospel book and the other a censer, or incense burner. To the emperor's immediate right is probably Belisarius, the empire's most successful general. A high-ranking court official stands slightly behind the general, and a second official stands slightly rear left of Justinian. Six soldiers stand to the emperor's far right, one of whom bears a shield with the Chi-Rho (X-P) monogram. Note that only one person has a halo, or nimbus.

Emperor Heraclius's Persian War, 624–28

A Sasanian army captured and pillaged Jerusalem in 614, reportedly killed tens of thousands, desecrated and severely damaged the Church of the Holy Sepulcher,[2] and carried thousands of captives back to Persia. Included among the booty was a piece of what was believed to be the True Cross of Christ. The Christian world was shocked, and in response, Emperor Heraclius embarked on a difficult but ultimately successful counterthrust in 624.

In the midst of his campaign, Heraclius offered his troops several morale-boosting exhortations. Almost two centuries later, a monastic chronicler,

---

2. The site of what is believed to be Jesus's Crucifixion and Tomb of Resurrection.

Theophanes, relying on now-lost dispatches from the field that Heraclius had sent to Constantinople and several imperially commissioned, postwar sources, inserted two short harangues into his chronicle. In a speech that Heraclius delivered in 624, Theophanes quotes him as stating:

> Men, my brethren, let us keep in mind the fear of God and fight to avenge the insult done to God. Let us stand bravely against the enemy who have inflicted many terrible things on the Christians. Let us respect the sovereign state of the Romans and oppose the enemy who are armed with impiety. Let us be inspired with faith that defeats murder. . . . The danger is not without recompense: nay, it leads us to the eternal life. Let us stand bravely, and the Lord our God will assist us and destroy the enemy.[3]

Recompense that "leads us to the eternal life" sounds like the promise of eternal salvation. The second speech, delivered when the army faced the threat of encirclement by three advancing armies, is more explicit. According to Theophanes:

> The emperor gathered his troops and gave them courage by assuaging them with these words of exhortation: "Be not disturbed, O brethren, by the multitude (of the enemy). For when God wills it, one man will rout a thousand.[4] So let us sacrifice ourselves to God for the salvation of our brothers. May we win the crown of martyrdom so that we may be praised in the future and receive our recompense from God."[5]

The promise of a martyr's crown sounds like a clarion call to holy combat, and in light of the sources available to Theophanes, we can reasonably conclude that the historian did not invent the speeches, contrary to normal practice since antiquity.

Curiously, 624 was the year of the Battle of Badr, Muhammad's first and most significant military victory. According to Islamic tradition, it was on this occasion that the dual promise of martyrdom and Paradise was extended to all Muslims who fell in battle against unbelievers. Perhaps it was a coincidence and has no wider significance. Regardless, the assurance of a martyr's crown is a powerful incentive for waging holy war, and there is good reason to conclude that Heraclius offered that enticement to his soldiers.

Heraclius's sole surviving dispatch, a proclamation of total victory sent to Constantinople in 628, provides additional evidence of how the emperor sacralized this war. It does not mention his soldiers' deaths and presumed martyrdoms,

---

3. *The Chronicle of Theophanes Confessor*, trans. Cyril Mango and Roger Scott (Oxford: Clarendon Press, 1997), 438–40.
4. Joshua, 23:10; Leviticus, 26:8; Deuteronomy, 32:30.
5. *Chronicle of Theophanes*, 442–43.

but it does place the defeated, dead shah into a satanic mold. "That God-abhorred Chrosroes" (Khusrau II) was "the blaspheming opponent of God," who "departed on the path of Judas Iscariot . . . to the unquenchable fire which had been prepared for Satan and his peers." And in that victory, "God and our Lady the Mother of God collaborated with us and our Christ-loving contingents beyond mortal understanding."[6] Empty rhetoric cynically offered to indulge the ignorant masses? One would have to be a harsh skeptic to conclude that.

Emperor Leo VI's Taktika

Between 843 and 1000, Byzantine warfare became increasingly sacralized, a development that should be understood within the framework of an evolving imperial ideology, namely, that defending the Orthodox Christian empire, and even expanding it at the expense of frontier peoples who threatened it, was God-assisted, sanctifying work. The reign of Leo VI (r. 886–912) was a milestone in this evolution insofar as he was the author of the *Taktika* (Chapters on Tactics), a military manual that allows us to see how the Byzantines conducted war around the year 900.

Leo begins by stating that the Devil has instituted warfare through sin, making it necessary for people to defend themselves using the diabolical instruments of war in order to cut out this evil.[7] War might involve the necessary use of "diabolical instruments," but as Leo's manual also makes clear, tenth-century Byzantines at war likewise employed many sacramental instruments.

A day or two before battle, priests bless the military standard, and before undertaking a campaign and on the night prior to battle, the army must be purified from sin and priests should offer up prayers and blessings. Thus sanctified, the army can be assured of God's assistance.[8] Back home, those who do not go off to war must support the troops with religious processions, and in this way they also campaign against those who blaspheme Christ and strengthen those who do the fighting on Christ's behalf.[9]

This might be dismissed as nothing more than morale-boosting. But Leo has more to say on the subject: "The priestly task is to deal with divine things properly and incessantly to perform these <rites> in the army piously and in a manner pleasing to God. . . . As a result the Divinity takes pity and *by their faith in*

6. Preserved in the contemporary *Easter Chronicle*: *Chronicon Paschale 284–628 AD*, trans. Michael Whitby and Mary Whitby (Liverpool: Liverpool University Press, 1989), 183–84.
7. *The Taktika of Leo VI*, rev. ed., trans. George Dennis (Washington, D.C.: Dumbarton Oaks, 2014), 4–5 (Prologue: 4).
8. Ibid., 279 (14:1), and 597 (20:172).
9. Ibid., 483 (18:123).

salvation [italics added] the souls of the soldiers are made ready to face dangers more firmly."[10] Apparently the priests were charged with assuring the soldiers that salvation was certain should they fall in battle. Therefore, as Leo also notes, "with God fighting along beside us, we charge them bravely . . . *on behalf of the salvation of our souls* [italics added]."[11]

By the Year 1000

It seems reasonable to conclude that by the end of the tenth century, Byzantium had in place its own version of holy war that differed to a fair degree from Islamic jihad and shared only some attributes of the crusade, as it later evolved in the Latin West. One key component of Byzantine holy war was that it was the emperor not the patriarch of Constantinople who set in motion holy war, and it was a war in defense of Christ's sacred empire. Perhaps source 1, portraits of two triumphant emperors, will help to clarify the way in which the ideal of holy war evolved from the mid-sixth to the early eleventh century.

A Prelude to the First Crusade

From the mid-eleventh century onward, Western Christians increasingly framed their growing efforts to defeat the weakened Islamic powers in the Iberian Peninsula as the continuation of a conflict that began with the Muslim invasion of the peninsula in 711. The struggle, which became known as the Reconquista, was a complex, often ambiguous process of "reconquest" that only ended in 1492, and it was anything but an unbroken series of conflicts between two competing religions and their champions. Yet, regardless of alliances of convenience that at times involved Muslims and Christians allied against one or the other's coreligionists, there was a growing sense in Latin Christendom that lands which were rightly Christian had been despoiled by Muslim conquest and domination and had to be reclaimed. Consequently, around 1050, both the papacy and the French Church and nobility began to take an active interest in Iberian affairs.

In this context, the king of Aragon sought French military aid and papal support in his effort to conquer Muslim-ruled Barbastro in 1064. Pope Alexander II responded by granting indulgences (remission of penalties due for forgiven sins) to Christians who participated in the campaign, citing the Muslim persecution of Christians as his justification. According to the pope, the war would be fought in defense of persecuted Christians and, consequently, it merited the indulgence. This was unusual at the time, as an indulgence was more typically offered

---

10. Ibid., 639 (Epilogue: 62).
11. Ibid., 485 (18:127).

to repentant, unarmed pilgrims, who sought to atone for their sins through the hardships of a pilgrimage to an often-distant shrine. Pope Alexander's extension of indulgences to armed combatants was the first time, of which we are aware, that such spiritual rewards were extended to armed men fighting in defense of the faith. Thus began a tradition that carried over to crusading and allowed the Western Church to promote the First Crusade as an armed pilgrimage to Jerusalem.

Crusading in Defense of Eastern Christians

During the eleventh century, there was a decided increase in the numbers of penitential pilgrims traveling to Rome, Compostela (the Spanish shrine of Santiago, the patron saint of the Reconquista),[12] and elsewhere in Europe, but most important for the development of crusading were pilgrimages to Jerusalem. Pilgrims who had traveled there and survived brought home news of the state of the Holy Land. Their reports were not often encouraging, with many reporting troubling circumstances, as conflicts between Shi'a Fatimids and Sunni Turks created difficulties and dangers for Christians. These reports of the abuse of Christian places and peoples in the Holy Land, dating back at least to Fatimid Caliph al-Hakim's destruction of the Church of the Holy Sepulcher in 1009, and continuing in various degrees throughout the century, alarmed many Western Christians.

On its part, from the mid-eleventh century onward, the Roman papacy sought to assert and extend its authority over the Church and by extension all of Christendom. One immediate consequence was a bitter conflict between the papacy and the Western Empire that turned violent, a contest known as the Investiture Controversy (1075–1122). In response, and as a means of justifying violence in defense of the Church, some militantly pro-papal theologians and church lawyers promoted new views of warfare that were based on the proposition that violence is morally neutral. Therefore, under the right circumstances, it is not inherently sinful, but can even be a positive good.

Around the same time, the Byzantine Empire suffered a crushing defeat in 1071 at the hands of the Seljuk Turks at Manzikert in Armenian eastern Anatolia. Letters and embassies from Byzantine and Armenian authorities to the West caused alarm at the highest levels in Latin Christendom.

---

12. Compostela in northwest Spain claims to have the remains of the apostle Saint James the Greater. According to legend, at the Battle of Clavijo in 844 (a battle that never happened), Saint James, or Santiago, miraculously descended from Heaven on a white horse and began beheading thousands of Muslim enemies, thereby becoming Santiago Matamoros (Saint James the Moor-killer). Around 1170, the military Order of Santiago was founded in León to further the Reconquista. The order's distinctive emblem, which is depicted on the cover of the paperback version of this book, is a red sword-cross.

In 1074, Pope Gregory VII took the extraordinary step of calling for the raising of an army of fifty thousand Western soldiers whom he would lead personally to aid Eastern Christians in their conflict with the Turks. The plan did not immediately materialize, as Gregory was distracted by the Investiture Controversy. Meanwhile, for the next two decades, the Byzantine Empire worryingly witnessed the fall of several major Byzantine cities and even total regions to the Turks. Most troubling of all was the loss in 1091 of Nicomedia, only fifty miles from Constantinople, leading to an intense effort by Emperor Alexius I Comnenus to reclaim it.

Alexius also embarked on a campaign to win military support from the West. His efforts included overtures to Count Robert of Flanders, King Zvonimir of Croatia, and Pope Urban II, among others. In each case, Alexius emphasized the suffering of Eastern Christians at the hands of the Turks, which incited outrage in the West.

Pope Urban had not forgotten Pope Gregory VII's plan for an expedition to the East. Channeling this outrage, he set in motion the First Crusade. Source 2 provides the text of a letter in which the pope summarized his reasons for initiating the crusade and exhorted the recipients to join the expedition. We leave it to you to decide whether the pope's letter presented this "military mission for the remission of all of their sins" as a defensive holy war. Suffice it for now to note that in a charter that two brothers signed before departing on that expedition, they noted they were participating "to wipe out the defilement of the pagans and the immoderate madness through which innumerable Christians have already been oppressed, made captive and killed with barbaric fury."[13]

Islam's Response to the Crusades

In 1105, the jurist Ali ibn Tahir al-Sulami (d. 1106) composed the *Kitab al-Jihad* (*Book of Jihad*) in reaction to the recent loss of Jerusalem and other Muslim lands. Connecting the crusaders' invasion with similar Christian offensives in Spain and Sicily, he argued that Allah was punishing Muslims for their moral and religious laxity, including their failure to wage holy jihad in the path of God against all infidels. They must repent, purify themselves with a spiritual jihad, and then undertake jihad against these Frankish invaders.

Because of deep political and religious rivalries within the House of Islam, his appeal went largely unheeded until two Sunni jihadists emerged in the latter half of the century: Nur ad-Din (r. 1146–74) and Saladin (r. 1171–93). A

---

13. Jonathan Riley-Smith, *The First Crusade and the Idea of Crusading* (London: Athlone Press, 1995), 23–24. Translated by the author.

contemporary of Saladin, the historian Ali ibn al-Athir, basking in the glow of the successful efforts of both men to win back major portions of the lands conquered by "the Franj" (Franks), picked up the argument that al-Sulami laid down more than a century earlier: the crusaders' incursions into Syria-Palestine constituted the third stage of an offensive against Muslim lands that began in Spain, continued in Sicily, and then advanced into the eastern Mediterranean. Consequently, any effort to expel the crusaders was a holy defense of the House of Islam.

And Ibn al-Athir was not the only Muslim intellectual to celebrate the defensive holy struggles of these two jihadists. In his description of Nur ad-Din's defeat of a Frankish army in northern Syria in 1155, the historian quotes a poem of Ibn Munir composed to commemorate that victory:

> In this resplendent age of yours you have repeated
> The victories of the Prophet and their times.[14]
> You have matched—how wonderfully!—their Uhuds
> And you have gladdened their Badrs with a Badr.[15]

These are strong sentiments. Nur ad-Din's victory rivals the Prophet's miraculous triumph at Badr and, by implication, any setbacks he suffers are equivalent to the defeat at Uhud in December 624, which Allah visited upon the Muslims as a "test." Both were significant events in the jihad in the path of God that led to the triumph of Islam in Arabia.

Ibn al-Athir died in 1233, fifty-eight years before the Mamluks of Egypt and Syria captured Acre, the last significant Frankish stronghold in Syria-Palestine, but he had no doubt about the eventual outcome of these holy jihads in defense of Islam.

Holy War in Ethiopia: Defending the New Zion

According to Sunni Hadith, Muhammad instructed his followers, "Leave the Abyssinians [Ethiopians] in peace as they leave you in peace." The reason for this reputed guarantee of security was that in 615 a group of Muslims, including the Prophet's daughter Ruqayya and son-in-law and future caliph, Uthman, found refuge in the Ethiopian kingdom of Axum (ca. 100–ca. 1050), where they remained safe from their Meccan enemies until departing for Medina in 628. Perhaps because of this act of hospitality, Christian Axum enjoyed immunity from Muslim armed invasion during the initial period of Islamic conquests (634–ca. 750).

---

14. "Their times" refers to the earliest Muslim community at Medina.
15. *The Chronicle of Ibn al-Athir for the Crusading Period from* "al-Kāmil fi'l-ta'rīkh," pt. 2, trans. D. S. Richards (Burlington, VT: Ashgate, 2007), 46.

3.5. Bete Giyorgis (House of [Saint] George), Lalibela, Ethiopia. The church's entrance is forty feet beneath the surface and reached by a narrow trench. According to tradition, God appeared in a vision to King Lalibela (r. 1181–1221), commanded him to build churches modeled on those of Heaven, and assured the king that angels would descend to assist in their construction. Consequently, Lalibela ordered the construction of ten rock churches in and around the town of Roha, which were carved out of volcanic tuff (with the constant assistance of a company of angels). Roha now became a new Jerusalem, or Zion, and subsequently this holy site of pilgrimage was renamed in honor of the king. In fact, the churches were created over a long span, from the seventh into the thirteenth century. This, the last and greatest of the rock churches, dates from the late twelfth to the early thirteenth century and is dedicated to the patron saint of Ethiopia. On his part, King Lalibela is revered as a saint by the Ethiopian Orthodox Tewahedo (United as One) Church. Ethiopia received its Christian faith in the fourth century from Egypt and accepted from it the doctrine that Christ's human and divine natures are perfectly "united as one." Tradition credits King Ezana (r. 320s–ca. 360) with making Christianity the official faith of the Axumite kingdom of Ethiopia.

Freedom from attack did not preclude Muslim incursions of another sort. Muslim merchants from nearby Arabia and later from other areas of Dar al-Islam, especially Iran, began to make serious inroads into coastal Ethiopia and then along the caravan routes of the hinterland by the mid-eighth century. In the mid-tenth century, Muslim merchants were a fixture in the main trading centers of north and central Ethiopia.

Conflicting desires to control Ethiopia's lucrative trade routes resulted in inevitable hostilities between Muslim enclaves on the coast and the Christian kingdom of the highlands, and almost reflexively Muslims and Christians alike shrouded these clashes in the cloth of religion. To what degree they were legitimate holy wars is anyone's guess. What we do know is that each side was essentially unable to overwhelm the other until the fourteenth century. The large armies of the

Christian kingdom, as well as the rugged topography of its mountainous heartland, made it essentially invincible, whereas the malaria-infested lowlands of the coast protected the Muslim emirates from the highlanders.

This balance of power ended in the reign of Amda Seyon (r. 1314–44). His given name translates as "Pillar of Zion," and his throne name, Gabra Masqal, means "Servant of the Cross." Together, they symbolized the dual self-image of the Solomonic dynasty, which had taken control of the throne around 1270 and would reign until 1974. Its emperors were orthodox Christians and claimed to be blood descendants of King Solomon of Israel. As such, they were the God-anointed defenders of the true religion and heads of the New Chosen People.

The emperor launched successful attacks on the emirate of Ifat and its allies—a conquest that seems to have been driven largely by his desire to dominate coastal trade but also to bring the territory under Christian rule. According to a fourteenth-century Ethiopian chronicle, when Emir Sabr ad-Din of Ifat rebelled in 1332, he declared, "I will make the Christian churches into mosques . . . and I will convert to my religion the king of the Christians together with his people."[16] In defense of the faith and his realm, Amda Seyon rose to the challenge, defeated Sabr ad-Din, ravaged his capital, and appointed Sabr ad-Din's brother as ruler of Ifat. Victories over other Muslim emirs in the lowlands followed, making the Ethiopian emperor the most powerful lord in the Horn of Africa. But was this holy war in defense of religion? At best it is an ambiguous case.

During the late fifteenth century, the Solomonic Empire of Ethiopia began to contract under pressure from the Muslim sultanate of Adal in present-day Somalia. In 1529, Imam Ahmad ibn Ibrahim al-Ghazi, known to his Christian enemies as Gragn (Lefty), initiated a series of invasions into the Ethiopian heartland that conquered about three-fourths of Christian Ethiopia, destroyed monasteries and churches, looted and defaced the rock churches of Lalibela, enslaved large numbers of Christians, forced conversions, and slaughtered those who refused.[17] Because Imam Ahmad's forces initially enjoyed overwhelming firepower due to arms and soldiers supplied by the Ottoman Empire, Ethiopia's emperors engaged the assistance of Portuguese crusaders and rallied for a defensive holy war.

---

16. *The Glorious Victories of 'Amda Şeyon, King of Ethiopia*, trans. G. W. B. Huntingford (Oxford: Oxford University Press, 1965); excerpted in Alfred J. Andrea and James H. Overfield, eds., *The Human Record: Sources of Global History*, 2 vols., 3rd ed. (Boston: Houghton Mifflin, 1998), 1:376.

17. One sixteenth-century Ethiopian chronicler noted that "it is doubtful if one in ten retained his faith." *The Ethiopian Royal Chronicles*, trans. Richard K. P. Pankhurst (Addis Ababa: Oxford University Press, 1967), 50.

The Portuguese, who had established themselves in the Indian Ocean and were facing off with the Ottomans in the area of the Red Sea, were searching for a Christian ally. Specifically, they sought Prester John, a mythical Christian priest-king of great power who, according to legend, resided somewhere in "the Indies," namely the area east and/or south of the well-known areas of western Asia and Egypt. The West had been looking for him expectantly since the twelfth century in the hope of crushing Islam with his aid. Because Western missionaries and merchants had failed to establish contact with him in East Asia during the period of the so-called Mongol Peace (ca. 1250–ca. 1350), the Portuguese sought him in Ethiopia.

There were sporadic diplomatic contacts between Ethiopia and the West throughout the fifteenth century, though nothing substantive came of them. But when Vasco da Gama anchored off Calicut, India, in 1498, it was new game on. Shortly after 1500, the Portuguese set up stations in the western Indian Ocean, from which they attacked and conquered several key Muslim strongholds. Commerce, crusade, and conversion constituted the three strategic goals of Portugal's emerging *Estado da Índia*.

In 1540, as the situation in Christian Ethiopia looked increasingly desperate, the emperor requested Portuguese assistance, which arrived in 1541 in the person of Vasco's son, Christóvão da Gama, and four hundred musketeers. After three battlefield victories, the Portuguese were soundly defeated, losing a major part of their soldiery and their leader, who was wounded, captured, tortured, and executed after refusing to convert. But the Ethiopians and the much-depleted Portuguese contingent were not through. On February 21, 1543, they met the army of Adal, which outnumbered them in soldiers and firearms. Given the fortunes of war, victory does not always go to the larger, better-equipped army. Imam Ahmad was killed by a Portuguese musketeer, and with his death, his army evaporated. Emperor Galawdewos then began systematically rolling back the Muslim enemy.

Although Ethiopia won back most of its lands, it was exhausted by the fourteen-year holy war, and its Muslim neighbors on every side remained a threat. Because the Ethiopian Church was independent of the Roman papacy, the Portuguese took this opportunity to "convert" Ethiopia to Roman Catholicism, and to that end Jesuit missionaries arrived in 1557. During the era of Catholic interlude that followed, Emperor Susenyos (r. 1607–32) converted to Catholicism in 1625, probably to curry favor with the king of then-united Portugal and Spain. But Susenyos's pro-Catholic policies set off a vicious civil war that broke out the next year, as defenders of Ethiopian orthodoxy rallied to their faith, their Church, and their distinctive religious traditions. Casualties on both sides of this five-year holy war were massive. Finally, seeing the impossibility of his position, the emperor abandoned his patronage of Catholicism and then abdicated in favor of his son Fasilides, who expelled the Jesuits in 1632. A second holy war in defense of the faith and religious culture of Christian Ethiopia had been won.

Ottoman Turks and European Christians: "There Is No Paradise for Cowards"[18]

In 1331 and 1337 respectively, a new Turkish power, the Ottomans, conquered the cities of Nicaea and Nikomedia, which left the Byzantine Empire with no strongholds in Anatolia. Before the century ended, Constantinople was flanked by Ottoman forces that were also entrenched in southeastern Europe, thanks to a serious miscalculation. Initially seeing the Orthodox Christian Serbians as the greater threat, Byzantium deployed Ottoman mercenaries against these Balkan coreligionists in the mid-fourteenth century. It was not prudent. Although the Serbian campaign was successful, the presence of Turkish mercenaries in the Balkans gave the Ottomans a foothold there. The gradual Ottoman encirclement of Constantinople culminated in the fall of the city to the army of Mehmed II, "the Conqueror," and the end of the Byzantine Empire in 1453. Constantinople (later renamed Istanbul) was now the capital of an expansionistic Ottoman Empire that had designs on the heart of Europe.

At the height of Ottoman power in the late seventeenth century, the empire controlled, either directly or through vassals, most of southeastern Europe, parts of central Europe, all of the eastern Mediterranean, Egypt and the rest of North Africa, Mesopotamia, and the holy cities of Mecca and Medina. Twice, in 1529 and 1683, Ottoman armies besieged Vienna, Austria, marking the farthest advance of Turkish forces into central Europe.

Although political concerns often dictated the varying alliances among Europe's states and, at times, of some European Christian powers with the Ottomans, many Western Christians promoted resistance to Ottoman expansion as a Christian holy war. Indeed, in the sixteenth century, popes still offered indulgences to crusaders who fought in defense of Christendom against the Turks. Such was the case when Pope Pius V encouraged the formation of the Holy League, a confederation of Catholic states united against the Ottoman threat, and subsequently blessed the banner of the league's naval forces before it ventured out to meet the Ottoman fleet in the eastern Mediterranean. Several months later, the pope joyously greeted the resulting victory at Lepanto in October 1571, the greatest naval battle of the century, by instituting the Feast of Our Lady of Victory.

---

18. Words ascribed to Don Juan of Austria, commander of the Holy League's fleet at Lepanto.

3.6. *Allegory of the Battle of Lepanto.* The artist Paolo Veronese created this memorial to the Venetian fleet's vital role in the victory at Lepanto. The Virgin Mary receives an allegorical Venice, represented by the kneeling woman with crown and dagger. Surrounding Lady Venice are four saints, from left to right Peter, Roch, Justina, and Mark the Evangelist (the patron of Venice). In the right corner of the heavenly cloud, an angel tosses fiery arrows onto the Turkish fleet.

Not everyone in the Christian West agreed with the idea of waging holy war against the Ottoman Empire. This included Martin Luther, whose rejection of the efficacy of "good works," such as pilgrimages and crusades, and the indulgences "earned" for undertaking them, stood at the heart of his revolt against the Church of Rome. In 1518, Luther saw himself as attempting to reform an errant Church and a sinful Europe, and so he initially interpreted Turkish military success in Europe as God's punishment for the sins of Christians. For this reason, he argued against resistance to the Turks, as it would be futile to resist God's just and rightful punishment.

Luther, however, eventually changed his view, and in his 1528/29 essay *On War Against the Turk*, he advocated for war but with important qualifications. He explained his earlier rejection of warfare against the Turks, noting the popes never seriously intended to wage such a war. Instead they used the call for holy war as a cover for their game of robbing Germans by means of indulgences.[19] Yet now, when the city of Vienna and other parts of central Europe were threatened by the Turks, Luther embraced a defensive effort against the Turks as long as it was a totally secular war led by lay Christian rulers rather than the pope, whom

---

19. Martin Luther, "On War Against the Turk, 1529," in *Luther's Works, Vol. 46: Christian in Society III*, ed. Robert C. Schultz (Philadelphia: Fortress Press, 1967), 164. Since the reign of Innocent III (r. 1198–1216), crusade indulgences had been given to persons who offered "free-will donations" in support of a crusade.

he called the Antichrist. Luther also emphasized that the conflict must be defensive for it to win divine approval, noting that he would "never advise a heathen or a Turk, let alone a Christian, to attack another or *begin* war."[20] Once this condition had been met, Luther argued, it is "God's command [to Christian rulers] to protect their subjects" and not let them "perish so terribly."[21] Finally, consistent with his theological vision that it is by faith alone that a person is justified, or made righteous, in God's eyes, he rejected the notion that fighting in such a war merits salvation or redemption in some form.

It is worth noting that Luther wrote at a time when some Protestants were supportive of the Turks, seeing them as potentially allowing greater opportunities for religious freedom than was the case under European Catholic rulers. Yet most European Christians, including Protestants, eventually, like Luther, came to see that the Turkish threat to Europe had to be repelled, and so Protestants often allied with Catholics and contributed to the military defense of Europe. As a general rule, while the Ottomans fought, at least formally, under the unifying banner of jihad during such conflicts, Christian views of the defense of Christian Europe varied. Catholics tended to see resistance to the Ottoman advances as holy war, whereas Protestants, even when they joined that resistance, were disposed to view it otherwise.

Protestant and Catholic Views of the French Wars of Religion

Protestant attitudes toward religious warfare had other sources of inspiration beyond the Turks, as Lutherans, Calvinists, and other Christian opponents of the Church of Rome engaged in multiple conflicts with "papists." In the case of Europe's internecine wars of religion, both camps—Protestants and Catholics alike—saw themselves defending God's Church and its sacred doctrines.

The French Wars of Religion (1562–98) are prime examples of arms taken up in defense of conflicting visions of the True Faith and fellow believers. The Huguenots, or French Calvinists, envisioned themselves as fighting for their right to exist as a religious minority in overwhelmingly Catholic France, whereas the Catholics saw themselves as defending Catholic society from the pollution of Huguenot heresy. In 1588, Louis d'Orleans, a pamphleteer for the Catholic League, which formed in 1576 to eradicate Protestantism, summed up the philosophy of the league's most radical elements: "If your brother, your friend, and

---

20. Ibid., 165.
21. Ibid., 186–87.

your wife, all of whom you hold dear, wish to strip you of your faith, kill them, cut their throats, and sacrifice them to God."[22]

At the same time, we would be hopelessly naïve if we dismissed as insignificant the political, social, and economic factors that contributed to these wars. Surely more than just religious ideology drove the infamous Saint Bartholomew's Day Massacre of 1572, in which tens of thousands of Huguenots were killed in Paris and a dozen provincial cities. But Catholic Counter-Reformation zeal, above all else, was a primary motivator.

The Thirty Years' War

Europe's most destructive war before the twentieth century was the Thirty Years' War (1618–48). A morbid memory of it lingered on well into the nineteenth century in Germany, which bore the brunt of the devastation. Depending on one's estimate of the death toll, anywhere from 25 to 40 percent of Europe's population perished, or somewhere between 19.5 and 31.2 million individuals, most being the victims of war-induced famines and epidemics. Beyond that, massive numbers of persons were displaced. Some regions lost upward of 60 percent of their people.

The war broke out in Hussite Bohemia in reaction to the religious and imperial policies of the Catholic Holy Roman Emperor. Although political factors played an important role in the Prague insurrection that sparked the conflict, the fact that German princes quickly lined up on either side of the battle lines according to sectarian allegiances indicates that initially combatants envisioned this war as a defense of their respective religious faiths. To be sure, the war ended as a complex, geopolitical conflict involving almost all the powers, great and small, of continental Europe that occasionally resulted in Protestants and Catholics fighting alongside each other against mutual opponents. This does not negate the fact that the Thirty Years' War was, for much of its course, Europe's greatest domestic holy war.

Defensive Holy Wars in North America

As Chapters 1 and 2 have already demonstrated, Native American societies had their own versions of holy war long before the arrival of colonists from Europe. Yet settlers from across the Atlantic brought with them new motives for holy war

---

22. Quoted in Dalia M. Leonardo, "'Cut off This Rotten Member': The Rhetoric of Heresy, Sin, and Disease in the Ideology of the French Catholic League," *Catholic Historical Review* 88 (2002): 247–62, at 247.

and were also the reason for uprisings against them that reached the level of sa-cred resistance by oppressed indigenes.

The Spanish Assault on Protestant Fort Caroline

The Spanish-French conflict for control of Florida during the sixteenth century, which assumed the character of a struggle between Spanish Catholics and French Huguenots, was a defensive holy war from the Spanish perspective. During the early stages of the French Wars of Religion, Gaspard de Coligny, a prominent Huguenot, who would be subsequently martyred in the Saint Bartholomew's Day Massacre, sought to establish a French colony in Florida. His efforts resulted in the settlement of Fort Caroline in June 1564. This alarmed Spain's Philip II, who regarded the overwhelmingly Protestant colonists as a cancer in his New World empire. Consequently, Admiral Pedro Menéndez de Avilés led the Span-ish effort to eradicate the Huguenot presence in Florida, resulting in the conquest of Fort Caroline in September 1565, the killing of most of its inhabitants, and the return of its survivors to Europe. Florida was now securely in Spanish Catholic hands and would remain so for two centuries.

Native American Defensive Holy War in the Nineteenth Century

The efforts of Native Americans to resist the influence of Christian settlers in North America resulted in their occasionally waging wars in defense of their reli-gious traditions. One compelling example is the struggle of the Sioux against the U.S. Army in the last quarter of the nineteenth century.

As part of a broader number of conflicts resulting from tensions between Na-tive Americans and U.S. citizens expanding westward, the resistance of the Sioux to settlers in their sacred ancestral lands was driven by religious devotion and vi-sions, as demonstrated in the circumstances leading up to the Battle of the Greasy Grass (also known as the Battle of Little Big Horn) in the Montana territory in June 1876.

In early June, members of the various Plains tribes in the region gathered to attend a Sun Dance, an important religious gathering. On this occasion, the re-spected Lakota chief and seer Sitting Bull had a vision of U.S. troops falling from the sky, which was interpreted by others, such as the Lakota war leader Crazy Horse, to be a sign of victory in any upcoming conflict with the U.S. Army.

Conflict was imminent as gold had been discovered in the Black Hills in 1874, prompting a gold rush and aggressive efforts by the U.S. government to gain con-trol of the region, even though it had previously signed a treaty with the Sioux exempting it from white settlement. Aside from the government's not respecting the treaty, this was offensive to the Lakota because the Black Hills are sacred lands, the womb of Mother Earth and central to their culture. More than anything else, the threat of losing those lands inspired their militant resistance to the U.S. Army, resulting in Custer's well-known defeat.

Defensive Holy War in the Twentieth Century

Defensive holy wars also carried over well into the twentieth century and beyond. Moreover, such wars were not unique to any one region of the world, taking place in India, the Central and Far East, and the Middle East.

Japanese Shintoism and World War II

Most persons undoubtedly view the Japanese effort prior to and during World War II as a war of aggression driven primarily by economic concerns and imperialist ambitions, but there is good reason for viewing it otherwise from the Japanese perspective. Evidence strongly indicates that many Japanese who fought in the war framed their efforts within the context of a Shinto-inspired ultranationalist worldview that envisioned Japan as threatened by Western secular democratic ideals. As historian Walter A. Skya has argued, "Shinto ultranationalists were convinced of the necessity of waging, to borrow the words of Benjamin R. Barber, an 'ethnic and religious jihad' against secularized Western civilization."[23] The only way that Japanese civilization could be "spiritually and physically" free of Western civilizational influence was to "destroy the Western secular democratic international world order and replace it with an emperor-centered hierarchical world order ruled by Japan's divine emperor."[24] From this perspective, Japan was waging no less than a holy war in defense of its spiritual traditions against an oppressive Western secular world order.

Tibetan Holy War against Communist China

One of the most interesting examples of holy war to come from the region where East and Central Asia meet is the Tibetan effort to resist the military aggression of communist China in the 1950s. Tibetans are known for their rugged toughness as mountain warriors who, for centuries, have fought to maintain their independence from foreign powers. Likewise, for more than a thousand years, their identity as a people has been intimately linked to the branch of Buddhism known

---

23. Walter A. Skya, *Japan's Holy War: The Ideology of Radical Shinto Ultranationalism* (Durham, NC: Duke University Press, 2009), 4.
24. Ibid.

as Vajrayana, which we saw in Chapter 1. Western observers often celebrate Buddhism for its commitment to nonviolence. While there is much truth in that view, it fails to take into account numerous wars, holy and otherwise, waged by Buddhists over the past twenty-five centuries. Certainly, the Tibetans never found the warrior norms of their culture at odds with their religion. During the 1950s, when the Chinese attempted to assert their authority over the small nation, about 25 percent of Tibet's fighting age men were Buddhist monks. These monks were not pacifists and became heavily involved in the effort to resist the Chinese invasion and occupation.

A skeptic might argue that although many Tibetan Buddhists, both monks and members of the laity, carried out acts of violence against the Chinese, this alone does not prove they were fighting a holy war. Such resistance could just as well be framed in a nationalist context, as they sought to defend their country from an outside invader. Yet there are two important points to consider. First, as noted, Tibetan identity cannot be separated from the Buddhist faith. Indeed, the historic ruler of Tibet is the Dalai Lama, who is considered to be a living bodhisattva (an incarnation of Avalokiteśvara) and the embodiment of Tibetan unity and culture. Second, as Mikel Dunham has demonstrated through interviews with numerous Tibetan Buddhists who fought against the Chinese invasion, defense of their religion was a major motivator of their efforts. From their perspective, they were fighting a war to defend Tibetan Buddhism as much as they were fighting in defense of their sacred land because the two are inseparable.[25] Of the exiled veteran warriors Dunham interviewed over a five-year period, in the United States, India, Nepal, and elsewhere, he makes clear that their willingness to fight should not be seen as an abnormality. He writes, "These men could not be dismissed as a few aberrant Tibetans. Whole monasteries, I would learn, armed themselves and went to war."[26]

In October 1950, Chinese troops moved into tiny Tibet in an invasion that the Chinese government described as the "peaceful liberation of Tibet," taking only around two weeks to defeat the Tibetan military forces sent to resist them. Facing a war that could ravage the tiny nation, the Dalai Lama's representatives were pressured into signing the so-called Seventeen Point Agreement, which recognized Chinese authority over Tibet, but allowed, at least on paper, for the nation's autonomy under the People's Republic of China, religious freedom, a

---

25. Mikel Dunham, *Buddha's Warriors: The Story of the CIA-Backed Tibetan Freedom Fighters, the Chinese Communist Invasion, and the Ultimate Fall of Tibet* (New York: Jeremy P. Tarcher/Penguin, 2004), 8.
26. Ibid., 10.

guarantee that the monasteries would not be molested, and assurance that the Dalai Lama would continue to oversee domestic affairs.

For a time, these concessions minimized violence between Tibetans and their occupiers. But in the years that followed, tensions increased, resulting in periods of intense violence. Tensions came to a head in 1956 when Tibetan militias in eastern Tibet rebelled against Chinese-imposed land reforms. The militias eventually united and, with backing from the U.S. Central Intelligence Agency, waged a rebellion against Chinese authority that spread to the Tibetan capital city of Lhasa in 1959.

During this period of resistance, which was often led by Buddhist monks, much of southern Tibet came under the control of the rebels, but at a bloody cost of tens of thousands of Tibetan lives. Consequently, because of the involvement of the monasteries in the rebellion, the Chinese government sought to suppress them and came to see the Dalai Lama as a threat, even seeking to take him into custody. When the fighting reached Lhasa, an uprising took place in response to a rumor that the Chinese planned to kidnap the Dalai Lama. The immediate result was a brutal Chinese crackdown on the city and the flight of the Dalai Lama into exile in neighboring India. In response, the Chinese executed the Dalai Lama's guards and destroyed the major monasteries in Lhasa, killing many monks in the process. Indeed, overall, by the time the repression ended, 95 percent of the monasteries and temples in Tibet were in ruins and 1.2 million Tibetans were dead.[27]

On his part, the Dalai Lama repudiated the Seventeen Point Agreement, established a government in exile in India, where scores of thousands of Tibetan Buddhists followed him, and advocated with world leaders on behalf of a free Tibet. Tibetan resistance fighters continued to make their presence felt against Chinese forces in the country for many years thereafter, but they would not be able to stop the consolidation of Chinese rule that came in the 1960s and 1970s.

In considering the motivations of the Buddhists who fought in this conflict, we invite the reader to carefully consider excerpts from Ani Pachen's *Sorrow Mountain: The Journey of a Tibetan Warrior Nun*, which serve as source 3.

Al-Qaeda's Holy War against the West

Al-Qaeda (The Base), founded in 1988 by Osama bin Laden (1957–2011), is one of the most well-known terrorist organizations in the world. Bin Laden, a member of a wealthy Saudi family and the self-proclaimed jihadist who struggled to preserve true Islamic values and ways of life, began in the early 1990s to argue that the United States is a major threat to the House of Islam. His

---

27. Ibid., 6.

fundamentalist religious views were born in the cauldron of the Soviet-Afghan War (1979–89), which ended with the expulsion of Soviet occupying forces. During the war, bin Laden served as a financier, funneling weapons and money to the *mujahideen* (they who are engaged in jihad). Because of the jihadists' success, bin Laden came to appreciate the ability of even poorly equipped holy warriors to gain victory over the most powerful foes. As a result, near the end of the war he founded Al-Qaeda, which based its ideology on Salafism, a fundamentalist Sunni movement that originated in nineteenth-century Egypt in reaction to Western imperialism and modernism. Its adherents seek to return Islam to the purity of the "Pious Predecessors" (*al-Salaf as-Salih*), the first three generations of Muslims. Additionally, bin Laden advocated the need for armed resistance to perceived aggression against Muslims.

When the war in Afghanistan ended, Al-Qaeda turned its focus to the Iraqi invasion of the tiny oil-rich nation of Kuwait in 1990. Bin Laden was distressed over the introduction into the Arabian Peninsula of hundreds of thousands of foreign, non-Muslim troops, who served in the successful U.S.-led effort to free Kuwait from the Iraqis. After all, the Arabian Peninsula, specifically Saudi Arabia, is home to Islam's two most sacred sites, Mecca and Medina, to which non-believers are denied access.

The fact that U.S. and other non-Muslim troops remained in Saudi Arabia after the Gulf War, and that this continued presence seemed to be welcomed by Saudi authorities, angered bin Laden and led him to publicly criticize Saudi leaders as betraying the global Muslim community. At one point, he claimed the Saudi authorities offered to pay him $400 million to silence his criticism and acknowledge the Saudi regime as a legitimate Islamic regime, but he refused.[28] Indeed, his continued criticism prompted the revocation of his Saudi citizenship in 1994, forcing him to spend time in Sudan and Afghanistan, where his anger toward the United States and Saudi Arabia grew. His initial outburst against the presumed crimes of the West against Islam, as laid out in his 1996 declaration of jihad against the United States, appears below as source 4.

We shall see more of bin Laden and Al-Qaeda in the Epilogue.

---

28. Peter L. Bergen, *Holy War, Inc.: Inside the Secret World of Osama bin Laden* (New York: Free Press, 2001), 93.

SOURCES

Source 1. Two Imperial Victors

The first source for consideration is a sixth-century relief sculpture on five inter-locking ivory panels from Constantinople. Known as the *Barberini Ivory* (after its seventeenth-century owner) and *The Emperor Triumphant*, it portrays a reign-ing emperor, probably Justinian I, who has been characterized as "the last Latin Roman emperor and the first Byzantine ruler." The emperor wears a helmet-like crown. His clothing is that of a military commander in chief, and he is seated on a rearing horse that leaps out of the tableau. In his right hand, the emperor holds the butt of a lance, with its spear tip planted into the ground. Hovering over the horse's mane is Nike, the Greco-Roman goddess of victory, whom we saw in Chapter 2. Her missing right hand probably held a crown; in her left hand she holds a palm, a symbol of victory. Her left foot rests on a globe inscribed with a cross. To the emperor's right, a Roman general presents him with a second image of Nike, who presents a laurel wreath, another Greco-Roman symbol of victory. At the general's foot is a bag (representing booty?). We can only imagine what was carved on the missing left panel. Beneath the emperor's horse is Gaia, the Greco-Roman allegorical figure who symbolizes Earth (note the fruits in the fold of her robe), who supports the emperor's foot.

3.7. *Barberini Ivory.*

Standing behind the emperor is a man wearing a soft conical cap, trousers, and boots, who grasps the emperor's lance with his right hand and raises his left hand. Peaked hats (known as Phrygian caps), trousers, and boots were the attire of the horse-riding peoples of Central Asia. There is good reason to infer that person represents the Sasanian Empire of Persia. In 532, in a period of momentary weakness, Khusrau I entered into an Eternal Peace with Emperor Justinian (an eternity that lasted less than eight years). Possibly this ivory celebrated that "triumph." Further, on the right side of the lower panel (our left), are two other men dressed like Central Asians; each carries something, and behind them is an Asian lion. Since at least the sixth century B.C.E., the lion was a symbol of Persian royalty.

On the lower panel's left are two men in turbans and *dhotis* (lower-body garments worn by male Indians). One carries an elephant tusk and the other bears a stave. Some Indian mendicants (begging holy men) were noted for carrying bamboo staves. Behind the two men are an elephant and tiger. Between the two sets of foreigners is another Nike, who holds a *tropaeum* (trophy), which is defined in Chapter 2, note 57.

In the upper panel a youthful, quite Greco-Roman Christ holds a scepter surmounted by a cross in his left hand and offers a blessing with his right hand.

3.8. The *Psalter of Basil II.*

Above his right shoulder is a symbol of the sun, and to his left are representations of the moon and a star. Two angels, who very much are modeled on Greco-Roman Nike figures, support or present the shield that frames Christ.

Our second image is an eleventh-century miniature from the *Psalter of Basil II*. Basil II (r. 976–1025) brought Byzantium to the heights of its military-political power in the East by extending imperial authority in the Balkans and into Mesopotamia, Georgia, and Armenia. Emperor Basil, who is identified in the illustration as "Basil the Younger, the faithful emperor of the Romans in Christ,"[29] stands on a pedestal, garbed in the armor of a general. Six warrior saints, each dressed like Basil, flank the emperor (the two Theodores, Demetrius, George, Procopius, and Mercurius), and the Archangel Gabriel crowns Basil. At his feet are eight persons representing various ethnicities; each performs the Byzantine court ritual of bowing low to the point of being prostrate. A poem on the facing page explains the scene:

> A new wonder is to be seen here: Christ extends from Heaven with his life-bearing right hand the crown, the symbol of power, to Basil, the faithful and mighty Ruler. Below are the first among the angels. One, having taken [the crown], has presented it and joyfully crowns [Basil]. The other, linking power to victories and bearing the lance, a weapon which terrifies enemies, places it in the hand of the emperor. The martyrs fight along with him as a friend, throwing down those lying at his feet.[30]

The term "martyrs" refers to the six military saints.

Although the psalter page is heavily damaged, it is still possible to compare these two works of art to see if we can discern any evolution in the imperial Byzantine attitude toward warfare.

Questions for Consideration

First consider the overall artistic style of each work. Are they similar or different? If different, how so, and what might that signify? Now on to specific elements of each. Consider the size of Heaven relative to Earth as well as the interaction of Heaven with the emperor in the two pieces. It has been said that Heaven is static in one and dynamic in the other. True or false? If true, what might that suggest? Consider the persons and other beings who flank each emperor. How do they differ? And what might those differences suggest? Consider the body language

---

29. Robert S. Nelson, "'And So, With the Help of God': The Byzantine Art of War in the Tenth Century," *Dumbarton Oaks Papers*, 65/66 (2011–12): 169–92 at 172. Translated by the author.

30. Ibid., 173.

and placement of each emperor in these pieces. What do those differences suggest? Consider the lance held by each emperor (it might be difficult to discern, but Basil's points upward). What do their differences suggest? In considering this question, review illustration 6 in Chapter 2 on page 57. How, if at all, do the suppliants differ in each work? Is there any significance to this? Consider the frames surrounding each of the six martyrs. What appearance do they give them? Is it significant? In summary, when we take into consideration all of this, are we able to perceive any meaningful differences in spirit, message, and even worldview?

Source 2. Holy War as an Act of Christian Fraternity

Pope Urban II, *Letter to All the Faithful in Flanders*[31]

In December 1095, a month after his sermon at Clermont, which we briefly considered in Chapter 2, Pope Urban dispatched this letter to the "Faithful in Flanders."

Questions for Consideration

According to Pope Urban II, what is the current state of Eastern Christianity? What, according to Urban, is the mission of the expedition? What did he urge the lords and subjects of France to do? What can we tell about the organization and recruiting process for the First Crusade from the pope's letter?

◆◆◆◆◆

Bishop Urban, servant of the servants of God, to all the faithful, lords as well as subjects, living in Flanders, greetings and grace and an Apostolic Blessing.

We believe that you, Brothers, already learned long ago from the reports of many people that a barbarous frenzy has devastated and miserably infested the Churches of God in the regions of the East. Even beyond that, and it is an abomination to say it, they have seized the holy city of Christ,[32] a city made illustrious by His Passion and Resurrection, subjecting it and its churches to an intolerable slavery. Devoutly reflecting on and grieving over this calamity, we visited the regions of France and, in a substantial way, we urged the lords and subjects of that land to liberate the Eastern Churches. At a council in Auvergne,[33] as is well

---

31. Pope Urban II, *Letter to All the Faithful in Flanders (December 1095)*, trans. A. J. Andrea, *Medieval Record*, 306–7.

32. Jerusalem.

33. The region in central France where the Council of Clermont was held from November 18th to the 28th in 1095.

known, we enjoined them to embark on such a military mission for the remission of all of their sins,[34] and we appointed in our place our most beloved son, Adhémar, bishop of Le Puy, as the leader of this expedition and effort.[35] Thus, they who strongly wish to undertake this expedition should obey his orders as if they were our own and should be totally subject to his "loosening and binding"[36] insofar as such orders are perceived as being relevant to this undertaking. If God should inspire any of you to take this vow, they should know that he will set out, with God's help, on the feast of Mary's Assumption[37] and that they can then join his company.

Source 3. Can a Buddhist Nun Be a Holy Warrior?

Ani Pachen, *Sorrow Mountain: The Journey of a Tibetan Warrior Nun*[38]

The following excerpts provide a detailed account of the author's involvement in the Tibetan war against communist China. Pachen sought a monastic life but was swept up in the conflict and helped lead Tibetan resistance from 1958 until 1960, when she was captured. She would spend the next twenty-one years in a Chinese prison.

In our first selection, Pachen describes how a man visited her father, Pomdha Gonor, an influential Tibetan chieftain, with news of how the Chinese were humiliating and attacking Buddhist religious leaders, including the man's Lama (a spiritual teacher and guide of Tibetan Buddhism).

---

34. The indulgence, or remission of the penances for forgiven sins, that the pope granted crusaders. Despite its ambiguity, this phrase did not mean remission of unconfessed, unforgiven sins or instant salvation.

35. Before traveling to the Council of Clermont, Urban appointed Adhémar of Le Puy (r. 1079/80–98) as his legate (special representative) to the expedition that he planned to launch. As early as 1086, Bishop Adhémar had supported sending southern French warriors to Spain to battle Muslim forces. He died at Antioch in 1098.

36. A reference to Matthew, 16:19, in which Jesus grants Peter the power to bind and loose on Earth. The papacy claimed (and claims) that Peter was the first pope, and all of his Petrine powers are inherited by each pope, who can delegate some of those powers to those who serve in their name.

37. August 15, 1096.

38. Ani Pachen and Adelaide Donnelley, *Sorrow Mountain: The Journey of a Tibetan Warrior Nun* (New York: Kodansha International, 2000), 106–7, 127–28, 130.

Questions for Consideration

According to Pachen, how did the Chinese soldiers harass and humiliate religious authorities in Tibet? In what other ways did the Chinese threaten Tibetan Buddhism? What gave Pachen a "new sense of purpose"? How far was she willing to go to defend the Buddha Dharma?

♦♦♦♦♦

"Oh Pomdha Gonor." The man, unable to contain himself anymore, burst into tears. My precious Lama Dhondun . . . my blessed Lama. . . ."

He was unable to continue, his body shaking with sobs. My father came over to him and gently guided him to a seat. Sitting beside him, he waited for him to regain composure.

"In Kyiedo, just two days ago, I saw a terrible thing," the old man said when he was able to speak. "I had come to the monastery to pray with Lama Dhondun when four Chinese soldiers broke in. They dragged him out of the temple. In front of a large group of monks and townspeople he was forced to kneel. His face kept its radiant calm, and he looked up into the eyes of the soldiers with a look of compassion, his eyes soft and caring.

"That seemed to unsettle one of the soldiers. Coming closer to Lama Dhondun, he raised his foot and brought it down several times on my poor Lama's head. When Lama Dhondun continued to look patiently at him, blood beginning to flow from his mouth, the soldier kicked him again and again, this time in the ribs. Lama Dhondun let out a soft moan and fell to his hands.

"At that, the soldier mounted him, put a cord around his neck and pretended to ride him as if he were a horse. He held the cord tightly, jerking it back several times. As he was doing this another soldier came over, unbelted his trousers, and urinated over my Lama's poor battered head. The other soldiers doubled over with laughter and gestured to the nearby monks as if this would be their fate too, if they continued their religious practices. Oh Pomdha Gonor . . . words cannot tell . . . it was awful!" His voice broke off again into sobs.

∞∞∞

Pachen then describes how her father helped coordinate military resistance against the Chinese in Tibet until his death. In the aftermath of her father's death, when she took over her father's leadership role for her kin group, she then sought spiritual guidance from her Lama. After advising her on how she could pray for her father, the Lama than offered the following advice.

∞∞∞

At the same time, he pointed out that under my father's leadership, our tribe was the best organized in all of Gonjo.

"Your leaders are able, the people are well-off, your men are strong, and your horses are swift," he said. "But now Buddha Dharma is facing extinction. It is a matter of the survival of the teachings."

Survival of the teachings! A new sense of purpose came over me when I heard the words. Centuries of wisdom, innumerable sacred texts, all threatened. If I can contribute something to protecting the great teachings of Buddha, I thought, I will do whatever is asked. Even kill.

∞∞∞

Pachen then took control of her late father's tribe and met with ministers to discuss what the Lama had told her and her plans to lead the effort to resist the Chinese.

∞∞∞

"I have just come from Lama Ratri," I said, hoping to roust them from their gloom. "He told me that it was up to us to offer aid. He said our religion and culture are imperiled. He asked us to lead the struggle."

I reminded them that before he died, my father had started sending men from Lemdha to fight the invading soldiers in Lower Gonjo.

Source 4. In Defense of Dar al-Islam

Osama bin Laden, *Declaration of Jihad against Americans Occupying the Land of the Two Holy Mosques of August 1996*[39]

After relocating himself and his family to Afghanistan in May 1996, bin Laden issued a number of pronouncements, beginning with his declaration of a jihad against the United States issued on August 23 of the same year. Tellingly titled *Declaration of Jihad against Americans Occupying the Land of the Two Holy Mosques*, this roughly twenty-page document contains an analysis of U.S. foreign policy in the Middle East; attacks on the Saudi regime, accusing it of being corrupt and un-Islamic; references to Islamic authorities and texts justifying the call for jihad; and a carefully crafted argument for why jihadists could defeat the Americans, which was largely based on the assumption that Americans did not

---

39. Osama bin Laden, "Declaration of Jihad against the Americans Occupying the Land of the Two Holiest Sites," Combating Terrorism Center at West Point (online) https://ctc.usma.edu /harmony-program/declaration-of-jihad-against-the-americans-occupying-the-land-of-the -two-holiest-sites-original-language-2/ (accessed August 18, 2020).

have the will to fight a prolonged conflict in the Middle East. Bin Laden's declaration was then picked up by various media outlets in the Middle East and Europe and eventually published around the world.

In the first part of the excerpt, bin Laden lays out the scope of the oppression of Muslims, as he sees it. In order to place this into a context that bin Laden does not provide, the UN's operation in Somalia (1993–95) and NATO's bombing campaign in Bosnia in 1995 were part of humanitarian efforts to prevent, respectively, famine among Muslim populations and war crimes against Muslims.

Questions for Consideration

What assumptions does bin Laden make that help frame his proposed war on the United States as a defensive war? Who are the "people of the cross," and what does that term suggest about bin Laden's worldview? What are bin Laden's goals in calling for the jihad? What does he hope to accomplish? Why does bin Laden claim it is important for Muslims to unify and put aside their internal quarrels? What will the impact be if they do not? What is the tone and message of the concluding prayer?

◆◆◆◆◆

It is not concealed from you that the people of Islam had suffered from aggression, iniquity and injustice imposed on them by the Jewish-Christian alliance and their collaborators to the extent that the Muslims' blood became the cheapest and their wealth and assets looted by the hands of the enemies. Their blood was spilled in Palestine and Iraq. The horrifying pictures of the massacre of Qana,[40] in Lebanon are still fresh in our memory. Massacres took place in Tajikistan, Burma, Kashmir, Assam, Philippine [sic], Fattani, Ugadin, Somalia, Eritrea, Chechnya and in Bosnia Herzegovina.[41] Massacring Muslims that sent shivers in the body

---

40. The Lebanese village of Qana, from where the Islamist organization Hezbollah launched rockets and mortars attacks against Israel in 1996. In response, Israel shelled the village, hitting a UN compound and killing over 100 people who had taken refuge there.

41. A civil war in Tajikistan (1992–97) pitted Islamists and their allies against the Russian-backed government, resulting in the deaths of tens of thousands and a number of massacres. In Myanmar (formerly Burma) there was (and is) the ongoing conflict between Rohingya Muslims and the Myanmar government, which heightened in intensity in the early 1990s (see the Epilogue). The Kashmir conflict is a territorial dispute between India and Pakistan that has been ongoing since 1947. Assam is a reference to the so-called Nellie massacre, which took place in northeastern India, on February 18, 1983. It resulted in the slaying of thousands of Muslim immigrants from East Bengal (today, Bangladesh) by rural peasants who were upset with the Indian government's decision to give immigrants voting rights. The reference to the Philippines

and shook the conscience. All of that happened and the world watched and heard, and not only did not respond to these atrocities, but also with a clear conspiracy between America and its allies prevented the weaklings from acquiring arms to defend themselves by using the United Nations as a cover. Muslims became aware that they were the main targets of the Jewish-Crusader alliance of aggression. The false propaganda regarding human rights have vanished under the tribulations and massacres that were committed against Muslims everywhere.

This last aggression was the worst catastrophe that was inflicted upon the Muslims since the death of the Prophet. That is, the occupation of the land of the two holiest sites, Islam's own grounds, the cradle of Islam, source of the Prophet's mission, site of the Ka'bah[42] was launched by the Christian army of the Americans and their allies.

∞∞∞

Bin Laden also devotes considerable space to the "duty" of the Muslims to unify and stop fighting wars among themselves so they can expel the Americans.

∞∞∞

Clearly after Belief there is no more important duty than pushing the American enemy out of the Holy land. . . . If it is not possible to push back the enemy except by a collective movement of the Muslim people, then it is a duty of the Muslims to ignore the minor differences among themselves. The ill effect of ignoring these differences, at a given period of time, is much less than the ill effect of the occupation of the Muslims' land by the main infidels. . . .

---

concerns an ongoing conflict between Abu Sayyaf (see the Epilogue) and the government, which in 1995 resulted in the Ipil massacre. "Fattani" refers to Muslim separatist violence in Thailand, which is based mostly in lands that once made up the Sultanate of Pattani (1457–1902). Urgadin refers to Ogaden, an ethnic Somali-Muslim region that Great Britain ceded to Ethiopia in 1948, engendering the rise of the separatist Ogaden Liberation Front (OLF). In 1994, an OLF insurgency erupted (with help from Al-Qaeda) against the Ethiopian government. In Somalia itself, the Somali Civil War saw the collapse of the government in 1991 and led the United Nations to intervene. UN peacekeeping forces, including troops from the United States, were unable to establish security or a central government and withdrew in 1995, leaving it as a failed state. Eritrea refers to incidents from the Eritrean War of Independence (1961–91). Chechnya refers to the First Chechen War (1994–96), which was a successful rebellion against the Russian Federation and resulted in the establishment of an Islamic state in 1997. Finally, Bosnia Herzegovina refers to the Bosnian War (1992–95). During that conflict, Bosnian Muslims were the victims of horrific massacres, such as the one at Srebrenica in July 1995.
42. Known also as the House of God, it is Islam's holiest site and located within Mecca's Sacred Mosque.

[To] push the enemy the greatest infidel out of the country is a prime duty. No other duty after Belief is more important than the duty of Jihad. Utmost efforts should be made to prepare and instigate the nation against the enemy, the American-Israeli alliance occupying the country of the two holiest sites, and the root of the Messenger[43] [Allah's Blessings and Salutations may be upon him]. Also to remind the Muslims not to engage in an internal war among themselves, as that will have grave consequences, namely:

1- Attrition of Muslims human resources as most casualties and fatalities will be among the Muslims.

2- Attrition of economic and financial resources.

3- Destruction of the country's infrastructure.

4- Disintegrating the society.

5- Destruction of the oil industries because of the presence of the American-Crusader military forces in the Islamic Gulf States thus threatening the largest oil reserves in the world.

∞∞∞

Bin Laden ends with a prayer.

∞∞∞

O God, people of the cross came with their men and arms and desecrated the land of the two holiest sites.[44] The Jews are spreading and causing havoc in Al Aqsa Mosque.[45]

O God, dispel them, divide them, shake the ground under their feet.

O God, place them under your immolation, and protect and deliver us from their evil.

O God, punish them and show them your great power.

O God, defeat them and grant us victory.

O God, you are our refuge and strength, you are our helper, and with you we fight.

---

43. Muhammad.

44. The second holiest site is the Mosque of the Prophet in Medina, which contains the tombs of Muhammad and the first two caliphs, Abu Bakr and Umar. As with the Ka'bah, it is a site visited by all pilgrims on hajj.

45. The mosque and surrounding land on the Temple Mount in Jerusalem and Islam's third holiest site. Muslims believe it as the place from which Muhammad made his Night Journey to Heaven.

Sufficient unto us is God, how good a trustee.

O God, those young men came to defend your faith and raise your banner high, O God, help and support them.

O God, give the Muslim youths strength and guide them.

O God, make peace between them and unite them, give us steadfastness and patience, strength and aid us to conquer the unbelievers.

O God, do not burden us with heavy laden that we cannot bear, like you gave our ancestors. Forgive and have mercy on us, you are our God, aid us to conquer the unbelievers.

Chapter 4

Holy Wars in Anticipation of the Millennium

4.1. General Gordon faces down the Mahdi's "dervishes." George William Joy, *General Gordon's Last Stand* (1893).

Holy wars that fall under the rubric "millenarian" have cut across all religious boundaries over the past several thousand years, even though, in the strictest sense, the religious concept behind the terms "millenarian," "millennialism," and "the Coming Millennium" is Christian in origin but with a Judaic foundation.

Definitions

Millennialism

Millennium derives from the Latin *millenarium* (one thousand years). In the context of Christian belief, millennialism is the expectation of Christ's thousand-year reign on Earth as foretold in the New Testament's Book of Revelation. Within the broader framework of non-Christian religions, millennialism is the belief that a savior or a supernatural event will usher in a fundamental and irrevocable transformation of the natural and supernatural spheres of the universe. The result will be the salvation or redemption of a righteous minority and the damnation or destruction (or both) of an unrighteous majority. The righteous minority can be passive recipients, who quietly await this coming event, or active agents in bringing it to pass. In the latter instance, that activity can be purely ritual and nonviolent, or it can involve the sanctified violence of holy war.

More Terms

A rare synonym for millennialism is *chiliasm*, derived from the Greek *chilioi* (one thousand). *Eschatology* and *eschatological* refer to any doctrine or belief concerning "last things," such as death, Heaven and Hell, and the End Times. In its biblical context, *Armageddon* is the site where demonic spirits will assemble the kings of Earth to fight Christ and his heavenly army.[1] By extension, an Armageddon is a decisive battle or catastrophe on a massive scale. And finally, there is *Apocalypse* (and *apocalyptic*), which derives from the Greek *apokalupsis* (a revelation). In its original Judeo-Christian sense, it meant any religious text produced in the period ca. 250 B.C.E. to ca. 200 C.E., such as the Judaic Book of Daniel or the Christian Book of Revelation (also known as the Book of the Apocalypse), that claimed to disclose some divine but up-to-then hidden truth regarding a future cosmic event or series of events and that was revealed through a dream, a vision, or a message transmitted by an angel. In addition to these two biblical books, the period produced a significant number of apocalyptic writings that never made it into the established Bible. Because the Christian Book of the Apocalypse deals with eschatological crises that will usher in the destruction of all evil forces and the end of history, "Apocalypse" came to denote the End Times, and "apocalyptic" came to refer to the signs and figures associated with the End. In everyday speech, they are convenient terms for any catastrophic event of immense magnitude.

The Judaic Roots of Millennialism

During and after the Babylonian Exile (ca. 587–ca. 537 B.C.E.), several biblical prophets proclaimed a future Day of Yahweh when the Lord would redeem the bloodied and battered people of Jerusalem, striking down all the peoples who had fought against the children of Israel. Around the year 520, Zechariah proclaimed, "a great terror will fall upon them . . . and they will fall to fighting among themselves." After that "all the survivors of all the nations which have attacked Jerusalem

---

1. Revelation, 16:16; 19:19. See also illustration 4.2.

will come up year after year to worship the King, Yahweh, Yahweh Sabaoth."[2] Significantly, "Yahweh Sabaoth," means "Yahweh, the Lord of the heavenly army."

Associated with the Day of Yahweh is the concept of a *messiah* (the anointed one). Originally the term was applied to anointed kings and, less so, priests, who were Yahweh's instruments of justice and guardianship on Earth. Beginning in the sixth century B.C.E., several prophets foretold of a new messiah, a kingly messiah who was a redeemer-to-come. Through this messiah, Yahweh would gather together his Chosen People from all alien lands to form a single kingdom that would last forever. Their exile, pain, and suffering wiped away, Yahweh's people would enter into a new and eternal Covenant with their God.[3]

Jewish prophecies of a climactic battle between Israel and its enemies reached their apogee, at least as far as the Hebrew Bible is concerned, in the Book of Daniel, which was composed at the time of the Maccabean War. According to Daniel, this battle, which will usher in the End, will initially be a period of great distress, but it will conclude with the sparing of all "whose names are written in the Book," and the Resurrection of the dead. Some will awaken to everlasting life and some to everlasting disgrace.[4]

The War Scroll

As noted, most Jewish apocalyptic texts never became part of the Hebrew Bible. One of the most interesting is the *War Scroll*. Discovered among the Dead Sea Scrolls in 1947, it was probably composed between 150 B.C.E. and 50 C.E. and was likely part of the library of the nearby Qumran religious community.

Although the scroll describes the organization, strategy, and tactics that the Sons of Light will employ in a coming forty-year battle with the Sons of Darkness, the army of Belial, it is not primarily a military manual. Rather, the author was concerned with offering hope—hope in the midst of current tribulations visited upon Israel by the "Kittim," a generic term for all of the Chosen People's adversaries. As the scroll proclaims: "On the day when the Kittim fall there shall be a battle and horrible carnage before the God of Israel, for it is a day appointed by Him from ancient times as a battle of annihilation for the Sons of Darkness."[5] In alliance with the Kittim, and accompanying them to destruction, will be Jews who violated the Covenant.

---

2. Zechariah, 14:13–16 (New Jerusalem Bible, 1590). See all of chapters 12–14, as well as Isaiah, 24–27, and 34–35; Ezekiel, 37–39; and Joel, 3–4.
3. Ezekiel, 37:20–28.
4. Daniel, 12:1–3.
5. Michael O. Wise, Martin G. Abegg, Jr., and Edward M. Cook, *The Dead Sea Scrolls: A New Translation* (San Francisco: HarperSanFrancisco, 2005), 148.

If the Qumran community was preparing itself in hopeful expectation for that final battle, it was doomed to disappointment. Just as the Romans annihilated the Sicarii and Zealots, so they wiped out Qumran in the midst of the Great Jewish Rebellion (66–73).

The Bar Kochba Rebellion, or Second Roman-Jewish War

The crushing of the Great Rebellion and the destruction of Jerusalem's Second Temple did not end Jewish faith in a war that would usher in the God of Israel's reign on Earth. In 132, in reaction to rumors that Emperor Hadrian planned to severely restrict Jewish religious practices and to construct a shrine to Jupiter on the Temple Mount, Simon bar Koseva led a massive revolt that took the Romans three and a half years to suppress. The Roman historian Cassius Dio estimated that 580,000 Jewish "men" were killed. We will never know the true number of deaths, but when we take into account deaths from disease and famine, as well as from combat and execution, the total number who perished must have been staggering. In addition, untold numbers of Jews were carried off into slavery.

Evidence is clear on one point: Bar Koseva claimed to be the messiah, and vast numbers of Jews accepted him as such. A leading biblical scholar of the day, Ahiva ben Yosef, declared Simon to be the promised King Messiah and called him Bar Kochba (Son of the Star) in reference to an ancient prophetic poem that claimed a star would arise out of Jacob to crush Israel's enemies.[6] And it is as Bar Kochba that he is memorialized by history.

The Consequences of the Bar Kochba Revolt

Following the crushing of the Bar Kochba Revolt, a mass scattering, or diaspora, of Jews into the lands of Rome, Persia, and beyond took place. A people separated in this manner lack the means to wage effective war. Moreover, a rabbinic tradition emerged that remembered Simon as Bar Koziba (Son of Lies), a pun underscoring his false messiahship. Indeed, throughout most of the centuries of the Diaspora, mainstream rabbinic teaching maintained that Jewish insurgents were not freedom fighters but criminals.

Given these realities, Jewish hopes for a messiah and renewed mastery over the Promised Land were now almost exclusively expressed in prayerful quietism and passive expectation of the Day of Yahweh. It was only in the modern era, with the struggle first to create a Jewish state in Palestine and then to preserve the nation of Israel, that thought and action turned to political activism and armed struggle on a significant, on-going scale.

---

6. Numbers, 24:17.

Diaspora Judaism's Holy Wars after Bar Kochba

Regardless of this general mood of watchful waiting for a messiah, on several occasions and within limited circumstances, Jewish communities engaged in uprisings that had all of the flavor of holy warfare. Two took place in Judaism's ancient homeland.

Rebellions in Roman Palestine

Despite Roman oppression and the choice of many Jews to leave Palestine, some—we know not how many—tenaciously stayed in their ancient homeland. In 351–52, persecuted by Roman imperial officials and the general Christian population, Jews in the Galilee region of northern Palestine rebelled, killing Christians, pagans, and Samaritans ("heretical" Jews) alike. Our limited sources, all Christian, do not provide any evidence of millenarian aspirations fueling this uprising, although the leaders of the rebellion employed Deuteronomic imagery to describe their enemies, and it is likely that messianic hopes impelled some of the rebels to action. Once again, Roman authorities suppressed the insurgency with bloody force.

Whatever the case in the fourth century, millenarian expectations were clearly part of the mix driving a seventh-century Jewish rebellion in the same region. According to our sources, about twenty thousand Jews, inspired by eschatological hopes, rose in support of an invading Sasanian army and assisted in the capture of Jerusalem in 614. Also, so the sources claim, the rebels massacred large numbers of Christians, but once the Persians vacated the region, the Jews were crushed by the avenging forces of Emperor Heraclius. We can question the reported number of Jews who participated; crowd estimation is an imprecise exercise. There is no reason to doubt, however, that the rebels viewed the Sasanians in the same light as the sixth-century-B.C.E. prophet Isaiah regarded the Persian king, Cyrus, a Zoroastrian, whom he characterized as Yahweh's anointed one (messiah), who rebuilds Jerusalem and brings the Lord's people home from Babylonian captivity.[7]

Millenarian Insurrection in Iran

The most significant apocalyptic insurrection by a Diaspora-era Jewish community took place in eighth-century Iran. It was sufficiently violent and long-lived to imprint itself in the traditions of both Islam and Judaism, but variant memories have caused confusion as to its precise dates and its leader's identity. The best reconstruction is that it began toward mid-century as the Umayyad Caliphate

---

7. Isaiah, 45:1 and 13.

(661–750) was breaking down and continued into the Abbasid Caliphate (750–1258 or 1517). Its leader was an Arabicized Jew whose given name was probably Ishaq ibn Ya'qub (Isaac the son of Jacob), but his followers bestowed on him the honorific Abu Isa al-Isfahani (The Father of Jesus from Isfahan), and it is by that title that history remembers him. Claiming to be the fifth and last of God's messengers, who included Jesus and Muhammad, he preached the imminence of the messiah (whom he did not claim to be) and the End Times that would follow.

Although his message was Jewish in essence and directed toward Jews, it appears to have been deeply influenced by contemporary Shi'a Islamic belief regarding the coming of the *Mahdi* (the Rightly Guided One). For the oppressed Shi'a, the Mahdi will establish a true Islamic state (as opposed to the false Umma of the Sunni Umayyads and Abbasids) and bring relief to the downtrodden, elevating them to the highest echelons. This powerful millenarian theme struck a respondent chord among the lowest elements of Jewish society, whose marginalization was especially acute in a time of social-political unrest. Although Ishaq ibn Ya'qub died around 750, his movement persisted for an unknown period of time after his death, but eventually Abbasid authorities crushed it.

Despite these setbacks and Judaism's general retreat from political-military involvement in the world after the mid-second century, messianism and apocalyptic expectations were a major current in Jewish thought throughout the centuries of the Diaspora and have remained so to today. Every century has had its proclaimed messiahs; all have failed the test.

Two Facts about Millenarian Religions and Movements

This survey of Jewish millenarianism illustrates two realities. First, although millenarian warfare is often exceedingly destructive, there is nothing inherently violent about millennialism as a religious belief. The vast majority of people who have embraced millenarian beliefs have not resorted to war to usher in the salvation, redemption, or New Age that they prayerfully await. Second, millenarianism has especially appealed through the ages to oppressed peoples, especially in times of crisis. Among those drawn to millenarian hopes are many colonial peoples, who find in apocalyptic promises hope for the defeat of a foreign oppressor and a return to or the creation of a golden age. Even though most anti-colonial millenarian movements do not endorse violence and have not turned violent, we shall study several examples of violent anti-colonial millenarianism in the holy wars that follow.

But first, let us look at Christian millennialism and several examples of Christian millenarian holy war.

Christian Millennialism

Early Christians obsessively anticipated the End Times. Around the year 95, a prophet named John wrote that upon Jesus's appearing to him in a vision, he was summoned to Heaven, where he viewed God enthroned. There follows a bewildering array of scenes revealing the events that will usher in the End of Time and the Last Judgment. Following a series of disasters that shock the cosmos and devastate humanity, the Devil in the form of a dragon is cast into the fiery pit, where he abides for a millennium, while Christ reigns in peace on Earth. After the thousand years, the Devil is released and proceeds to lead astray the nations, mobilizing them for war against the saints. In a climactic battle, the Devil is defeated and cast again into the lake of fire and sulfur—this time for eternity. A Resurrection of the Dead and the Last Judgment follow, and a Heavenly Jerusalem, with no more suffering or death, replaces the old Earth and Heaven. The book ends with John being told not to keep these prophecies secret because the Time is near.

By the fifth century, the Church's theologians largely rejected literal millennialism and the imminence of the Second Coming, preferring to understand this complex and disturbing book as an allegory that clothes divine truths in symbolic imagery. Yet, rejection of a literal reading of the Book of Revelation did not mean rejection of a belief in the End Times or an end to searching for signs of its arrival, despite the New Testament's warning that only God knows the day and the hour, and when it arrives it will come like a thief in the night.[8]

Well before the Age of the Crusades, one theory regarding the signs that would herald the Second Coming of Jesus revolved around two apocalyptic individuals. One was the Last World Emperor, a military hero who would defeat all of God's earthly enemies, especially Muslims, convert all the Jews, and vindicate righteousness, but who would also open the way for the second figure, Antichrist, a pseudo-messiah. Antichrist is the one enemy whom the Last World Emperor cannot defeat, but Jesus and a celestial army of angels will defeat him and thereby usher in the Millennium.

A Millenarian First Crusade?

Crusading did not end with the First Crusade nor did it cease evolving. It was not until the early thirteenth century that crusading reached its full development as an institution of the Roman Church. Nevertheless, the First Crusade was *the*

---

8. Matthew, 24:36–44; 1 Thessalonians, 5:1–3.

crusading model and ideal of the West for centuries after the capture of Jerusalem in 1099, and so we should inquire whether it was millenarian in any way whatsoever.

The Vision of Pope Urban II

The first issue to address is how Pope Urban II framed the crusade in 1095–96. As noted in Chapter 2, six twelfth-century versions of the pope's sermon exist. None is a verbatim transcript, but each supposedly offers, in the author's words, the essence of the pope's sermon. Most emphasize the centrality of Jerusalem, which demanded liberation from "the gentiles," the need to rescue Eastern Christians from these same enemies of Christ, the penitential nature of this holy war, and the spiritual rewards offered to those who heeded the call. Only one version of the sermon, in a history of the crusade by Guibert, abbot of Nogent, places the expedition to Jerusalem into an apocalyptic context.

Guibert, who had not been at Clermont and did not go on the crusade, wrote in the period 1106–9, with the intention of "correcting" and rewriting in a more theologically correct and artful style an anonymous participant's account known as the *Gesta Francorum* (*The Deeds of the Franks*). The *Gesta* collapses Urban's call for a crusade into the brief statement that one must be prepared to suffer for Christ in order to be rewarded in Heaven. This brevity did not deter Guibert. In a rather rambling sermon that he ascribes to Urban, Guibert writes that the time of Antichrist and the end of the world is near at hand, but Jerusalem has been taken over by pagans with scarcely any Christians remaining there. Consequently, "according to the prophecies, it is necessary, before the coming of Antichrist in those parts, either through you or through whomever God wills, that the empire of Christianity be renewed, so that the leader of all evil, who will have his throne there, may find some nourishment of faith against which he may fight."[9] In other words, Christians must rescue Jerusalem so that Antichrist can reign there briefly.

When we turn to the few extant letters of Urban regarding crusading (and you read one among Chapter 3's sources), we find no references to Antichrist or any other aspect of the Last Days. So, it is likely that Urban did not publicly present this expedition to Jerusalem as a means of ushering in the Second Coming of Christ. The best explanation for Guibert's turning Urban's sermon into an eschatological call to arms is that he was writing from a post-crusade perspective. Jerusalem had been liberated. Apparently he believed that with that victory, the first steps leading to the Millennium had been taken. Supporting this interpretation is

---

9. *The Deeds of God through the Franks: A Translation of Guibert de Nogent's "Gesta Dei per Francos,"* trans. Robert Levine (Woodbridge, UK: Boydell Press, 1997), 44.

the fact that toward the end of his history, Guibert reports that prior to the crusade Muslim astrologers had foretold the conquest of the Holy Land by Christians, but they also read in the stars that in time the Christians would be driven out by military force—the very prophecy regarding Antichrist that Guibert ascribed to Pope Urban.

Despite the pope's probable silence at Clermont on the issue, there is reason to conclude that Urban set in motion a holy war believing that the Christian people whom he summoned would be the agents of God, "who changes times and seasons and transfers and raises up kingdoms" (Daniel, 2:21). Thus God, by transferring Jerusalem from the hands of Saracens into those of his Christian agents, would raise up a New Israel.[10] And that New Israel would be the last empire on Earth.

That verse from the Book of Daniel comes from a laudatory prayer that the prophet utters upon receiving a vision in which God reveals to him King Nebuchadnezzar's dream. Later, Daniel informs the king that his dream foretells the rise and fall of four world empires and the rise of a fifth that would last forever. Medieval Christian commentators on the Bible interpreted that fourth empire as Rome, which they believed still existed but was in its senescence. The fifth, eternal empire was clearly a future Kingdom of God.

As far as we know, Urban employed Daniel 2:21 only three times in his eleven-year pontificate, in three separate letters. One letter, in 1091, concerned the reconquest of a portion of Spain, and two letters, in 1093 and 1098, focused on the reconquest of Sicily. Both lands, as he noted, had been lost centuries earlier to the Saracens because of Christian sin. Now, however, a repentant and renewed Christian people, serving as God's agent, was regaining these lands. Note that it was not kings or emperors who had lost and were now recovering the lands. It was the entire Christian people who were now re-winning the lands with a penitential heart. In very much the same way, in his letter to the faithful of Flanders, quoted in Chapter 3, Urban noted that he had "visited the regions of France and . . . we urged the lords and subjects of that land to liberate the Eastern Churches." It would not be the lords alone, but all the faithful, who would regain Jerusalem. In other words, Christian offensive operations in Spain, Sicily, and the Holy Land were all part of the same mission, and that mission was assisting in God's work of transferring and raising up kingdoms.

So, it appears that Guibert, who did not pretend to be a scribe who faithfully set down the pope's words, saw himself as communicating a higher truth. He might have been incorrect in placing Urban's vision into the framework of the

---

10. What follows depends on the insightful work of Matthew Gabriele, "The Last Carolingian Exegete: Pope Urban II, the Weight of Tradition, and Christian Reconquest," *Church History* 81 (2012): 796–814.

Book of Revelation, but he did not err in perceiving that the pope was acting on millenarian expectations.

Emicho of Flonheim, the Last World Emperor?

Raymond of Aguilers, a crusader and the author of source 1, employed apocalyptic imagery to give context to the crusaders' capture of Jerusalem in 1099, but one wonders how typical this viewpoint was. Getting into the minds of the more than one hundred thousand participants in the several waves of the First Crusade to the Holy Land is an impossible task. The vast majority left no trace of the motives that drove them, although it is more than reasonable to infer that most were impelled by some degree of piety and religious fervor. But piety and religious fervor take many forms, and we cannot say what percent framed their piety in millenarian terms. That noted, there is evidence that at least one crusade leader placed this expedition into an apocalyptic framework.

At the beginning of his journey eastward, Count Emicho of Flonheim led a contingent of an estimated twelve thousand soldiers and others that attacked the Jews of Mainz in May 1096, offering them the choice of conversion or death. Most opted for death, with many committing suicide to avoid profanation. Two sources, one Christian and one Jewish, offer clues as to what seems to have motivated the count. Writing sometime after 1102, Ekkehard of Aura, a German monk, reports that Emicho had a religious conversion and claimed that he was called by divine revelation to be a second King Saul, the first king of Israel, and thereby to defend his religion. Consequently, his band sought to either annihilate the "accursed Jewish people . . . or . . . drive them into the fold of the Church."[11] Solomon bar Simson, who around 1140 compiled several early Jewish sources of the massacres of the Jews of the Rhine and Mosel Valleys in 1096, recorded that Emicho "concocted a tale that an apostle of the crucified one had come to him and made a sign on his flesh to inform him that when he arrived at Magna Graecia,[12] he [Jesus] himself would appear and place the kingly crown upon his head, and Emicho would vanquish his foes."[13] If this Jewish account is correct, Emicho thought himself to be the Last World Emperor. This dream, if it was his dream, did not get him far. His band was almost totally wiped out by Christian forces when it tried to force its way through Hungary, and Emicho and several fellow nobles beat a hasty retreat home.

---

11. Ekkehard of Aura, *Hierosolmita*, trans. A. J. Andrea in Andrea, *Medieval Record*, 311.
12. Southern Italy.
13. The *Chronicle of Solomon bar Simson* in *The Jews and the Crusaders: The Hebrew Chronicles of the First and Second Crusades*, ed. and trans. Shlomo Eidelberg (Hoboken, NJ: KTAV Publishing House, 1977), 28.

Rumors of Wars[14]

Despite the paucity of the evidence, it appears probable that Emicho is emblematic of apocalyptic rumors and expectations that were subcurrents within the ranks of the First Crusade, but they are subcurrents that defy quantification because those moods and hopes are obscured in the records. Such undertones seem to have been especially true for the misnamed Peasants' (or People's) Crusade, which set off in the spring of 1096, and of which Emicho and many other trained warriors were an integral part. A glimmer of this apocalypticism peeks though in another passage in Ekkehard of Aura's history of the crusade. According to him, at this time, rumors abounded of resurrected persons, including Charlemagne, who would participate in the expedition. Shades of the Last World Emperor prophecy!

Moreover, significant numbers of persons from the lower orders of society participated in both the First Crusade's initial wave (the so-called Peasants' Crusade) and second wave (the Nobles' Crusade), excited by popular preachers, who reached out to all classes. Although evidence for their harboring explicit millenarian dreams is scanty at best, it is reasonable to assume that they had often heard sermons focusing on Jesus's statement that the lowly in spirit would possess the Kingdom of Heaven.[15] And their priests, often from the same social order, told them that as the poor, they were especially loved by God, whose Son came into the world and died there a poor man, before ascending to celestial Glory. As beloved agents of God, surely some saw themselves as fighting to usher in the Kingdom of God on Earth.

This theory seems all the stronger when we consider four popular crusades that arose largely in France and Germany in the thirteenth and fourteenth centuries. The Children's Crusade of 1212, the Shepherds' Crusades of 1251 and 1320, and the Crusade of the Poor of 1309 were mass movements inspired by crusade preaching and news of events overseas that attracted large numbers of youths and adult men and women from the lower and middle ranks of society. Each crusade clearly had an apocalyptic tenor. There is evidence that some elements of the Children's and the First Shepherds' Crusades expected that the waters would part when they reached the sea, and they would walk dry-shod to Jerusalem, where they would rescue the Holy Sepulcher. In the crusade of 1251, the shepherds and allied participants carried banners emblazoned with the Lamb of

---

14. Matthew, 24:6.
15. Ibid., 5:3. The Latin Vulgate text is at https://www.sacred-texts.com/bib/vul/mat005.htm (accessed April 15, 2020).

God (Revelation, 5:9) and their leader, the Master of Hungary, claimed to carry a letter sent from Heaven by the Virgin Mary.

None of these unauthorized crusades made it to the East, but whereas the several branches of the Children's Crusade appear to have been peaceful, the other three turned violent with murderous attacks on the clergy and Jewish communities. In the case of the two Shepherds' Crusades, evidence strongly indicates that the acts of violence were attempts to cleanse society prior to the coming of the Kingdom of God. All of them failed.

Although the Church did not recognize these four crusades as legitimate, the participants thought otherwise, because the highest of all authorities had called them to a world-changing mission. But even official crusades were taking on unambiguous apocalyptic overtones as the Age of the Crusades grew older.

The Fifth Crusade (1217–21)

The army of the Fifth Crusade attempted to reconquer Jerusalem, which Saladin had retaken for Islam in 1187, by first destroying the Ayyubid sultanate's power base in northern Egypt. In the midst of the crusade's military operations in Egypt, millenarian prophecies ran wild throughout the crusaders' camp, and their sheer volume and intensity suggest that crusade millenarianism was not a new phenomenon. Oliver of Paderborn, a cleric who was involved with almost every aspect of the crusade, reports one example. A book in Arabic by an author who was not Jewish, Muslim, or Christian came to the crusaders' attention, and in that book the author predicted that

> a certain king of the Christian Nubians[16] was to destroy the city of
>
> Mecca and cast out the scattered bones of Muhammad, the false
>
> Prophet, and certain other things which have not yet come to pass.
>
> If they are brought about, however, they will lead to the exaltation
>
> Of Christianity and the suppression of the Agarenes.[17]

---

16. Christians in Sudan and the Horn of Africa, especially Ethiopia.

17. Muslims are the descendants of Ishmael, Abraham's first son whose mother was Hagar, the servant of Abraham's wife Sarah. The excerpt is from John Gavigan's translation of Oliver of Paderborn, *The Capture of Damietta* (1948), reprinted in *Crusade and Christendom: Annotated Documents in Translation from Innocent III to the Fall of Acre, 1187–1291*, ed. Jessalynn Bird, Edward Peters, and James M. Powell (Philadelphia: University of Pennsylvania Press, 2013), 188–89.

4.2. An Apocalypse fresco. Located in the crypt of the Cathedral of Saint-Étienne in Auxerre, France, the painting depicts the Risen Christ astride a white horse and flanked by four mounted angels. According to traditional interpretation, Jesus is the horseman of the Apocalypse who leads a celestial army of white-clad angels on white horses to wage war on the kings of Earth.[18] The jeweled cross, which serves as Christ's background, has been a symbol of Jesus's triumph over death since the fourth century. Bishop Humbaud (r. 1092–1114) probably commissioned the fresco around 1100 to celebrate the triumph of the First Crusade. The bishop, a close friend of Pope Urban, had almost certainly been at Clermont in 1095 when the pope preached the crusade. A patron of crusading and the Latin presence in the Holy Land, Humbaud traveled on pilgrimage to Jerusalem while in his sixties or seventies and drowned in a shipwreck on the voyage home.

The anonymous "heathen gentile," as Oliver characterizes him, failed to predict the encircled crusaders' humiliating surrender in the wetlands of the Nile delta.

Anabaptism

Like the crusades, the sixteenth-century Protestant Reformation took numerous forms. On the more conservative side there was Lutheranism and Anglicanism, in the middle was the Reformed Protestantism of Zwingli and Calvin, and on the radical fringe there was Anabaptism.

Anabaptism was not a single sect or church but an assortment of evangelical Christian communities that shared many beliefs and drew adherents from all socioeconomic strata. Their commonly held convictions included refusal to associate with any government and a commitment to radically reform the lives of all true Christians. The term "Anabaptist," imposed on them by their critics, means "one who re-baptizes" and refers to the doctrine that no one should be

---

18. Revelation, 19:11–16, and 19.

baptized before reaching the age of understanding and true faith. Consequently, Anabaptists re-baptized all converts. Catholics and mainstream Protestants alike considered second baptism a sacrilege and the Anabaptists' rejection of government subversive of God's divinely mandated order. Consequently, they deemed Anabaptists worthy of eradication.

The first Anabaptists were pacifists, and most believed in an imminent Second Coming of Jesus, which they expected to occur in 1533, the fifteen-hundredth anniversary of Christ's death, Resurrection, and Ascension into Heaven.

The Anabaptists of Münster: Apocalyptic Warfare in the Age of the Reformation

The year 1533 came and went with no Second Coming but with intensified oppression of "the Saints." In reaction to persecution, several hundred Anabaptist immigrants from the Netherlands arrived in Münster, a town in northwestern Germany, in 1534. The numbers of Dutch immigrants soon swelled to about twenty-five hundred. Under the leadership of Jan Matthijs, the now-dominant Anabaptists expelled several thousand of the city's Catholics and Lutherans. In expectation of the Second Coming, which Matthijs prophesied would now occur on Easter Sunday 1534, they declared the town to be the New Jerusalem. The local Catholic bishop, who was the lord of Münster, consequently besieged the town. On the expected day of Christ's coming, Matthijs, thinking himself a latter-day Gideon, who could defeat thousands with a handful of soldiers and Yahweh's aid,[19] led twelve men out of the city to fight the bishop's mercenaries. Matthijs and his band were immediately cut down, the prophet's body was decapitated, and his head was placed on a pole for all to see.

The siege continued, and a new prophet arose in the town, Jan van Leiden, who claimed to receive continuous visions. In August, he was declared King of the New Zion and instituted a community that was radically communistic, polygamous (he took sixteen wives), banned all books except for the Bible, and was governed by his interpretation of biblical mandates. He held together and "purified" this theocratic millennial kingdom through a reign of terror in which numerous inhabitants were beheaded for the slightest infraction, including questioning his judgment.

As 1534 drew to a close, and the Second Coming had not yet arrived, Jan van Leiden's ally and fellow visionary, Bernard Rothmann, offered a reassuring message that placed what was happening at Münster into a new eschatological

---

19. Judges, 7:4–7.

4.3. Jan van Leiden's coffin. Replicas of the cages that were suspended from the steeple of the Cathedral of Saint Lambert and held the dismembered bodies of Jan van Leiden and two colleagues, who were executed in the town square in January 1536. The rotted corpses remained in the cages for fifty years.

context. He proclaimed that following the Christian Church's first century of existence, fourteen hundred years of steady decline and desolation ensued. Now, however, the world was entering the Third and Last Age, a time of vengeance and the triumph of the Saints. And it had already begun at Münster. From there, under the leadership of the new David, Jan van Leiden, the Children of God would go forth to conquer the world with an avenging Sword of Justice. Armed with supernatural strength, they would march to the Holy Land and usher in a new Heaven and Earth.

The New Jerusalem did not last long. After sixteen months of besiegement, the town finally succumbed to the bishop's forces. The victors entered Münster in June 1535, and the reprisals began, including Jan van Leiden's public execution by torture in January 1536. The town had held about 10,000 inhabitants in 1534; a year after it was retaken, its population stood at 216.

In many respects, the defeat of the Münster uprising was a turning point for Anabaptists. Many fled to more welcoming lands in the East, such as Moravia, Poland, and Ukraine, where they, as well as the Anabaptists who remained in the West, rejected violent apocalypticism and returned to millenarian quietism.

Archaic Millenarianism in the Colonial Americas

The term "archaic millenarianism" describes movements, both peaceful and violent, that arise out of a desire to return to an original, purer form of religion, often in opposition to a religion imposed from outside. The histories of colonized peoples around the world are filled with examples of this phenomenon. Although global in scope, it was especially prevalent throughout the colonized Americas. Two blood-soaked examples deserve our attention.

Po'pay and the Pueblo Revolt

Native resistance to Spanish colonial rule throughout the North and Central American portions of the Viceroyalty of New Spain was deep-seated and extensive. Much of that resistance was a reaction to inhumane policies and horrific abuses, but an equal or greater reason for resistance was the Spaniards' heavy-handed attempts to suppress Native religious beliefs and rituals. On numerous occasions resistance turned violent, and one of the most successful, but ultimately doomed, rebellions was the Pueblo Revolt of 1680–92, which broke out in northern New Mexico under the prophetic leadership of a spiritual healer of the Tewa people known as Po'pay (also spelled Popé).

The Native pueblo peoples (village-dwellers) of the present-day states of New Mexico and Arizona had suffered grievously since the arrival of the Spaniards. Spanish-introduced diseases alone had devastated the population. Of roughly 130 pueblos before 1600, fewer than twenty were inhabited by 1680. Between 1667 and 1672, the region was beset by drought and famine, and in 1671, an outbreak of pestilence attacked the severely weakened Natives. Added to that, ancient en-

4.4. Po'pay. Carved by Cliff Fragua at Jemez Pueblo, New Mexico, this statue was installed in the visitor center of the U.S. Capitol Building, Washington. D.C., in 2005. In his hand is the knotted cord that he sent to the pueblos as a means of coordinating the revolt. Source 2 further explains the cord. No contemporary image or description of Po'pay has survived.

emies, Apaches and Navaho, raided their lands in 1672. By 1675, at least six more pueblos had been wiped out, and in that same year, the governor began a concerted effort to eradicate pueblo "sorcery." Forty-seven spiritual leaders and healers, including Po'pay, were hauled into court, tried, and found guilty of witchcraft and devil worship. Three were hanged, one committed suicide, and the rest were flogged and sentenced to slavery. The governor later relented and freed the surviving healers. Following this public humiliation, Po'pay, a native of San Juan Pueblo, took up residence at Taos Pueblo, where he plotted the destruction of those whose assaults on the *kachinas* had brought misery to his people.

The Franciscan missionaries were uncompromising in their attempts to eradicate what they considered to be devilish idolatry and made no attempt to accommodate Native religious traditions to their interpretation of Christian Truth. The pueblo peoples believed that their roughly five hundred kachinas, or spirits of nature and the ancestors, maintain cosmic order and balance, if properly venerated. Consequently, the pueblos' most important religious ceremonies consisted of men dressed as kachinas performing ritualized dances. Without such dances, chaos would ensue, as had obviously happened when the kachina ceremonies were banned.

Taos was the perfect place from which to launch a rebellion because it had long been a center of Native resistance to the Spaniards and their religion. The uprising broke out on August 10, with almost all of the northern pueblos participating. The depth of the Natives' focus on religion can be seen by the fact that out of thirty-three missionary priests, they killed twenty-one, and destroyed every mission church they could seize. An additional 375 colonists were killed, and about 2,500 surviving Spaniards, mestizos (persons of mixed blood), and Natives who chose not to rebel straggled into places of refuge in the south.

Spanish attempts to reconquer New Mexico in 1681 and 1687 failed. It was probably soon thereafter, in 1688, that Po'pay died in unknown circumstances. Prior to his death, possibly as early as 1681, Po'pay had been stripped of his leadership because of a general attitude that he had turned into an autocratic despot, squeezing tribute from the pueblos and imposing excessive religious obligations. Even had Po'pay lived longer and not been deposed, it does not seem likely that the pueblos' freedom from Spanish control could have lasted much longer than it did.

The pueblos had never been united in any political sense, and with increasing Apache pressure and inherent disunity, the confederation that Po'pay had created grew feeble. Seizing upon that reality, the new governor, with a small force of Spanish troops and loyal Natives, reoccupied most of the north in 1692, effectively ending the rebellion despite continuing pockets of resistance. The fact that he offered amnesty helped his cause.

Taos, the epicenter of the revolt, did not submit until 1695, and in 1696, it briefly rose up again. Despite the military-political failure of the Great Revolt, the pueblos' fight had not been in vain. Spanish policies regarding enforced labor and Native religious traditions relaxed, and a synthesis of Native religious beliefs and ceremonies and Spanish Catholicism developed over the coming years, and has persisted to our day.

Tupac Amaru II

As noted in the introduction to source 4 of Chapter 2, the neo-Incan state at Vilcabamba, the last major center of Incan resistance, fell to the Spaniards in 1572, but with its fall a myth arose: a once-defeated *Inkarri* (Inca king) would return from the distant past to liberate his people. An eighteenth-century rebellion that began in Peru and spread outward carried that strong messianic message.

In November 1780, José Gabriel Condorcanqui, who claimed direct descent from the Incas, initiated an insurgency known as the Tupac Amaru Rebellion. The first Tupac Amaru was the last Inca of Vilcabamba, whom the Spaniards beheaded in 1572. Two centuries later, in the midst of deep socioeconomic inequities, Condorcanqui assumed the title Tupac Amaru II. His rebellion, which attracted large numbers of Native peasants, women, and artisans, began quite conservatively. Claiming that he had the blessing of King Charles III of Spain and that he was the most loyal son of the Catholic Church, Tupac Amaru II initially insisted he was only attempting to punish corrupt governmental officials. Soon enough, however, he metamorphosed into the messiah of Andean redemption, whom the divine will had chosen as its agent of justice—an agent who would drive out the Spaniards and establish an egalitarian society. But he did not stop there. He ultimately rejected Jesus because Jesus was the Son allied with the Spaniards. Asserting that he was the Inca-Jesus, he demanded to be addressed as "God and Lord" and claimed it was his divine wrath that was scourging the Spaniards.

Some historians have theorized that the sixteenth-century Taqui Onqoy movement, which we saw in Chapter 2, had never died out and resurged as a force within the Tupac Amaru Rebellion. We cannot say with any degree of certainty that this was the case, but what is certain is that at its height in early 1781, the rebellion raged over an area from present-day southern Columbia to northern Argentina and throughout much of Peru. Only five months after his uprising began, Tupac Amaru II was captured and judicially tortured to death. The rebellion, however, continued into late 1782, and there were even sporadic outbreaks of violence by Tupac's rebels well into 1783. A conservative estimate is that by the time the fighting and reprisals had ended, the dead totaled somewhere between 110,000 and 140,000.

As great as those numbers are, they are insignificant when compared with the death tolls from millenarian wars waged elsewhere, especially in China.

Utopian Holy War in China

Over the more than 2,100 years of Chinese imperial history, the Middle Kingdom experienced numerous rebellions, many fueled by utopian religious dreams. From the sixth century onward, Buddhist theology played a major role in shaping and expressing those rebellious hopes, but Buddhism did not have a monopoly on millenarian violence. Whenever natural disasters, nomadic invasions, or both occurred or government became too oppressive, there was always someone ready to announce that the emperor had lost the Mandate of Heaven (the right to rule bestowed by Heaven), and rebellion was now the will of Heaven. A case in point was the Yellow Turban Rebellion.

The Yellow Turban Rebellion, or the Way of the Great Peace

Several centuries before Buddhism became a major force in China, the Taiping Dao (the Way of Great Peace) Rebellion of 184 C.E. erupted. It is also known as the Yellow Turban Rebellion because of the distinctive headgear that many rebels wore. In Chinese culture, yellow is a symbol of power, prosperity, and harmony, and according to the ideology driving this uprising, a yellow sky, the manifestation of a new Heaven, would soon replace the blue sky.

The person preaching this message was a faith healer, Zhang Jue, who styled himself "Great Teacher" and "Lord General of Heaven." Inspired by the *Taipingjing* (*The Classic of Great Peace*), a text that purports to teach the methods for achieving universal harmony, he promised that a mystical new order was imminent in which heavenly agents, known as the Celestial Masters, would renew the world—a world in which all would share equally in the plenty that was unending. A step on that path was toppling the corrupt palace eunuchs who controlled an incompetent Han dynasty (206 B.C.E.–220 C.E.). In response, large numbers of peasants rose in revolt in central and eastern China.

The Hán emperor conscripted a huge army to suppress the revolt. Although Zhang and his two brothers were dead shortly after 184, and major elements of the rebellion were soon crushed, it took two decades to stamp out the last vestiges of the revolt. About fifteen years later, in 220, the Han dynasty collapsed and a disjointed China was thrown into disorder. In the midst of the troubles that accompanied this disunity, a salvific religion from outside—Mahayana Buddhism—began to take root.

The Maitreya Buddha and Buddhist Millenarian Wars in China

Buddhism's messiah-to-come is an enlightened being, or bodhisattva, known as the Maitreya (loving-kindness) Buddha, or the Buddha of the Future. Currently he resides in the Tushita (Contented) Heaven, where he awaits the moment when the Dharma, or Law, of the historic Shakyamuni Buddha (Siddhartha Gautama of the Shakya clan) has degenerated to the point that it and all of society have been taken over and totally corrupted by demons. He will then descend to Earth to reteach and re-establish the Dharma. Unlike the historic Buddha, he will become a world ruler who presides over an earthly paradise in which there is no suffering or strife.

4.5. The Maitreya Buddha. This sculpture from Gandhara (present-day northern Pakistan and eastern Afghanistan) dates to ca. 300 C.E. The jewelry indicates the regal nature of this bodhisattva, whereas his monastic robe, elongated earlobes, and third eye of transcendent wisdom signify his imminent Buddhahood. Two characteristic symbols associated with the Maitreya are the pot in his left hand, which holds the water of creation and life, and his topknot, which signifies his abandonment of worldly possessions. The statue's muscular, well-defined body and sharp facial features, as well as the artful use of drapery, indicate the strong influence of Greco-Roman statuary on the Gandharan sculptor. Inasmuch as Gandhara was an early, possibly the first, center of the cult of the Maitreya Buddha, there is good reason to suspect that Christian and Zoroastrian messianic beliefs to the west influenced its emergence.

The cult of the Maitreya Buddha appears to have emerged in the third century C.E., and he is the sole messiah-to-come who has a place of honor in the scriptures of the three major branches of Buddhism. As such, he has been the focal point of almost-countless millenarian movements, some of which have broken out in violent rebellion.

Maitreyan Rebellion in China: The Dacheng Rebellion of 515

During the era of Chinese disunity (220–589), a non-Chinese people from the steppe lands of Central Asia, the Tuoba Xianbei, established the Northern Wei kingdom (366–534) in North China, where they played a key role in introducing Buddhism into the Middle Kingdom. Moreover, their art displays a special devotion to the Maitreya Buddha. Ironically, a short-lived but widespread Maitreyan Buddhist rebellion severely shook the kingdom in 515.

Faqing, a renegade monk, proclaimed that he was *Dacheng* (Mahayana—the Great Vehicle), the true vehicle who would lead all to Enlightenment, as opposed to the false Mahayana teachings that then prevailed. Moreover, he was the promised Buddha of the Future, and he would eradicate the demons, namely the Northern Wei and all members of the Buddhist sangha, or monastic community.

Consequently, Faqing informed his followers that whoever killed one "demon" would become a first-stage bodhisattva; whoever killed ten would enter the tenth stage. Spurred on by this promise, and supposedly the hallucinogenic drugs that he prepared and freely distributed, the rebels destroyed monasteries and convents, butchered monks and nuns, and burned sacred sutras and images. One sixth-century source reports that an army of one hundred thousand needed three months to capture and kill Faqing and his wife, a former nun, and to suppress the main body of their fifty thousand followers. There is no way to verify those numbers, but it is likely that tens of thousands were killed or died of rebellion-related causes in that quarter year. Even with this imperial victory, rebel remnants continued to cause trouble into 517.

Maitreyan Rebellion in China: The Red Turban Rebellion, 1351–68

The cult of the Maitreya cut across all social, political, and religious strata in China, including the imperial court. Despite widespread devotion accorded the Buddha of the Future by mainstream Buddhists, Maitreyism continued as an underground movement spawning countless moments of unrest and numerous rebellions. One of the most significant was the uprising of the Red Turbans in 1351.

Before the Mongols had completed their conquest of China, Kublai Khan (r. 1260–94) established the Yuan dynasty (1271–1368), which ruled the Middle Kingdom for almost a century. Although the Yuan emperors worshipped the Buddha and assumed most of the traditional symbols and rituals of imperial rule, they were deeply resented by most ethnic Chinese, who looked upon them as foreign demons. Consequently, between 1279 and 1350, twenty or more local uprisings ravaged portions of China, and at least four of them centered on the insurgents' belief that they were preparing the way for the Maitreya Buddha. All of these insurrections were suppressed, but that was not the case with a rebellion that began in southern China in 1351, became an empire-wide civil war by 1354, and ended Mongol dominance of China in 1368.

In early 1351, Han Shantong, who claimed imperial blood, proclaimed that the Maitreya Buddha had arrived to restore right order in China. His followers, known as the "incense army" because they burned incense as an act of worship, wore distinctive red turbans, because red, the symbol of fire, wards off evil and consumes demons. When the Yuan government seized and executed Han, the Red Turbans reacted with a general insurrection that within a few months controlled most of South China. With Han Shantong dead, several other leaders emerged and jockeyed for position, including his son Han Lin'er, who assumed the title "Young King of Radiance" and claimed to be the incarnation of the Maitreya Buddha.

Han Lin'er's most competent commander was a former monk of peasant origin, Zhu Yuanzhang, who had joined the Red Turbans in 1352 as a common soldier and within four years was a major power in South China. In 1367, Han Lin'er drowned under suspicious circumstances while on his way to visit Zhu. The following year, the Yuan emperor fled from his palace at Dadu (today Beijing) and retreated into Mongolia. Zhu entered the imperial city in triumph and assumed the title of Emperor Hongwu, thereby establishing the Ming imperial dynasty (1368–1644).

The White Lotus Society

The White Lotus Society, an outlawed religious sect that anticipated the imminent arrival of the Maitreya, probably played a role in initiating or fueling the Red Turban Rebellion, but we lack solid evidence to say so with certainty. What we do know is that various millenarian incarnations of the White Lotus Society emerged across China over the centuries that followed. It would be wrong to see the White Lotus as a coherent religion or as a single, one-of-a-kind organization that persisted across generations. "White Lotus" was a convenient tag that adherents and opponents alike applied to numerous millenarian sects, even though they differed greatly in regard to ideology, myths, and makeup. The sole element that bound together the numerous White Lotus societies was a belief in the impending arrival or the immediate presence of a Buddha-savior.

Most White Lotus movements were peaceful, but some turned violent. In 1420, 1622, 1774, 1794–1804, and 1813, White Lotus uprisings threatened the stability of the empire. One of the most threatening was a revolt whose members, mindful of the fourteenth-century rebellion that threw out the hated Mongols, sported red turbans. The insurrection broke out in 1854, in Guandong Province in southeastern China, set in motion by a secret White Lotus faction known as the Heaven and Earth Society. The society had a religious core—faith in the coming of the Maitreya Buddha—but it was more than a religious sect. It was a mutual-aid organization that attracted people who shared deep social, political, and cultural grievances and sought to re-establish the Ming dynasty, which had been overthrown by foreigners from Manchuria, who created the Qing dynasty (1644–1912). By the time the Qing quelled the rebellion in 1857, about one million people were dead. However, because this second Red Turban Revolt was a subset, or sideshow, of the Taiping Civil War of 1850–64, it has largely been overlooked as a distinct millenarian war. But it was, as was the Taiping.

The Taiping Civil War, 1850–64

Taiping (Great Peace) has been a popular term throughout Chinese history. We have already seen the Taiping Dao Rebellion of 184, and from the third to mid-fourteenth century, at least seven emperors, warlords, and rebels designated the eras over which they presumably reigned as Taiping. But the one period that immediately comes to mind when the term arises is the great civil war that tore China apart in the mid-nineteenth century. The oft-cited low estimate of twenty million dead rivals that of World War I, and the equally believable high estimate of forty million is roughly half the number of persons who perished in World War II. And at least one historian argues for seventy million dead before the Taiping Heavenly Kingdom was crushed. By any standard, the Taiping Civil War (or Rebellion), which devastated southern China, ranks as one of history's greatest mass slaughters, and it was millenarian from start to finish. It seems that whenever violence is used to usher in a millenarian utopia, the result is dystopia.

The person who set the Taiping Civil War into motion was Hong Xiuquan (1814–64), originally named Hong Huoxiu. Hong, who came from a well-to-do family, was a Confucian scholar and schoolteacher, who had failed the second level of the imperial civil service examinations four times. He was also an ethnic Hakka.

The Hakka (guest people) were a Chinese minority that had migrated into southern China beginning in the late thirteenth century but maintained its distinctive identity. Although many Hakka prospered, especially as merchants, its poorer elements—peasants, charcoal-burners, and miners—were disconnected

4.6. A Taiping battle flag. The crew of the British gunboat HMS *Hardy* captured this flag on May 10, 1862, when they stormed Ningpo, along with French and imperial Chinese forces. The character in the center is "Chen," which probably refers to General Chen Yucheng, who bore the title *Ying Wang* (Hero King). The Eight Auspicious Buddhist Symbols, including two golden fish, a lotus flower, and an endless knot, surround the central character. Chen was captured and executed by the Qing shortly after this flag was lost.

from their neighbors, aggrieved, and ready recruits for revolt. The core of the Taiping leadership came from the Hakka.

Hong's third examination failure sparked a nervous breakdown in 1837, during which he dreamed he journeyed to Heaven, where his celestial Father informed him that Earth had been overtaken by demons. Hong received permission to lead a heavenly army against them. With the assistance of his Elder Brother, he defeated them but, at his Father's insistence, he allowed Yan Luo, the king of Hell, to escape. Hong then rested with his wife, First Chief Moon, after which his Father instructed Hong to return to Earth to continue the war against the demons. Before Hong departed, however, his Father offered him the opportunity to change his given name to Xiuquan (exhibiting completeness) because Huoxiu (exhibiting fire) violated taboos. The Father also bestowed on him the title "Heavenly King, Lord of the Kingly Way, Quan." Upon awakening, Hong insisted on his new name but otherwise continued preparing for the provincial-level examination.

He failed for the fourth time in 1843, and abandoned pursuit of a civil-service post. Meanwhile, Great Britain's victory in the First Opium War (1839–42) and several imposed treaties opened China to Protestant missionaries. Hong had been introduced to Christianity earlier, but now he began to explore it in detail and concluded that his Heavenly Father was the Judeo-Christian God the Father. Moreover, Hong's Elder Brother was Jesus. Thus, Hong was God's Younger Son. With this realization, he began preaching, destroying "idols," and purging the region of Confucian texts and statuary, arguing that Confucius and a corrupt imperial system had destroyed China's original religion of compassion that he was now restoring. That religion was a mixture of traditional Chinese Buddhism, Daoism (a complex ethical and metaphysical Chinese philosophy and religion that focuses on becoming one with the rhythms of the universe), and Euro-American evangelical Christianity. Hong articulated these ideas in several religious tracts and the *Authorized Taiping Version of the Bible*, a severely edited version of the Bible that reflected his theological message and was, therefore, a purer form of God's message.

All the while, he and several relatives gathered converts to eradicate the demons, in essence all idolaters and unbelievers. In addition to large numbers of Hakka followers, he attracted many Zhuang, a Tai-speaking, non-Chinese ethnic group in southern China, as well as numerous Heaven and Earth Society members, who had no doubt that the demons were the Manchus who ruled China.

In 1849, the government imprisoned two of his converts, who died in captivity, thereby confirming that the Manchus were the primary demons that must be exterminated. In early 1850, an army of believers was on the move in South

China. Soon thereafter, Hong began occasionally wearing an imperial yellow robe sent by his Heavenly Father. In early 1851, he declared himself Heavenly King of the Heavenly Kingdom of Great Peace. It was to be an eternal Paradise embracing all who believed in Jesus and his Younger Brother and worshipped the Lord of Heaven. When the Taipings captured Nanjing in March 1853, and Hong declared it to be the New Jerusalem and the Heavenly Capital of his kingdom, open rebellion became a civil war.

Imperial armies and local militias organized by defenders of the traditional ways and religions were now arrayed against the growing Taiping forces that, by 1853, numbered around a half million. By then the Taipings held most of southeastern China and were making incursions into the north. As the conflict evolved into total war, both sides committed atrocities on a massive scale, especially on an ever-suffering peasantry.

In the midst of the conflict, Hong became increasingly erratic and arbitrarily executed many former loyalists. Meanwhile Taiping fortunes slipped away, especially as Great Britain and France began to support the Qing and to intervene militarily. By May 1862, Nanjing was under siege and two years later, after a lingering illness, Hong Xiuquan returned to Heaven to request that his Heavenly Father and Elder Brother send a celestial army to rescue Nanjing. That was the official statement to cover the fact that he had died. But the celestial army never appeared. On July 19, 1864, victorious Qing soldiers entered Nanjing and slaughtered everyone. Hong Xiuquan's son and successor, Hong Tianguifu, fled south but was captured on October 25. He was executed by slow slicing on November 18, five days before his fifteenth birthday.

The war was essentially over, but several thousand loyalists escaped into the mountains and were not wiped out until 1871. Although victorious, the Qing Empire's weaknesses were made clear and exacerbated by this millenarian civil war.

Islamic Eschatology

Judaism, Christianity, and Islam are known as the "Three Abrahamic Faiths" because each claims descent from the patriarch Abraham—Judaism through his son Isaac, Islam through his son Ishmael, and Christianity through faith. Consequently, they share many beliefs and modes of worship. Most important of all is their devotion to a single God of the universe who demands a high standard of moral conduct on the part of "the faithful" and requires them to oppose evil. Islam, like Christianity, also has a detailed eschatology. In fact, it has two eschatologies, one Sunni and one Shi'a.

Both visions of the End Times (The Hour) have some basis in the Qur'an, which mentions that violent events will precede the Resurrection of the Dead, but mainly depend on later collections of Hadith. Both Sunnis and Shi'as agree that Jesus the Messiah, a major Muslim Messenger of God, did not die on the cross. Rather, he awaits in Heaven the days of crises and universal injustice that will precede the End of Time when he will reappear to battle and defeat the false messiah *al-Daijal* (the Deceiver). Then he will establish a forty-year reign of peace and justice to be followed by the Resurrection of the Dead and the Last Judgment. Accompanying Jesus will be the *Mahdi* (the rightly guided one), and here Sunni and Shi'a traditions diverge.

For Sunnis, the Mahdi, is a military figure from the family of the Prophet who will battle the forces of evil on Earth. For Shi'as, the Mahdi is a direct descendent of Muhammad through his daughter Fatima and son-in-law Ali. Unlike the unlawful Sunni caliphs, the Mahdi is the Imam, the rightful head and teacher of the Muslim community, who went into mystical "occultation" in the eighth or ninth century (depending on one's Shi'a sect) in order to escape persecution and who resides hidden somewhere within the Shi'a community. He will return to establish his rightful and righteous reign of peace and justice and usher in the Last Days.

Just as Judaism has produced would-be messiahs over the centuries and Christianity has seen self-proclaimed agents of God come and go, so Mahdis have risen and fallen for more than a thousand years. Among them was the Sudanese mystic Muhammad Ahmad ibn as Sayyid Abdullah (1844–85).

Mahdist Jihad in the Sudan

In 1820, Khedive (viceroy) Muhammad Ali Pasha, who ruled Egypt autonomously but in the name of the Ottoman Empire, sent a small army of conquest up the Nile into the vast region known as the Sudan (the South), and by 1822, the Khedivate of Egypt had more than doubled in size. The Sudanese did not take kindly to Turco-Egyptian rule. Much of that governance was exploitive, which only exacerbated the deep ethnic, cultural, and religious schisms that separated the Sudanese from their new overlords. Sufi brotherhoods, which emphasized the mystical aspects of Islam, had a profound impact on Islamic devotion in the South. Added to that were reformist movements that contrasted the Islamic purity of the southern desert to the cosmopolitan adulterations of the Egyptian and Turkish northern cities. Moreover, a popular legend circulated in the Sudan that in the year 1300 A.H. (After the Hijra), which translated to 1862, the Mahdi would appear. Thinking that the khedive in Cairo was either al-Daijal or his henchman, many Sudanese were ready for a deliverer.

4.7. Muhammad Ahmad ibn as Sayyid Abdullah, the Mahdi. A nineteenth-century etching.

4.8. Charles George Gordon. A watercolor
by Lady Julia Abercromby.

In June 1861, Muhammad Ahmad ibn as Sayyid Abdullah, a Sunni Muslim
who claimed direct descent from the Prophet Muhammad, proclaimed he was
the Mahdi who would purify Dar al-Islam by creating a fundamentalist Mahdiyya (Mahdist state). Holy war against the khedivate was inevitable. Moreover, Great Britain would be drawn into the conflict because of another religious
zealot, Major General Charles Gordon, known to his admiring public as Chinese
Gordon.

Charles George Gordon, a deeply devout but eccentrically unorthodox evangelical Christian, was a career soldier, who battled two millenarian states, the
Taiping Tianguo and the Mahdiyya. No novelist could have imagined a more
suitable foil for Muhammad Ahmad al-Mahdi.

In 1863, Major Gordon assumed command of the Ever-Victorious Army, a
militia of Europeans and Asians in the employ of the Qing emperor that played a
critical role in the last stages of the Taiping War. A decade later, eager to join the
crusade against slavery and with the blessing of the British government, Colonel
Gordon accepted the khedive of Egypt's offer to serve as governor of the Sudanese province of Equatoria (present-day South Sudan and northern Uganda). He
assumed the post in 1874, remaining there until October 1876. Falling out with
the Egyptian governor-general of the Sudan because of his attempts to suppress
slavery, Gordon left for home. But he returned in 1877, convinced by the khedive
that he should serve as governor-general of the entire Sudan. Ruling from Khartoum, Gordon won widespread respect for his incorruptibility and zeal, but he

resigned and left for England in early 1880, out of frustration with the powers that had obstructed his attempted reforms.

Within a year and a half following his departure, rebellion broke out in the Sudan as the Mahdi declared jihad against the Turco-Egyptian government to the north that, among its many sacrileges, had appointed Jewish and Christian administrators and military officers over pious Muslims. In August 1881, Mahdist forces ambushed a force of two hundred that had been sent to arrest Muhammad Ahmad, killing 60 percent of the khedive's soldiers. The Mahdi, who had assumed the persona of the Prophet Muhammad, declared this victory to be his Battle of Badr, the Prophet's first battlefield triumph.

Against this background of rebellion in the South, the khedivate was losing its grip on Egypt due to rising religious and ethnic unrest and its inability to repay European creditors. An attempted coup against the khedive led to Great Britain's intervention and its unofficial but firm control of Egypt. The next step was for the British to be drawn into the Mahdist conflict.

In November 1883, an Egyptian force of about nine thousand, sent out to put down the uprising in the Sudan and under the command of retired Colonel William Hicks, was cut to pieces by Mahdists at El Obeid. Among the fallen were Hicks, all of his European officers, and two English journalists. Under pressure from the British, the khedive's government decided to abandon the Sudan, leaving it to the Mahdi. In the midst of this pullback, Prime Minister William Gladstone's government was unable to withstand the insistence of the press and the public that Gordon, who had recently been promoted to major general, be dispatched to Khartoum to oversee the evacuation of British subjects.

When Gordon arrived in Khartoum in February 1884, he became convinced that a withdrawal was not appropriate. In April, an estimated thirty thousand Mahdists besieged the city. Despite Gordon's offers of peace, the Mahdi refused to retire. By September, some sixty thousand warriors were besieging a bit more than half that number at Khartoum. Meanwhile, Gordon's plight aroused popular sympathy in Britain, and a relief force was dispatched, which arrived in the Sudan in early January 1885. With a column of the relief force pressing to Khartoum, the Mahdists decided on a frontal assault, which they launched on the night of January 25/26, 1885. Upon breaching the city's wall, the Mahdists wiped out the Egyptian force that originally had numbered about seven thousand, massacred an estimated four thousand civilians, and enslaved the rest. Gordon was killed under circumstances that vary according to the surviving reporter. His head was sent to the Mahdi and his body dumped into the Nile. The relief force arrived within sight of Khartoum two days later, and then retired, seeing it could do nothing to change the situation.

The Mahdi, who now controlled the Sudan, retired to Omdurman, which he transformed into the capital of the Mahdiyya, naming it *Asimat al-Islam* (Capital of Islam), a title reserved for Mecca until that moment. Five months later he was dead. Prior to death, he had, in imitation of the Prophet, named a caliph, or deputy successor, Abdullah ibn Muhammad. Bearing the title *khalifat al-Mahdi* (the Mahdi's deputy), Abdullah challenged the claim of the Ottoman sultan to be Islam's true caliph, the deputy of the Prophet.

In death, Gordon was hailed at home as a Christian martyr and gallant holy warrior, and there was an outcry for revenge. Revenge was slow in coming, but it was total and devastating when it arrived. In 1896, Prime Minister Lord Salisbury dispatched a British expeditionary force to join forces with the Egyptians to reconquer the Sudan. Although the invasion was largely for geopolitical reasons, "Remember Gordon" became its rallying cry. In November 1899, an Anglo-Egyptian army destroyed the last substantial remnant of the Mahdiyya at the Battle of Umm Diwaykarat, and killed Caliph Abdullah.

With that victory, Great Britain effectively controlled the entire Sudan. But at what cost? The lives lost between 1881 and 1899 numbered at least in the tens of thousands, but a greater cost was to come.

The Somali Dervishes

Between 1899 and 1920, Mohammed Abdullah Hasan led a religious war against the Christian empires of Great Britain, Italy, and Ethiopia from the southeastern corner of the Sudan that today is Somalia. Deeply influenced by both a puritanical branch of Sufism and an ultraconservative branch of Sunni Islam out of the Arabian Peninsula known as Wahhabism, he preached against all other forms of Islam, as well as against all Christian interlopers. The coalition of jihadists that he formed became known as the Somali dervishes.

Dervishes (poor people) are mainly Sufi holy men who live lives of poverty, self-denial, and charity and practice a form of mystical devotion known as *sama*. Sama consists of ritual music, dance, prayer, recitation of poetry, and meditation that free the devotee to transcend the ego and all other distractions, thereby allowing one to have an immediate but brief contact with the Almighty. Given the jihadist zealotry and fighting abilities of the Somali dervishes, however, the British came to understand, quite incorrectly, that "dervish" meant exclusively an Islamic warrior of color of the Sudan, who was noted for fanatical bravery, cruelty, and a desire for martyrdom.

The Somali dervishes became far less aggressive with the death in 1920 of the "Mad Mullah," as the British termed him, but by the time the fighting abated, the Somali population had been reduced by an estimated one-third and the region was devastated. Arguably today's problems in Somalia, a land rent by warlords, beset by humanitarian crises, and bedeviled by an entrenched terrorist organization known as al-Shabaab, can be traced, at least in part, back to these dervishes.

SOURCES

Source 1. "Sing a New Song unto the Lord"[20]

Raymond of Aguilers, *A History of the Franks Who Captured Jerusalem*[21]

In collaboration with the knight Pons of Balazun, who was killed early in 1099, the priest Raymond of Aguilers coauthored one of the earliest eyewitness histories of the First Crusade, which he probably completed before the end of 1101. Raymond was well situated to write this history. Prior to the crusade he served as a canon (administrative cleric) at Notre Dame du Puy, the cathedral church of Bishop Adhémar, Pope Urban's legate to the crusade. Raymond was also associated with the household of Count Raymond IV of Toulouse, who led the largest contingent of the crusade's second wave.

The overriding theme of Raymond's account is that God expresses his Will in human history, and that Will is discernible. Consequently, his narrative is laced with visions, miracles, prophecies, and other phenomena that affirm the hand of God. Prior to the capture of Antioch in 1098, a beaten, discouraged army receives a message from Andrew the Apostle through the mouth of a young, unlettered visionary, who instructs the crusaders: "But know certainly that those days are at hand that the Lord promised ... saying that He would raise up the kingdom of the Christians, after the kingdom of the pagans had been cast down and ground into dust."[22]

For Raymond, the capture of Jerusalem signaled the grinding down to dust of the kingdom of the pagans, and he expressed his joy and certainty regarding its meaning by referencing two biblical passages: Revelation, 5:9, and Psalm 118. The more significant is the reference to the Book of Revelation, where Jesus, the Lamb of God, takes a sealed scroll from God the Father, a scroll that contains God's final settlement of the affairs of the universe, and a choir "sings a new song"

---

20. Psalms, 96:1.
21. August C. Krey, *The First Crusade: The Accounts of Eyewitnesses and Participants* (Princeton, NJ: Princeton University Press, 1921), 261–62. Revised by A. J. Andrea.
22. Ibid., 186.

that proclaims Jesus worthy to take the scroll and open the seals because he has redeemed the world.

Questions for Consideration

How does Raymond interpret the capture of Jerusalem? Does his vision conform to the pattern of events set out in the Book of Revelation? If not, what is his vision, and is it millenarian?

◆◆◆◆◆

Now that the city was taken, it was well worth all our previous labors and hardships to see the devotion of the pilgrims at the Holy Sepulcher.[23] How they rejoiced and exulted and sang a new song to the Lord! For their hearts offered prayers of praise to God, victorious and triumphant, which cannot be told in words. A new day, new joy, new and perpetual gladness, the consummation of our labor and devotion, drew forth from all new words and new songs. This day, I say, will be famous in all future ages, for it turned our labors and sorrows into joy and exultation; this day, I say, marks the justification of all Christianity, the humiliation of paganism, and the renewal of our faith. "This is the day that the Lord has made, let us rejoice and be glad in it,"[24] for on this day the Lord revealed Himself to His people and blessed them.

On this day, the Ides of July,[25] Lord Adhémar, Bishop of Puy, was seen in the city by many people.[26] Many also testified that he was the first to scale the wall, and that he summoned the knights and people to follow him. On this day, moreover, the apostles were cast forth from Jerusalem and scattered over the whole world.[27] On this same day, the children of the apostles regained the city and fatherland for God and the fathers. This day, the Ides of July, shall be celebrated to the praise and glory of the name of God, who, answering the prayers of His Church, gave in trust and benediction to His children the city and fatherland which He had promised to the fathers. On this day we chanted the Office of the Resurrection,[28] since on that day He, who by His virtue arose from the dead, revived us through His grace.

---

23. The Church of the Holy Sepulcher, which contained what was believed to be Christ's Tomb of Resurrection.
24. Psalms, 118:24 (117:24 in the Latin Vulgate).
25. July 15, 1099.
26. Adhémar had died from disease in 1098.
27. The Church celebrates the Dispersion of the Apostles on July 15 to commemorate the apostles' leaving Jerusalem to spread the Gospel throughout the world.
28. The special hymns for Easter Sunday. Easter had fallen on March 31 in 1095.

Source 2. The Pueblo Revolt of 1680

Declaration of Pedro Naranjo of the Queres Nation[29]

Between December 18, 1681, and January 1, 1682, Spanish authorities interrogated nine Native captives in an attempt to understand the factors that led to the Pueblo Revolt. On December 19, Pedro Naranjo provided the following information.

Questions for Consideration

Explain the background to the revolt, with particular attention to Po'pay's vision at Taos. Explain the actions that Po'pay and the inhabitants of the pueblos took after their successful uprising. Explain the role that the three spirits of the Taos kiva played after the revolt's initial success. And what were the people promised once the Spaniards and their religion were overthrown? In light of your answers, do you judge this to have been a millenarian holy war?

◆◆◆◆◆

His lordship[30] caused to appear before him an Indian prisoner named Pedro Naranjo, a native of the pueblo of San Felipe, . . . who was captured in the attack and siege of the pueblo of La Isleta.[31] . . . He took the oath in due legal form in the name of God, our Lord, and [with] a sign of the cross, under charge of which he promised to tell the truth concerning what he knew and what was asked of him, and having understood the seriousness of the oath and as he was made to understand through the interpreters, he spoke as indicated. . . .

Asked whether he knows the reason or motives that the Indians of this kingdom[32] had for rebelling, forsaking the law of God and obedience to his majesty, and carrying out and committing such grave and atrocious crimes, and what was the motive, who were the principal movers, and by whom and how it was ordered; and why they burned the images, churches, crosses, rosaries, and other things for divine worship, committing so many atrocities, such as killing priests, Spaniards, women, and children, and the rest that he might know touching the question.

---

29. Charles Wilson Hackett, ed., and Charmion Clair Shelby, trans., *Revolt of the Pueblo Indians of New Mexico and Otermín's Attempted Reconquest, 1680–1682*, 2 vols. (Albuquerque: University of New Mexico, 1942), 2:245–49. Revised by A. J. Andrea.

30. Antonio de Otermín, the governor and captain general of the province of Santa Fe.

31. Governor Otermín led an unsuccessful attempt to reconquer the northern pueblos in 1681 and in the process occupied La Isleta Pueblo in central New Mexico without a fight.

32. Nuevo Mexico, a province of the Viceroyalty of New Spain, was sometimes referred to as a *reino* (kingdom).

He said that . . . they have planned to rebel on various occasions because of the urgings of the Indian sorcerers, and that although in some pueblos the messages were accepted, others would not agree to it; and that it is true that . . . seven or eight Indians were hanged for this reason, whereupon the unrest subsided.

Sometime thereafter, the conspirators sent from the pueblo of Los Taos throughout the pueblos . . . two deerskins with some pictures on them signifying their conspiracy . . . , in order to incite the people to a new rebellion, and the said deerskins passed to the province of Moqui,[33] where they refused to accept them. The pact that they had been forming ceased for the time being, but they always kept in their hearts the desire to carry it out, so as to live as they are living today.

Finally, in the past years, at the summons of an Indian named Popé who is said to communicate with the Devil, it happened that in an estufa[34] of the pueblo of Los Taos there appeared to the said Popé three figures of Indians who never came out of the estufa. They made the said Popé to understand that they were going underground to the lake of Copala.[35] He saw these figures emit fire from all the extremities of their bodies, and that one of them was called Caudi, another Tilini, and the other Tleume. These three beings spoke to the said Popé, who was in hiding from the secretary, Francisco Xavier, who wished to punish him as a sorcerer.[36]

They told him to make a cord of palmilla[37] and to tie some knots in it which would signify the number of days that they must wait before the rebellion. The said cord passed through all the pueblos of the kingdom so that each pueblo that would join the rebellion would untie one knot as a sign of obedience, and from the other knots they would know the [number of] knots that were missing. This was to be done on pain of death to those who refused to join in. As a sign of agreement and notice of having concurred in the treason and perfidy, they were to send up smoke signals to that effect in each one of the pueblos. The said cord was taken from pueblo to pueblo by the swiftest youths under the penalty of death if they revealed the secret.

---

33. The land of the Hopi.
34. Literally "a stove." This was the *kiva*, a room, usually below ground, in which a sacred fire was kept burning and to which only members of the secret brotherhood were normally admitted. A pueblo would usually have multiple kivas, one for each brotherhood. There they held religious ceremonies, especially relating to the kachinas. At this time, the Spanish government was attempting to destroy the kivas.
35. The lake from which the Tewa ancestors emerged.
36. Captain Francisco Xavier, secretary of government and war, was second-in-command of the province and the person in charge of suppressing idolatry and sorcery.
37. A plant harvested for its fiber.

Everything being thus arranged, two days before the time set for its execution, because his lordship had learned of it and had imprisoned two Indian accomplices from the pueblo of Tesuque,[38] it was carried out prematurely that night, because it seemed to them that they were now discovered; and they killed religious,[39] Spaniards, women, and children. This being done, it was proclaimed in all the pueblos that everyone in common should obey the commands of their father whom they did not know. They do not know if it was said by El Caydi [Caudi] or Popé. . . .

As soon as the Spaniards had left the kingdom an order came from the said Indian Popé, in which he commanded all the Indians to plow the lands and enlarge their cultivated fields, saying that now they were, as they had been in ancient times, free from the labor they had performed for the religious and the Spaniards, who could not now be allowed to live. He said that this was the legitimate cause and the reason they had for rebelling, because they had always desired to live as they had when they came out of the lake of Copala. . . .

Asked for what reason they so blindly burned the images, temples, crosses, and other things of divine worship, he stated that the said Indian Popé came down in person . . . from the pueblo of Los Taos, and other captains and leaders and many people who were in his company, and he ordered in all the pueblos through which he passed that they instantly break up and burn the images of the holy Christ, the Virgin Mary and the other saints, the crosses, and everything pertaining to Christianity, and that they burn the churches, break up the bells,[40] and separate from the wives whom [the Christian] God had given them in marriage and take those whom they desired. In order to take away their baptismal names, the water, and the holy oils, they were to plunge into the rivers and wash themselves with *amole*,[41] which is a root native to the country, washing even their clothing, with the understanding that thereby they would rid themselves of the essence of the holy sacraments.

They did this, and also many other things that he does not recall. Popé made it understood that this mandate had come from El Caydi [Caudi] and the other two who emitted fire from their extremities in the said estufa of Taos, and that they thereby returned to the state of their antiquity, as when they came from the Lake of Copala, and that this was the better life and the one they desired, because the God of the Spaniards was worth nothing and theirs was very strong, the

---

38. Te Tesugeh Oweengeh, also known as Tewa Pueblo, is about ten miles from Santa Fe.
39. Franciscan friars.
40. The church bells tolled at regular times throughout each day, signaling times of prayer and all other activities in a pueblo mission.
41. The so-called soap plant, the juices from its bulbous root act as a detergent.

Spaniards' God was rotten wood. These things were observed and obeyed by all except some who, moved by the zeal of Christians, opposed it, and such persons the said Popé caused to be killed immediately.

They then erected and rededicated their houses of idolatry, which they call estufas, and made very ugly masks in imitation of the Devil in order to dance the dance of the kachina, and he [Naranjo] said likewise that the Devil had given them to understand that living thus in accordance with the law of their ancestors, they would harvest a great deal of maize, many beans, a great abundance of cotton, very large squashes and watermelons and cantaloupes; and that their houses would be filled and they would enjoy abundant health and leisure. As he has said, the people were very much pleased, living at their ease in this life of their antiquity, which was the chief cause of their falling into such shamelessness.

Following what has already been stated, in order to terrorize them further and cause them to observe the diabolical commands, there came to them a pronouncement from the three demons already described, and from El Popé, to the effect that he who might still keep in his heart a regard for the priests, the governor, and the Spaniards would be known from his unclean face and clothes, and would be punished. And he stated that the said four stopped at nothing to have their commands obeyed. Thus he replies to the question.

Asked what arrangements and plans they had made for the contingency of the Spaniards' return, he said that what he knows concerning the question is that they were always saying they would have to fight to the death, for they do not wish to live in any other way than they are living at present. The demons in the estufa of Taos had given them to understand that as soon as the Spaniards began to move toward this kingdom they would warn them so that they might unite, and none of them would be caught. He having been questioned further and repeatedly so in respect to the case, he said that he has nothing more to say except that they should be always on the alert, because the said Indians were continually planning to follow the Spaniards and fight with them by night, in order to drive off the horses and catch them afoot, although they might have to follow them for many leagues.

[Naranjo said] that what he has said is the truth, and what happened, on the word of a Christian who confesses his guilt. He said that out of fear he had passed through the pueblos to teach the idolatrous dances, for which he has a heavy heart for offending God. Now, having been absolved and returned to the fold of the Church, he has spoken the truth in everything that he has been asked. His declaration being read to him, he affirmed and ratified all of it. He declared himself to be eighty years of age, and he signed it.

Source 3. The Missions of the Elder and Younger Brothers

Hong Xiuquan, *Annotations to the New Testament*[42]

Hong Xiuquan inserted notes into the Taiping Bible's Old and New Testaments
that interpreted various passages in accord with his religious vision. The excerpts
that follow are several of his commentaries on the Gospel of Saint Matthew. The
translator's bracketed notes that precede each commentary indicate which passage Hong is commenting on.

Questions for Consideration

According to Hong, what relationship do the Elder and Younger Brothers have
with God? Where if anywhere, do you find millenarian ideas in these commentaries? Can you identify any commentary that might indicate a Maitreyan influence? What other indications are there of the syncretistic nature of this religion?
Consult the New Testament passages that Hong annotates. How well has he understood the theological messages contained in them?

◆◆◆◆◆

[3:13–17, *on Christ's baptism*] The Holy Ghost is God, and the Elder Brother
is God's heir apparent. When the Elder Brother comes, God also comes. So it is
that God and Christ have now descended into the world. Respect this. . . .

[4:1–22, *on Christ's preparation for his ministry*] God is flame; the sun also is
flame.[43] Therefore God and the sun both come. Respect this. . . . God is flame;
therefore there is Holy Light. The Elder Brother is flame; therefore he is the
Great Light.[44] I am the sun; therefore I am also light. Respect this.

[5:13–48, *on the Sermon on the Mount*] To speak of one great kingdom is to
include both heaven above and earth below. In heaven above there is the Heavenly
Kingdom. On earth below there is the Heavenly Kingdom. Heaven and earth
both are the Spiritual Father's Heavenly Kingdom. Do not make the mistake of
believing that this indicates only the Heavenly Kingdom in heaven. Therefore the

---

42. Franz Michael, ed., and F. Mote, trans., *The Taiping Rebellion. History and Documents*, 3
vols. (Seattle: University of Washington Press, 1966–71), 2: 227–29, passim.
43. In Daoist thought, fire is the element of power.
44. Manichaeism, a dualistic faith from Iran, had taken root in Central Asia and various provinces of China, where it influenced the teachings of the fourteenth-century White Lotus Society. Manichaeism's core teachings focused on the struggle between the spiritual and divine forces
of light and the material and demonic forces of darkness.

Elder Brother's prophecy says: "The Kingdom of Heaven approaches."[45] For the Kingdom of Heaven will come on earth. It is the Kingdom of Heaven which the Heavenly Father and Heavenly Elder Brother now have descended to earth to establish. Respect this. . . .

[13:24–43, *on the parable of the tares of the field*] Now the Sabbath has come for heaven and earth. The Father and the Elder Brother descend into the world to destroy the heterodox[46] and preserve the orthodox, to gather the wheat and burn the tares. It is fulfilled. The righteous enjoy good fortune in the Heavenly Father's kingdom. It is fulfilled. Respect this. . . .

[24:29–39, *on the signs of Christ's coming to judge*] The Elder Brother feared to divulge it; therefore he issued a secret proclamation that I am the sun and have descended to become a person of the world; therefore it has become darkened. My wife is the moon and has descended to become a person of the world; therefore it issues no light.[47] The heavenly generals and heavenly soldiers are stars and constellations which have descended to become persons of the world; therefore they have fallen from heaven to earth.[48] Now the Father and the Elder Brother have ascended and come forth on the clouds of heaven.[49] They gather together all the people; they come from the four quarters and from one end of heaven to the other. All things have been fulfilled. Respect this.

Source 4. The Clash of Two Holy Warriors

Letter of March 10,1884, from the Mahdi to General Gordon;[50] *Entry of September 11, 1884, in General Gordon's Khartoum Journal*[51]

Shortly after his arrival at Khartoum on February 18, 1884, General Gordon sent a message and a gift to the Mahdi. In response, the Mahdi sent the first of

---

45. Matthew 3:2, 4:17, and 10:7; Mark, 1:15.

46. Persons who believe any teaching that is counter to the orthodox, or correct, doctrine.

47. The sun god and goddess of the moon are important deities in the Shangqing (highest light) sect of Daoism.

48. Some Buddhist sects revere twelve heavenly generals; Daoism has numerous heavenly commanders (one sect has thirty-six), most of whom were historical or legendary generals.

49. For Daoists, the clouds that ring mountains are sacred because they are where Earth and Heaven connect.

50. Translated by Francis Reginald Wingate in *Mahdiism and the Egyptian Sudan*, ed. F. R. Wingate (London: Frank Cass & Co, 1891), 111–15, passim. Modified by A. J. Andrea.

51. Godfrey Lord Elton, ed., *General Gordon's Khartoum Journal* (New York: Vanguard, 1961), 34–35.

three known letters to Gordon. The Mahdi's communications with Gordon were lengthy and repetitious, and for that reason we have heavily edited the letter that appears below. On his part, Gordon maintained a journal during the siege, which contained his musings on a number of issues, as well as military details. The entry excerpted here concerns the defeat and death of Gordon's top lieutenant, Muhammad Ali Pasha (not to be confused with Khedive Muhammad Ali Pasha of Egypt), on September 5, 1884.

Questions for Consideration

What had been the tone and message of Gordon's overture to the Mahdi? What is the overall tone and core message of the Mahdi's letter? Place into context the Mahdi's statement "I shall not therefore deprive them of Paradise and send them to affliction and trouble." To whom does he refer and what principle, which we saw in Chapter 2, lies at the heart of this response? Although lines of communication would remain somewhat open, when Gordon received this letter, he responded that now he could not have any further communications with the Mahdi. Why? How did Gordon interpret the events that were unfolding at Khartoum, and what does this tell us of his personality and beliefs? Now study George W. Joy's *General Gordon's Last Stand* on page 102. Taking into consideration their weapons, clothing, demeanor, and body language, how does Joy contrast Gordon's assailants with the general? What is the message? Does that message have any religious overtones?

◆◆◆◆◆

The Letter of the Mahdi to General Gordon, March 10, 1883

FROM THE SERVANT OF HIS GOD, MUHAMMAD EL MAHDI IBN ES SAYID ABDULLAH, TO THE DEAR ONE OF BRITAIN AND OF THE KHEDIVE, GORDON PASHA.[52]

In the name of God. . . . —Your letter has been received and its contents have been read and understood. You say you wish the progress of the Muslims, and that you are desirous of opening up the road to enable them to visit the tomb of the Prophet.[53] You also express your desire to establish friendship between us and you, and ask us to set free the Christians and Muslims, promising also to declare

---

52. A Turkish title of honor accorded generals, governors, and others of like rank.
53. The Mahdi's uprising had closed down the road to the Red Sea that Africans took on the hajj, the holy pilgrimage that brought them to Mecca and Medina (where the Prophet's tomb was).

me ruler of Kordofan.[54] In reply I state that while I confess that the order is with God, I have preached to the people in order to reform them and to make them come nearer to God, to teach them to distinguish between the vanities of this world, and of the world to come, and to make known to them those things that must lead to their salvation.

When at Aba,[55] I wrote to the government of Khartoum, informing them about my call to the true faith, and that my Mahdiism comes direct from God and His Prophet and is not a stratagem whereby to gain property, money, and influence.

I am a humble servant, a lover of poverty and of the poor, one who hates the pride and haughtiness of those rulers whom I wish to lead into the way of truth. These rulers have been brought up to love money, power, and children,[56] all of them grave obstacles in the way of reformation, and deprive them of the blessings that they might otherwise have obtained from God. They seek after things that vanish, instead of those things that remain forever. . . .

God has therefore chosen me as an exponent of true Mahdiism, in order that I may show them the path to God. . . . I do not think that he who hankers after the pleasures of this world can believe in his heart that he is pleasing to God, nor can he hope to have a share in the world to come. . . .

How is it possible for one who is not a follower of the Prophet of God to wish to open the road to his tomb for pilgrims? The Prophet has no desire to be visited by dogs, for it is said that this world is a carcass, and those who seek after it are dogs. The Prophet cares not for those to visit him who worship other gods and who forget that God is over all and knows every word he says, and is one who seeks the vanity of this world. If you pity the Muslims you should pity your own soul first, and save it from the anger of its Creator, and make it a follower of the true religion, by following our lord the Prophet Muhammad, who has by his coming renewed that which was destroyed and had fallen into disuse. . . . God will not accept any religion except that of the Prophet. Come, therefore, and join his religion, and then you can pity his people and guide them in the fulfillment of his laws, then only can you be considered a man of pity. Unless you do so, no true believer can be your companion. . . .

We have therefore obeyed the orders of God. We believe in Him, and in His Prophet, and in His followers, and we shall be victorious as God has promised.

---

54. The central and southern areas of the Sudan.
55. Aba, an island in the White Nile, lies south of Khartoum and was the Mahdi's home. It was there that he declared the Mahdiyya, on June 29, 1881.
56. Fathering numerous children with their wives and many concubines.

God has promised victory to the true followers, and therefore none other can gain the victory. . . .

As regards the Muslims and Christians whom you wish me to set free and send to you, I am desirous of their good, and that they obtain the blessings of God and the inheritance of eternal life, just as I wish the same for you and for all of God's creatures. I shall not therefore deprive them of Paradise and send them to affliction and trouble. God has endued me with the feeling of mercy for His creatures and has sent me to save them from the destruction that would have been their lot had not God in His mercy sent me to them.

Be it known to you that I am without pride, the promised Mahdi and the successor of the Prophet. There is no need for me to be sultan or king of Kordofan or any other country, nor have I any desire for the benefits or adornments of this world. I am a servant, and my duty is to show the way to God and to His kingdom. He who wishes to be happy should hear and follow me, but he who wishes to be miserable should turn away from my guidance; him shall God remove from his position, destroy, and torment perpetually.

God has given me the power to revive His religion, assisted by the prophets, messengers,[57] angels, and all saints and believers. The Prophet has informed me that those who declare enmity against me shall fail and be conquered by the power of God, even should both the human race and the race of jinns[58] combine. Deceive not yourself, else you will perish like your brethren. Take heed, therefore, and give yourself up to us that you might be saved.

As regards the present you sent me, if it is sent in good feeling, God will reward you with His blessing and guide you to righteousness. But let be known to you that as I have already said, I do not care for the good things of this world, nor for its adornments, which worldly people strive after, and which have nothing to do with God. Your present is therefore returned to you, and I am sending you some articles of the dress worn by me and my followers,[59] who look for eternal life, and who shall gain happiness in Paradise. This was the dress taken into use by all the prophets and messengers of God and by all His pious servants. . . .

---

57. Islam recognizes as many as 124,000 prophets (*nabis*). Each, under the inspiration of Allah, preached the Oneness of God to a discrete group of people. Of these, only twenty-five, including Abraham, Moses, Jesus, and Muhammad, were special prophets, known as messengers (*rasuls*). Of them, Muhammad was the "Seal of the Prophets," the last and greatest prophet, who alone received the fullness of revelation for all humanity.

58. Spirits who rank below angels.

59. A *jubbah* (a gown-like garment with long sleeves), a full-length coat, a turban, a prayer cap, a belt, and prayer beads.

Be it known to you, Pasha, that all who have been killed through me received due warning beforehand. . . .

If after all this explanation you will deliver yourself up and become a follower of true religion, you will gain honor in this world and in the world to come, and by so doing you will save yourself and all those under you. Otherwise you shall perish with them, and your sins and theirs will be on your head. . . .

May God lead us and all His creatures into the right path.

∞∞∞

General Gordon's Khartoum Journal

September 11.— . . . I put down our defeat . . . to two things—1. A lot of Khartoum peddlers went out to loot, and they broke the square.[60] 2. Mahomet Ali Pasha captured a lad of twelve or fourteen years of age and the little chap spoke out boldly, and said he believed Mahommed Ahmed was the Mahdi, and that we were dogs. He was shot! Before I heard of our defeat I heard of this, and I thought "THAT will not pass unavenged." There was an old belief among old Christians that every event which happens on earth is caused by some action being taken in heaven; the action in heaven being the cause of the event on earth, *vide*[61] Revelations, when at the opening of seals the trumpet sounds, &c., &c., all events exercised in heaven are followed by events on earth.[62] This being the case, how futile are our efforts to turn things out of their course. Vials are poured on earth whence events happen.[63] To me, it seems little what those events may be, but that the great object of our lives is how we bear those events in our individuality. If we trust in the flesh, thus saith the Lord, we are cursed; if we trust in Him we are blessed.[64] I cannot think that there are any promises for answers to prayer made for temporal things; the promises are to hear prayer and to give strength to bear with quiet what may be the Will of God. A vial is poured on earth; events happen; one is furious with the British Government for these events; but if we were logical, we would be furious with the pourer out of the vial, and that we shrink from being, for He is the Almighty who pours out the vial.

---

60. The standard defensive tactic of British infantry when attacked on open ground was to form a square with several ranks of soldiers on each side and a hollow center. If the square could maintain its integrity, without soldiers leaving to loot or in panic, it was essentially unbreakable.
61. "See!" in Latin.
62. Revelation, 8–11.
63. Ibid., 16.
64. Jeremiah, 17:5.

Epilogue

Holy Wars Today and Tomorrow

Many people perceive holy war as something born in a less rational past that today is embraced, advocated, and pursued by small numbers of fanatics devoted to their faiths in perverse ways. It is not something that the mainstream faithful of any major religion would embrace. Such a view is mistaken. Multiple variations of holy war, in both traditional and new forms, are evident throughout the globalized world of the twenty-first century, and their advocates are neither few nor marginal. Religious believers willing to use violence include fundamentalist Hindus who view their Muslim neighbors as a threat to their religious traditions; advocates of jihad in the Middle East, Africa, South, Southeast, and Central Asia, and even Western Europe and the United States; militant Buddhist monks willing to use violence to establish the superiority of their sacred beliefs over non-Buddhists in Sri Lanka and Myanmar; and Jews who justify their expansion of the nation of Israel as a continuation of the people of Israel's commitment to divine mandates given over three thousand years ago. The list could be multiplied several times over, and the impact of these holy warriors is especially acute today because of globalization and the weapons at their disposal. They who promote and wage holy war have traditionally depended upon two types of weapons—arms that destroy bodies and messages that infect minds—and weapons of the latter sort are more lethal and far-reaching today than ever before.

Technology, the Internet, and Modern Holy War

The internet has had a profound effect on religion and holy war in the modern era. On one level, it allows believers throughout the world to join online communities in which they can discuss and instruct one another on matters of spirituality, faith, and religious practice. At the same time, it is an effective medium for the transmission of militant messages, often justified by claims of oppression, that are intended to provoke violent acts by true believers.

Holy War on the Internet and in Social Media

Perhaps the most disturbing and ironic example of the use of social media and the internet to promote holy war is evident in the efforts of the so-called Islamic State (ISIS/ISIL), which dedicated an entire division to maintaining a powerful presence on the internet and on which it effectively fought a propaganda war with the U.S. State Department. The irony is that an archaic millenarianism drives the Islamic State, whose leaders adhere to an ideology that advocates a return to the purity of the earliest days of the caliphate, a repudiation of all later corruptions of Islam, a rejection of Western materialism and modernism, and holy warfare against all disbelieving persons and polities, "infidel" and Muslim alike. In service to its ushering in the promised New Age of the caliphate, the Islamic State has employed the most up-to-date technology in an exceedingly sophisticated manner.

After ISIS established itself in Iraq following its conquest of

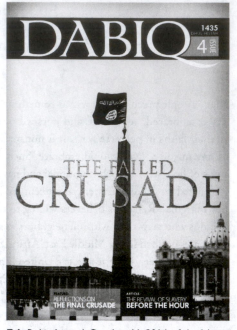

E.1. *Dabiq.* Issue 4, October 11, 2014, of the Islamic State's English language magazine. Many issues contain references to the crusades or explicit counter-crusading rhetoric.

Mosul in 2014, thereby occupying land in both Syria and Iraq, it instituted a media department that published its own glossy English language magazine, *Dabiq*, and made it available online in PDF. The title choice is significant. Dabiq is a town in northern Syria, which, according to Sunni Hadith, is one of two possible places where, on the authority of Muhammad, the *Malahim* (bloody battle) will take place. This long-anticipated, apocalyptic battle between Muslims and infidels will result in a Muslim victory that ushers in the End Times.

Just as noteworthy, ISIS's media department kept the internet cafes of its capital city, Raqqa, operational twenty-four hours a day, staffing them with jihadists who continuously posted the self-declared caliphate's messages supporting its legitimacy and inviting recruits for jihad. This propaganda was further shared worldwide by dedicated followers numbering in the tens of thousands. According to one estimate, these efforts resulted in as many as two hundred thousand supportive tweets, Facebook posts, and other types of online messages per day that reached up to one hundred million people.[1] If accurate, this would represent an

---

1. Anna Bruzgulis, "Stanley McChrystal: ISIS Reaches 100 Million People a Day Through

unprecedented marketing machine for any holy war. The fact that ISIS success-fully drew jihadists from all over the world to serve under its banner in Iraq and Syria, with estimates ranging from thirty thousand to eighty thousand recruits, suggests the effectiveness of such efforts.

Recognizing the powerful effects of the use of social media by ISIS, the U.S. State Department's response was to counter with its own social media presence. It had developed a division in 2010 to combat messaging from extremist groups, and after 2014, it devoted most of its efforts to *Think Again Turn Away*, a now-defunct campaign to defang ISIS's propaganda. The division posted in various online forums, including Twitter and Facebook, as well as in various languages, including English, Arabic, Somali, and Urdu. When ISIS posted images on so-cial media claiming Western soldiers raped Arab women, the U.S. State Depart-ment responded on Twitter by arguing the images were fake and pointed out that at least one image was taken from a Hungarian pornography movie.[2] The State Department also actively emphasized the suffering of Muslims and brutality to-ward women at the hands of ISIS members. Yet for all of these efforts, the cam-paign, staffed by dozens of State Department employees, could not keep up with the volume of online postings by the thousands of supporters of ISIS. Moreover, its critics argued that the campaign was counterproductive because it legitimated and strengthened the jihadists whom it sought to neutralize.[3]

The Islamic State is not the only entity to use social media to fan the flames of religious violence and division. Like ISIS, Al-Qaeda calls for a return to a pure/puritanical past and a total rejection of Western modernity, but embraces modern technology to spread its message. A notable example is Al-Qaeda's glossy English language publication *Inspire*. Like *Dabiq*, it appears in sharable PDF documents online.

One might also consider the use of technology in the ongoing conflict between Hindus and Muslims in India, where social media outlets have often turned

---

Social Media Campaign," PolitiFact.com, June 25, 2015, https://www.politifact.com /factchecks/2015/jun/25/stanley-mcchrystal/stanley-mcchrystal-isis-reaches-100-million -people/ (accessed June 14, 2020).

2. Adam Withnall, "ISIS Propaganda Image Showing 'Abuse of Muslim Women by Soldiers' Is Actually Taken from Hungarian Porn Film," *Independent*, November 23, 2014, https:// www.independent.co.uk/news/world/middle-east/isis-propaganda-image-showing-abuse-of -muslim-woman-by-soldiers-is-actually-taken-from-hungarian-9877993.html (accessed June 14, 2020).

3. Adam Edelman, "State Department's 'Embarrassing' Think Again Turn Away' Twitter Campaign Could Actually Legitimize Terrorists," *New York Daily News*, September 16, 2014, https://www.nydailynews.com/news/politics/state-department-embarrassing-turn-twitter -campaign-legitimizes-terrorists-expert-article-1.1941990 (accessed June 17, 2020).

Epilogue

E.2. *Think Again Turn Away.* Cover photo of the defunct Facebook page for the U.S. State Department's campaign. Image captured November 2014.

localized violence into a national affair. A recent article by journalist Neelanjan Sircar describes how acts of aggression by one community toward another do not inflame just local or regional populations, but the "fog of rumours, innuendo, and hate that act as kindling in a local communal clash immediately spread across India through social media."[4] The availability of capturing video on smartphones and sharing it online ensures a rapid spread of material that is often incomplete and without context. In such instances, consumers of social media are confronted with competing and incomplete narratives from which they must choose, and often such decisions appear to be based on which side of the religious divide they fall.

Contemporary Holy War and the Past

Another issue to consider when contemplating twenty-first-century holy war is the use of the past, or at least varying interpretations of the past, to justify today's grievances. Historians know that the past—what actually happened—and history—the narrative we construct about the past—are two different things. The past is unchangeable. What happened, happened. But history is different. There are multiple stories, or histories, we tell of the past that can be influenced by a huge variety of factors, from the sources we use to cultural and social stimuli that shade the lens through which we view the past.

---

4. Neelanjan Sircar, "Not All Communal Riots Are Local; Social Media Is Now Making Them National," ThePrint.com, March 4, 2020, https://theprint.in/opinion/not-all-communal -riots-local-social-media-is-making-them-national/375277/ (accessed June 14, 2020).

Religious histories are essential to the faiths that promote them, and memories of past religious persecution, real or imagined, often become justifications for holy war in all of its forms, including terrorism and mob violence. Crusade historians Edward Peters and Mona Hammad have highlighted how the modern Muslim memory of the medieval crusades, a remembrance of the past that is deeply flawed, is used by radical Islamist groups to win both sympathy and recruits to their cause.[5]

Holy Mob Violence in India

The Republic of India is home to more than 207 million Muslims, almost 15 percent of its population, giving it a Muslim population that ranks third in size among the world's nations. At the same time, 80 percent of the population, a bit more than one billion people, self-identify as Hindu. The remainder identify as Christian, Sikh, Jain, Parsi, Buddhist, or "no religion" (less than 1 percent).

Most Indians live in peace with one another, but religious animosities, especially between fundamentalist Hindus and fundamentalist Muslims, have become quite sharp over the past three decades. Religion is a major factor in these bitter and all-too-often bloody conflicts, but it is not the sole component. Hatred engendered by historical memories of mutual victimhood imposed both by the other as well as by outside forces, such as British colonialism and Western secularism, also plays an important role in fueling the conflicts. Regardless of mutual grievances, it is no stretch at all to label as holy wars these instances of violence. One example must suffice, the struggle over the holy site of the Babri Mosque.

The Babri Masjid (Babur's Mosque) was constructed in Ayodhya, a city in northern India, during the reign of the first Mughal emperor of India, Babur (r. 1526–30). Hindus believe that the site chosen, a hill on which there was an ancient structure, is the birthplace of Rama, the seventh avatar of the god Vishnu and one of India's most revered hero-deities. They further believe that the earlier structure on the hill, which was razed for construction of the mosque, was a sanctuary dedicated to Rama.

In India politics and religion have all too often been inextricably intertwined despite the efforts of secularists to separate them. In February 1989, Hindu activists resolved to reclaim the site and rebuild a temple dedicated to Rama. In 1991, in a series of virulent anti-Muslim speeches, Sadhvi Rithambara, the founder of Vahini Durga (Durga's Army), the female wing of the Hindu nationalist party

---

5. Edward Peters and Mona Hammad, "Islam and the Crusades: A Nine Hundred-Year-Long Grievance?" in *Seven Myths of the Crusades*, ed. Alfred J. Andrea and Andrew Holt (Indianapolis: Hackett Publishing, 2015), 127–49.

Rashtriya Svayamsevak Sangh (National Volunteer Association), whipped up Hindu fervor against the mosque, and it bore fruit.

On December 6, 1992, a mob, estimated at more than 150,000 persons, tore down the mosque. Riots across India followed. Nearly a decade later, on February 27, 2002, a mob of about two thousand Muslims firebombed a train from Ayodhya carrying Hindu activists who had been demanding that a temple to Rama be constructed on the site of the demolished mosque. Fifty-eight died in the conflagration. Several months of violence ensued across India. In the state of Gujarat, Hindus rioted for three days, with a combined death toll of Muslims and Hindus estimated at two thousand. It was alleged that the chief minister of the state, Narendra Modi, who rose to the office of India's prime minister in 2014, allowed and even encouraged the attacks on Muslims, but he was cleared of all charges in an official inquiry in 2012.

Mass killings and rapes of thousands across India, perpetrated by Hindus and Muslims alike, marked 2002, a year of mutual massacre. In the end, well over a hundred thousand Indians were displaced, and about five hundred mosques and Muslim shrines were destroyed, along with nineteen Hindu temples and three Christian churches. The god of holy war drank deeply from the blood spilled across the land.

Following a long legal dispute over the site at Ayodhya, where a temporary temple had been erected, the Supreme Court of India ruled in October 2019 that the land belonged to the government, but that the site would be handed over to a trust fund to build a new temple to Rama. An alternate five-acre tract would be given to the Sunni Waqf Board (a religious charitable trust) for a mosque. This judicial decision did little or nothing to lessen religious tensions. On February 23, 2020, rioting Hindus in Delhi killed approximately thirty-six Muslims and injured hundreds more. About half that number of Hindus were murdered in reprisal.

A month later, on March 25, 2020, despite a nationwide lockdown of all religious sites due to the COVID-19 pandemic, the chief minister of Uttar Pradesh participated in a solemn ceremony in which the statue of Ram Lalla (infant Rama) was carried out of the temporary temple that had been thrown up in the wake of the mosque's destruction and placed on a silver throne in another temporary structure, in preparation for the construction of a new, much grander temple. Despite accelerating concerns over the coronavirus, on August 5, Prime Minister Modi laid the cornerstone for the future temple, now a symbol of Hindu supremacy. Once again ultranationalism has been joined to a radical religious ideology to create a toxic mixture that threatens the rights and lives of a religious minority.

Other Twenty-First-Century Proponents of Jihad

Contemporary movements dedicated to jihadism are not the sole purview of the so-called Islamic State. Thomas Friedman of the *New York Times*, commenting on the jihadists' special hatred of the United States, asserted that there is a global "Narrative," consisting of a "cocktail of half-truths, propaganda and outright lies about America that have taken hold in the Arab-Muslim world since 9/11."[6] The United States is not the sole target of a narrative of hatred and its terrible consequences, as the efforts of terrorists groups such as Abu Sayyaf in the Philippines bear witness, but America suffered a singular attack by dedicated holy warriors on September 11, 2001.

Al-Qaeda, 9/11, and Its Aftermath

In Chapter 3, we saw the emergence of Al-Qaeda as a force for holy war during the 1990s, but Al-Qaeda did not cease functioning at the close of the millennium. After issuing his declaration for a jihad against the United States in 1996, Osama bin Laden and Al-Qaeda's efforts culminated in the attacks on the United States of 9/11. Suicidal jihadists using hijacked commercial airliners caused the deaths of roughly three thousand Americans and foreign nationals and immediately injured another six thousand. Interestingly, in a speech given shortly after the attacks, President George W. Bush referred to the U.S. effort to combat the jihadists as a "crusade," a comment that caused consternation in the West as well as in the Muslim world, forcing a rhetorical retreat on the president's part.

If bin Laden or his pronouncements were not widely known before 9/11, the events of that day made him a household name all over the world. In response to the attacks, the United States engaged in a lengthy war in Afghanistan and an invasion of Iraq, with a significant U.S. troop presence remaining in both nations even at the time of this writing nearly two decades later. During this time, the United States also engaged in a worldwide manhunt for bin Laden. He was finally located in Pakistan, where U.S. Navy Seals killed him on May 2, 2011. If bin Laden assumed the attacks of 9/11 would drive the United States out of the Middle East, he was mistaken.

Muslim Terrorists in the Philippines

In 2014, the leaders of Abu Sayyaf (Bearer of the Sword), an insurgent movement in the southern Philippines, openly pledged the group's allegiance to the Islamic

---

6. Thomas L. Friedman, "America vs. The Narrative," *New York Times*, November 28, 2009, https://www.nytimes.com/2009/11/29/opinion/29friedman.html (accessed June 17, 2020).

State of Iraq and the Levant. Since its formal founding in 1991, Abu Sayyaf has, in serial fashion, aligned itself with the most extreme militant jihadists, adopted their goals, and implemented their methods. Early on it received generous financial support from Al-Qaeda, which influenced the movement's ideological formation. In imitation of both Al-Qaeda and ISIL, Abu Sayyaf has issued calls for the establishment of an independent Islamic State in the southern Philippines founded upon the principles of Salafism, an ideology covered in Chapter 3. To further this goal, its jihadists have carried out campaigns of violence and terror against Christians, government troops, officials, and tourists alike.

State-Sponsored Persecution of Religious Minorities

Suppression by a state of a religious minority, sometimes rising to the level of ethnic cleansing, was all too common in the twentieth century and has continued into the twenty-first. In some cases, this "ethnocide" has occasioned armed resistance; in others it has spurred mob violence against the religious minority.

The Uyghurs of China

The Turkic Uyghurs (Uighurs), who reside largely in Xinjiang Province, in China's far northwest, are resisting what they perceive as the central government's attempts to destroy their culture and very identity, much of which centers on their Islamic faith, but their hopes seem forlorn. The Chinese Empire conquered this vast region in the mid-eighteenth century and gave it the name Xinjiang (New Frontier). In 1956, the People's Republic of China (PRC) renamed it Xinjiang Uyghur Autonomous Region. Although officially an "autonomous" province, it has been anything but semi-sovereign, especially since the government instituted a policy of flooding the province with ethnic Han Chinese in the later years of the twentieth century. Today, about 40 percent of the province's inhabitants are non-Muslim Chinese.

The result was resistance during the first two decades of the twenty-first century, marked by on-the-street stabbings and suicide bombings. In July 2009, rioting broke out in the capital city of Ürümqi, with an estimated two hundred fatalities, most of them Han Chinese. Hoping to take advantage of this discontentment, on October 7, 2009, high-ranking Al-Qaeda official Abu Yahya al-Libi released an online video informing the Muslims of "East Turkestan" to prepare for a holy jihad "against the ruthless brutal invader thugs," and further called upon

Muslims around the world to support the Uyghurs.[7] Nothing much came of this summons to holy war, and al-Libi was killed in a U.S. drone strike in June 2012.

Although there are some jihadist elements under the collective umbrella of the East Turkestan Independence Movement, to date Xinjiang has not experienced anything approaching a widespread holy war or even a revolution for political independence, nor is it likely to. The main reason appears to be the PRC's crackdown on all suspected dissidents, which began in earnest in 2017. Today concentration camps, euphemistically called "political training centers," hold at least eight hundred thousand and possibly as many as two million Uyghurs prisoner. China's official explanation is that it is combating terrorism and religious extremism through re-education.[8]

The Rohingya of Myanmar

In Buddhist Myanmar (formerly Burma), state-sponsored persecution has combined with apparently spontaneous but state-ignored mob violence against the country's Muslim minorities, especially the largest group known as Rohingya. And this atrocity has been growing in intensity since the 1990s, although the roots of official policies, as well as unprompted violence, against Myanmar's Muslims are much older and deeper. Here, as has often been the case throughout recent history, we have state-inspired and mob-activated sanctified violence. The result has been ethnic cleansing, the crisis of mass Rohingya exodus beginning in 2015, and a simultaneous armed-Muslim resistance in parts of the country.

Holy War in Defense of Modern Israel

When the modern state of Israel was founded in the wake of the Holocaust, the goal was to create a Jewish state that was free from religious persecution and discrimination and would promote and protect the Jewish faith and culture. Amid great jubilation and hope for the future, on May 14, 1948, David Ben-Gurion, chairman of the Jewish Agency for Palestine, declared the establishment of a Jewish state in Eretz Israel (the land of Israel). On the same day, Arab armies, whose leaders rejected the newborn nation's legitimacy, invaded it, thereby inaugurating hostilities, mistrust, and animosity that reverberate to today.

---

7. "Al-Qaida Leader Urges Uighers to Launch Holy War against China," *VOA News*, November 7, 2009, https://www.voanews.com/archive/al-qaida-leader-urges-uighurs-launch-holy-war-against-china (accessed June 12, 2020).

8. "China Uighurs: Detained for Beards, veils and internet browsing," *BBC News*, February 17, 2020, https://www.bbc.com/news/world-asia-china-51520622 (accessed September 23, 2020).

Hamas

Since its foundation, Israel has fought several wars with neighboring Arab states
and engaged in smaller conflicts with organizations such as the Palestinian Liberation Organization (PLO) and Hamas (the Islamic Resistance Movement),
which claim to represent the Arab populations living under Israeli control. Consider the Hamas Covenant of 1988, containing numerous anti-Jewish canards
and calling for a jihad to "obliterate" the State of Israel.[9] In 2007, Hamas assumed
leadership of the Gaza Strip and since then has overseen thousands of rocket
and mortar attacks on Israel, leading Israel to respond militarily. Although the
violence between Hamas and Israel ebbs and flows, it does not seem that it will
end any time soon. As a result of such long-standing conflicts, criticism of the
policies of Israel is often intertwined with hatred of Jews throughout much of
the Islamic world.

Israeli Settlers in Occupied Territories

Israeli settlements in the West Bank and Gaza, which came under Israeli control
as a result of the Six-Day War of 1967, remain a flashpoint for continuing animosity between Israel and its Arab neighbors. Palestinians and their allies see the
settlements as a theft of land and property, but the Israeli government and supporters of the settlements argue they are necessary for long-term security. Moreover, so the argument goes, they are historically Jewish lands, part of Eretz Israel
since biblical times.

While Israel is far from a theocracy, religious identity was intricately tied to
its founding and is integral to its continued existence. By no means are all Israeli
leaders or members of its military religious, yet a significant and influential component of both are quite religious. If anything, during the twenty-first century
the members and leadership of combat units have reportedly become increasingly
religious. This concerns some more secular-minded Israelis worried about issues
such as the troops' willingness to follow orders to remove Jewish communities
from settlements in the West Bank or Gaza, especially from sacred lands such as
Hebron, which is believed to contain the tombs of the Hebrew patriarchs, Abraham, Isaac, and Jacob, and their wives.[10] Jewish inhabitants of the settlements
can at times be even more militant than the troops, calling on Israeli soldiers to

---

9. The Covenant of the Islamic Resistance Movement, August 18, 1988, can be found at the
Avalon Project, https://avalon.law.yale.edu/20th_century/hamas.asp (accessed June 15, 2020).
10. Eyal Press, "Israel's Holy Warriors," *New York Review of Books*, April 29, 2010; republished
with permission on the Middle East Channel, https://foreignpolicy.com/2010/05/13/israels
-holy-warriors/ (accessed June 15, 2020).

disobey orders to remove them and engaging in low-level conflicts with nearby Palestinians. Indeed, one of the authors of this book, while spending time in Israel and the West Bank in 2016 and speaking with both Israeli Jews and Palestinian Muslims, was told on multiple occasions that recently arrived settlers, often religiously inspired in their purpose for moving to Israel, can be among the most militant, as seems confirmed by extensive reporting on the region.[11]

One of the best-known acts of settler violence was committed by Baruch Goldstein, an Israeli-American physician, army reservist, and settler. A religious extremist, Goldstein lived and worked in the Israeli settlement of Kiryat Arba near Hebron, where he reportedly refused to treat non-Jewish patients. Then, on February 25, 1994, the feast of Purim that commemorates the saving of the Jewish people whom an ancient Persian official plotted to kill, Goldstein carried out an attack on Muslims praying in a room set aside as a mosque at the Cave of the Patriarchs in Hebron, a site sacred to Jews, Muslims, and Christians. He shot to death 29 people and wounded over 125 before being beaten to death by survivors. In the aftermath, the Israeli government under Prime Minister Yitzhak Rabin made every effort to condemn the attack, but Goldstein's grave nevertheless became a place of pilgrimage for Jewish extremists, receiving thousands of visitors. A slab of marble at the site was inscribed with the words, "To the holy Baruch Goldstein who gave his life for the people of Israel, its Torah and land." In 1999, the government, in support of its law prohibiting monuments to terrorists, ordered the army to bulldoze the shrine and prayer area. Regardless, Goldstein's memory remains a dividing line within Israeli society. On their part, some radical settlers dress themselves or their children as Goldstein on Purim.[12]

Syncretic Millenarianism and Its Violence in the Twentieth and Twenty-First Centuries

There is nothing new about syncretic religions. In fact, all religions are syncretic insofar as they feed on pre-existing spiritual and ritual traditions, even as they

---

11. See Loveday Morris and Ruth Eglash, "Attacks by Israeli Settlers Surge as West Bank Tensions Boil," *Washington Post*, March 6, 2019, https://www.washingtonpost.com/world /middle_east/attacks-by-israeli-settlers-surge-as-west-bank-tensions-boil/2019/02/17/5c69 f176-2a30-11e9-906e-9d55b6451eb4_story.html (accessed June 15, 2020).

12. Ayelet Waldman, "The Shame of Shuhada Street," *The Atlantic*, June 12, 2014, https:// www.theatlantic.com/international/archive/2014/06/the-shame-of-shuhada-street-hebron /372639/ (accessed June 16, 2020); Rich Wiles, "Remembering the Ibrahimi Mosque Massacre," Al Jazeera, https://www.aljazeera.com/indepth/inpictures/2014/02/remembering-ibrahimi -mosque-ma-2014223105915230233.html (accessed June 17, 2020).

head off in new, often radical directions. With the ever-accelerating pace of globalization over the past several centuries, however, syncretic religious and spiritual movements have proliferated around the world at what seems to be an unprecedented tempo. Although many, perhaps most, of these hybrid religions have emerged within groups that have suffered real or imagined socioeconomic and political marginalization and whose members might even be the victims of ethnic or racial prejudice, most have chosen to express their suffering and religious hopes for a better world in prayer and other nonviolent ways. Some, however, have turned to violence or harbor within their midst terrorist elements.

Consider two contemporary examples, one in Japan and one in sub-Saharan Africa. Combined, they underscore the fact that millenarian violence, which many might dismiss as "medieval madness," is very much with us in the twenty-first century.

Aum Shinrikyo

In 1984, the charismatic Japanese preacher Shoko Asahara (1955–2018) founded Aum Shinrikyo (Universal Supreme Truth). Perceiving himself as the messiah who could save the world and appropriating the age-old title for Christ, "Lamb of God," Asahara promulgated a creed that is an admixture of Indian, Tibetan, and Japanese varieties of Buddhism, forms of esoteric yoga, and the Hindu cult of Shiva, the god of destruction, of whom Asahara claimed to be the incarnation. Beyond that, his message borrowed heavily from Christian eschatological theology and prophecies ascribed to the sixteenth-century French astrologer Nostradamus. Such a mishmash of strands could not fail to produce a creed that contains many contradictions and obscurities, but ambiguity aside, the essence of Aum Shinrikyo is clearly a doomsday message. Its core teaching is that a third world war is imminent, a nuclear conflagration that will be triggered by the United States, which is the Beast of the Apocalypse who appears in the Book of Revelation as a seven-headed, ten-horned enemy of the Lamb. All humanity will be killed except for members of Aum Shinrikyo. To usher in this age, Asahara further taught that mass murder would be a "cleansing karma."

Aum Shinrikyo planned murder on a global scale using nerve gas as its medium of destruction, and to that end established branches in at least seven nations, including the United States. Before launching a planned attack on New York City, members of the movement released sarin gas in the Tokyo underground rail system on March 20, 1995. The attack was largely botched, but it still managed to kill twelve people and sickened thousands, many of whom suffered life-altering disabilities. Asahara and a number of his leading confederates were arrested in May of that year and condemned to death for this outrage, and several other murders including an earlier sarin attack in 1994 that had killed seven and left at least 150 injured. The death toll charged against Aum Shinrikyo's leaders was twenty-nine persons, but it is likely that this was not a full count.

Shoko Asahara and twelve others were hanged in July 2018. Regardless of these executions and the failure of the prophesized Apocalypse, several thousand members of the movement remain active adherents of the faith in Japan, although they have changed the name of the sect to Aleph, the first letter in the Hebrew and Arabic alphabets. The organization continues to win new adherents, mostly through an online presence of supporters who promote the organization and its goals.[13]

The Lord's Resistance Army

Three years after Asahara began preaching his gospel of destruction and thousands of miles away, the Lord's Resistance Army (LRA; originally known as the United Holy Salvation Army) took shape as a militant religious movement in 1987 in northern Uganda under the leadership of Joseph Kony (ca. 1961–). Kony, a self-proclaimed prophet who claims to be a spokesman for God as well as a spirit medium, crafted a religion that mixes fundamentalist Christian beliefs with indigenous Ugandan spiritual beliefs and practices. His avowed aim is to create an equitable, democratic theocracy in Uganda that is governed according to the precepts of the Ten Commandments. Many outsiders, however, have cast doubts on Kony's avowed religiosity and goals, seeing him as simply a thug who uses religion as camouflage to mislead supporters and confuse opponents.

Whatever the truth about his motives, Kony's LRA initially focused its terror on mainstream Christian communities in Uganda, especially the Catholic Church. Forced out of Uganda in 2006, the LRA found refuge in the neighboring states of the Central African Republic, South Sudan, and the Democratic Republic of Congo. According to UNICEF, the LRA has abducted more than twenty thousand children, whom it has turned into child soldiers and sex slaves. Its soldiers have also been guilty of numerous other abductions, mass murders, and systematic rapes.

Over the past decade, attacks on the LRA by various African national forces have greatly reduced its numbers and ability to carry out terrorist assaults, but as of today Joseph Kony and a LRA remnant remain at large, probably having found refuge in South Sudan.

---

13. Tomohiro Osaki, "Aum Cultists Inspire a New Generation of Admirers," *Japan Times*, March 20, 2014, https://www.japantimes.co.jp/news/2014/03/20/national/social-issues/aum-cultists -inspire-a-new-generation-of-admirers#.XuEsTkVKiUk (accessed June 18, 2020).

Holy War Tomorrow

In closing, it is incumbent on us to offer brief musings on what we see as potential sacred battlegrounds in the future. To be clear, historians are not oracles, although sometimes their pronouncements rival in opaqueness the divinations of the oracle at Delphi. We hold that, given the role of accident, happenstance, and sheer human stupidity, history has no predictive qualities. A careful study of the past does, however, help us place our current situation into a fuller context and even allows us to say, with little or no sense of certitude, what might happen under similar circumstances, but that is it. We understand from our study of the past, for example, that the lethal mixture of social, cultural, and political alienation when combined with a religion that offers inflexible certainties and an "us versus them" mindset can but does not necessarily result in holy war. So with this uncertainty principle in mind, we will hazard some thoughts on current circumstances or situations around the globe that could, but might not, contribute to the outbreak of future holy wars.

Holy warriors are currently engaged in violent actions on behalf of their religious beliefs throughout the world, with no sign of letting up. In just the last six months, from January 1 to July 1, 2020, Islamic militants have killed or injured, by our count, people in thirty-six countries.[14] Much of this violence is concentrated in a small number of countries, largely Iraq, Afghanistan, Nigeria, Pakistan, and Syria. It is also often carried out by the groups we have considered here, such as ISIS/ISIL. We are hardly engaging in groundless speculation when we conclude that religiously inspired violence in these regions and by the types of religiously militant organizations we have considered in this book will continue well into the future.

As we hope the reader has realized by now, it will not be exclusively Islamic militants who will engage in violence for religious purposes. Holy warriors have perpetrated violence in the name of nearly all religions at one point or another, and this fact of life and history is likely to continue.

Just as religious violence is not something confined to the distant past, so it is also not restricted to lands far from the shores of the United States. Consider the growing violent ideology of white nationalists known as Christian Identity, who in the United States currently number somewhere between twenty-five thousand

---

14. News reporting on violence by Islamic militants during this period extends to Nigeria, Afghanistan, India, Iraq, Kenya, France, Mozambique, Philippines, Burkina Faso, Pakistan, Sudan, Syria, Cameroon, Mali, Yemen, Somalia, Niger, Democratic Republic of the Congo, Chad, Iran, Egypt, Thailand, South Sudan, Bangladesh, France, Maldives, Israel, Uganda, Canada, Tunisia, Turkey, Guinea, Lebanon, Indonesia, Ivory Coast, and the United States of America.

and fifty thousand, according to an estimate by the Anti-Defamation League.[15] If that estimate is correct, it indicates enormous growth for an organization that, according to the Federal Bureau of Investigation, had a membership of fewer than two thousand in 1989.[16] Whatever their numbers, Christian Identity adherents hold racist and anti-Semitic views and have committed hate crimes, bombings, murders, and other acts of terrorism. They also hold millennial beliefs that diverge significantly from traditional Christian views of the End Times in that they believe Christ's Second Coming will result in a holy race war in which their members will be God's chosen defenders of the white race and Christian America. The FBI has cited the movement as a significant future concern, describing its followers as "fanatics."[17]

Half a world away, in Sri Lanka, the Bodu Bala Sena (BBS, or Buddhist Power Force) was founded by Theravada Buddhist monks in 2012 and has been involved in harassment, threats, kidnappings, and inciting anti-Muslim riots that resulted in death and injury. A nationalist group that heavily emphasizes religion, the BBS has a history of aggressive advocacy on behalf of Buddhist or nationalist causes, with its leadership even condemning the Fourteenth Dalai Lama in 2014 after he called for Buddhist monks to stop committing acts of violence against Muslims in Sri Lanka and Myanmar.

From 1983 to 2009, Sri Lanka was torn apart by a civil war between the Tamil Tigers, who represented an ethnic and largely Hindu minority, and a government that empowered its Sinhalese and Buddhist majority. Is this island nation on the verge of another civil war, a civil war that will now pit Buddhist extremists against Muslims?

We end by noting what is obvious at this point: religious believers willing to use violence to further religious goals can be found in all of today's major faith systems and in some "designer," or syncretic, religions that have emerged in the maelstrom of globalization. While it is not certain that all of the religious organizations, groups, or states that we have considered here will continue to engage in religiously inspired violence, current circumstances lead us to conclude that holy war will be part of the human condition well into the future.

---

15. "Christian Identity," ADL.org, n.d., https://www.adl.org/resources/backgrounders/christian -identity (accessed June 14, 2020).
16. Federal Bureau of Investigation, "Christian Identity Movement," April 28, 1989, https://vault.fbi.gov/Christian%20Identity%20Movement%20/Christian%20Identity%20 Movement%20Part%201%20of%201/view (accessed June 14, 2020).
17. Ibid.

FURTHER READING

This is not a comprehensive bibliography of the best academic books on holy war. More limited in scope and ambition, it is a brief catalog of available books in English that should stimulate thought and further investigation by our intended audience—students and general readers.

Introduction: What Is Holy War?

Bellamy, Alex J. *Just Wars from Cicero to Iraq*. Cambridge: Polity, 2006.

Eller, Jack David. *Cruel Creed, Virtuous Violence: Religious Violence across Culture and History*. Amherst, NY: Prometheus Books, 2010.

Hashmi, Sohail H., ed. *Just Wars, Holy Wars, & Jihads: Christian, Jewish, and Muslim Encounters and Exchanges*. Oxford: Oxford University Press, 2012.

Jerryson, Michael K., and Mark Juergensmeyer, eds. *Buddhist Holy War*. Oxford: Oxford University Press, 2010.

Juergensmeyer, Mark. *Terror in the Mind of God: The Global Rise of Religious Terrorism*. 4th ed. Berkeley: University of California Press, 2017.

Juster, Susan. *Sacred Violence in Early America*. Philadelphia: University of Pennsylvania Press, 2016.

Lynn II, John A. *Another Kind of War: The Nature and History of Terrorism*. New Haven, CT: Yale University Press, 2019.

Victoria, Brian Daizen. *Zen at War*. 2nd ed. Lanham, MD: Rowman & Littlefield, 2006.

Wellman, Jr., James K., ed. *Belief and Bloodshed: Religion and Violence across Time and Tradition*. Lanham, MD: Rowman & Littlefield, 2007.

Chapter 1: Holy Wars in Mythic Time, Holy Wars as Metaphor, Holy Wars as Ritual

Farrar, D. S., ed. *War Magic: Religion, Sorcery, and Performance*. New York: Berghahn, 2016.

Murphy, Andrew R., ed. *The Blackwell Companion to Religion and Violence*. Chichester, UK: Wiley-Blackwell, 2011.

Renard, John, ed. *Fighting Words: Religion, Violence, and the Interpretation of Sacred Texts*. Berkeley: University of California Press, 2012.

Chapter 2: Holy Wars of Conquest in the Name of a Deity

Afsaruddin, Asma. *Striving in the Path of God: Jihad and Martyrdom in Islamic Thought*. Oxford: Oxford University Press, 2013.

Block, Thomas. *A Fatal Addiction: War in the Name of God*. New York: Algora, 2012.

Bonner, Michael. *Jihad in Islamic History: Doctrines and Practice.* Princeton, NJ: Princeton University Press, 2006.

Firestone, Reuven. *Holy War in Judaism: The Rise and Fall of a Controversial Idea.* Oxford: Oxford University Press, 2012.

Hamblin, William J. *Warfare in the Ancient Near East to 1600 BC: Holy Warriors at the Dawn of History.* London: Routledge, 2006.

Murawiec, Laurent. *The Mind of Jihad.* Cambridge: Cambridge University Press, 2008.

Tyerman, Christopher. *God's War: A New History of the Crusades.* Cambridge, MA: Belknap Press, 2006.

Chapter 3: Holy Wars in Defense of the Sacred

Bergen, Peter L. *Holy War, Inc.: Inside the Secret World of Osama bin Laden.* New York: Free Press, 2001.

Cobb, Paul M. *The Race for Paradise: An Islamic History of the Crusades.* Oxford: Oxford University Press, 2014.

Dunham, Mikel. *Buddha's Warriors: The Story of the CIA-Backed Tibetan Freedom Fighters, the Chinese Communist Invasion, and the Ultimate Fall of Tibet.* New York: Jeremy P. Tarcher/Penguin, 2004.

Housley, Norman. *Crusading and the Ottoman Threat, 1453–1505.* Oxford: Oxford University Press, 2012.

Knecht, Robert Jean. *The French Wars of Religion, 1559–1598.* 2nd ed. New York: Longman, 2010.

Nevin, Sonya. *Military Leaders and Sacred Space in Classical Greek Warfare: Temples, Sanctuaries, and Conflict in Antiquity.* London: I. B. Tauris, 2017.

Skya, Walter A. *Japan's Holy War: The Ideology of Radical Shinto Ultranationalism.* Durham, NC: Duke University Press, 2009.

Wilson, Peter H. *The Thirty Years' War: Europe's Tragedy.* Cambridge, MA: Belknap Press, 2009.

Wright, Lawrence. *The Looming Tower: Al-Qaeda and the Road to 9/11.* New York: Vintage, 2006.

Chapter 4: Holy Wars in Anticipation of the Millennium

Cohn, Norman. *The Pursuit of the Millennium: Revolutionary Millenarians and Mystical Anarchists of the Middle Ages.* New York: Oxford University Press, 1970.

Filiu, Jean-Pierre. *Apocalypse in Islam.* Translated by M. B. DeBevoise. Berkeley: University of California Press, 2011.

Kaplan, Jeffrey, ed. *Millennial Violence: Past, Present, and Future.* London: F. Cass, 2002.

Landes, Richard. *Heaven on Earth: The Varieties of the Millennial Experience.* Oxford: Oxford University Press, 2011.

Spence, Jonathan D. *God's Chinese Son: The Taiping Heavenly Kingdom of Hong Xiuquan.* New York: Norton, 1996.

Wessinger, Catherine, ed. *Millennialism, Persecution, & Violence: Historical Cases.* Syracuse, NY: Syracuse University Press, 2000.

Epilogue: Holy Wars Today and Tomorrow

Atwan, Abdel Bari. *Islamic State: The Digital Caliphate.* Oakland: University of California Press, 2019.

Conway, Maura, and Stuart Macdonald, eds. *Islamic State's Online Activity and Responses.* London: Routledge, 2020.

Fernandes, Edna. *Holy Warriors: A Journey into the Heart of Indian Fundamentalism.* New York: Penguin, 2006.

Gerges, Fawaz A. *ISIS: A History.* Princeton, NJ: Princeton University Press, 2016.

Lehr, F. Peter. *Militant Buddhism: The Rise of Religious Violence in Sri Lanka, Myanmar, and Thailand.* London: Palgrave Macmillan, 2019.

Lewis, Bernard. *The Crisis of Islam: Holy War and Unholy Terror.* New York: Modern Library, 2003.

Rashid, Ahmed. *Jihad: The Rise of Militant Islam in Central Asia.* New Haven, CT: Yale University Press, 2002.

Sageman, Marc. *Leaderless Jihad: Terror Networks in the Twenty-First Century.* Philadelphia: University of Pennsylvania Press, 2008.

IMAGE AND SOURCE CREDITS

Except where noted below, all images and sources are in the public domain.

Introduction

I.1 Photo courtesy of Alfred J. Andrea.

I.2 Wellcome Library, London. Wellcome Images (images@wellcome.ac.uk http:// wellcomeimages.org). First World War: two soldiers, one badly wounded, being comforted on the battlefield by a vision of Christ. Color halftone of an oil painting by George Hillyard Swinstead, 1915. Copyrighted work available under Creative Commons Attribution only license CC BY 4.0. http://creativecommons.org/licenses/by/4.0/.

I.4 Eccekevin (https://commons.wikimedia.org/wiki/File:Corby_Statue.jpg), https:// creativecommons.org/licenses/by-sa/4.0/legalcode.

Chapter 1

1.1 Photo courtesy of Alfred J. Andrea.

1.2 Unknown artist, Rama (https://commons.wikimedia.org/wiki/File:Stele_of _Adad_0233.jpg), "Stele of Adad 0233," https://creativecommons.org/licenses /by-sa/2.0/fr/deed.en.

1.5 Tonii (https://commons.wikimedia.org/wiki/File:Vajra.jpg), "Vajra," https:// creativecommons.org/licenses/by-sa/3.0/legalcode.

1.6 Wonderlane from Seattle, USA (https://commons.wikimedia.org/wiki /File:Yamantaka,_Fear-Striking_Vajra,_Lord_of_Death_on_a_water_buffalo, _Vajrayana_Buddhism.jpg), "Yamantaka, Fear-Striking Vajra, Lord of Death on a water buffalo, Vajrayana Buddhism," https://creativecommons.org/licenses/by/2.0/legalcode.

1.7 © José Luiz Bernardes Ribeiro / CC BY-SA 4.0 (https://commons.wikimedia.org /wiki/File:Christ_treading_the_beasts_-_Chapel_of_Saint_Andrew_-_Ravenna_2016. jpg), https://creativecommons.org/licenses/by-sa/4.0/legalcode.

1.9 Transity (https://commons.wikimedia.org/wiki/File:2004-05-06_07 _-_Petroglyph,_NM.jpg), "2004-05-06 07 - Petroglyph, NM", https://creativecommons. org/licenses/by-sa/3.0/legalcode1.10 olekinderhook

1.10 (https://commons.wikimedia.org/wiki/File:Asmat_bis_poles_from_Indonesian _New_Guinea_-_the_poles_are_named_for_deceased_people_and_the_huge _phalluses_on_top_represent_fertility._-_panoramio.jpg), "Asmat bis poles from Indonesian New Guinea - the poles are named for deceased people and the huge phalluses on top represent fertility. – panoramio," https://creativecommons.org/licenses /by/3.0/legalcode.

1.11 Wellcome Library, London. Wellcome Images (images@wellcome.ac.uk http://wellcomeimages.org). Buddha, resisting the demons of Mara, who are attempting to prevent him from attaining enlightenment, as the angels watch from above.

Sri Lanka, between 1800 and 1899. Copyrighted work available under Creative Commons Attribution only licence CC BY 4.0 http://creativecommons.org/licenses/by/4.0/.

1.12 Photo, Dharma from Sadao, Thailand (https://commons.wikimedia.org/wiki/File:040_Mara's_Three_Daughters_try_to_Seduce_the_Buddha_(9270770845).jpg), "040 Mara's Three Daughters try to Seduce the Buddha (9270770845)," https://creativecommons.org/licenses/by/2.0/legalcode.

1.13 Photo courtesy of Alfred J. Andrea.

Sources

1. *Bhagavad Gita*, trans. Stanley Lombardo (Indianapolis, IN: Hackett Publishing, 2019), 11–12, 14–15, 19, 27–28.

4. Franz Boas, *Kwakiutl Ethnography*, ed. Helen Codere (Chicago: University of Chicago Press, 1966), 109–10.

Chapter 2

2.1 Unknown artist (https://commons.wikimedia.org/wiki/File:Stele_of_Vultures_detail_01.jpg), "Stele of Vultures detail 01", https://creativecommons.org/licenses/by-sa/3.0/legalcode.

2.3 Eric Gaba, Wikimedia Commons user Sting (https://commons.wikimedia.org/wiki/File:Stele_of_Vultures_detail_01_reverse.jpg), "Stele of Vultures detail 01 reverse," https://creativecommons.org/licenses/by-sa/3.0/legalcode.

2.6 Photo courtesy of Alfred J. Andrea.

2.7 Used by permission of Giovanni Dall'Orto, Wikipedia. (Roma, Museo Ara Pacis - Calco di Roma con Vittoria - Foto Giovanni Dall'Orto, 30-Mar-2008.jpg).

Sources

3. Translated by Alfred J. Andrea.

Chapter 3

3.1, 3.2, 3.3 Photos courtesy of Alfred J. Andrea.

3.4 Roger Culos (https://commons.wikimedia.org/wiki/File:Sanvitale03.jpg), "Sanvitale03," https://creativecommons.org/licenses/by-sa/3.0/legalcode.

3.5 Photo courtesy of Alfred J. Andrea.

Sources

2. Pope Urban II, *Letter to All the Faithful in Flanders (December 1095)*, trans. A. J. Andrea, *Medieval Record* (Indianapolis, IN: Hackett Publishing, 2019), 306–7.

3. Ani Pachen and Adelaide Donnelley, *Sorrow Mountain: The Journey of a Tibetan Warrior Nun* (New York: Kodansha International, 2000), 106–7, 127–28, 130.

4. https://ctc.usma.edu/harmony-program/declaration-of-jihad-against-the-americans -occupying-the-land-of-the-two-holiest-sites-original-language-2/.

Chapter 4

4.2 PMRMaeyaert (https://commons.wikimedia.org/wiki/File:Auxerre,_Cathédrale _Saint-Etienne_F_198.jpg), "Auxerre, Cathédrale Saint-Etienne F 198," https:// creativecommons.org/licenses/by-sa/3.0/legalcode.

4.3 Dietmar Rabich (https://commons.wikimedia.org/wiki/File:Münster,_St. -Lamberti-Kirche,_Turm_--_2017_--_2068.jpg), https://creativecommons.org /licenses/by-sa/4.0/legalcode.

Sources

3. Franz Michael, ed., and F. Mote, trans., *The Taiping Rebellion. History and Documents*, 3 vols. (Seattle: University of Washington Press, 1966–71), 2: 227–29.

INDEX

Bold italics indicate an image or image caption. **Regular bold indicates a definition.**